Theories of Globalization

BARRIE AXFORD

polity

First published in 2013 by Polity Press

Polity Press
65 Bridge Street
Cambridge CB2 1UR, UK

Polity Press
350 Main Street
Malden, MA 02148, USA

ISBN-13: 978-0-7456-3475-3
ISBN-13: 978-0-7456-3474-6(pb)

A catalogue record for this book is available from the British Library.

Typeset in 9.5 on 13 pt Swift Light
by Toppan Best-set Premedia Limited
Printed and bound in Great Britain by Clays Ltd., St Ives plc

For further information on Polity, visit our website: www.politybooks.com

Contents

Acknowledgements

During the course of writing this book I have incurred many debts, not the least of which is the forbearance shown by Louise Knight, David Winters and others at Polity. Readers for the Press also offered strong support for the book in manuscript form, while pointing to the virtues of severe editing. Magnus Ryner and Tina Miller at Brookes read a draft of the book and I am grateful for their encouraging opinion of it and for their useful criticisms. Part of the argument in chapter 1 was based on an article in the journal *Globalizations* in 2007, and on a special issue I edited in that journal in the same year. Justin Rosenberg's response to the former, also in *Globalizations*, was a model of succinct critique, and enormously helpful in reframing chapter 1. I have been fortunate to present early versions of chapter 6 to research seminars at Oxford Brookes, at the annual conferences of the Global Studies Association in 2008, and at the ISA in San Francisco in the same year. The interpretation of world society found in chapters 2 and 8 is trailed in an article in *Protosociology* in 2012.

Barrie Axford
Oxford, December 2012

Introduction

This book offers a critical examination of the concept of globalization as it has been deployed across the social sciences and of its impact on social-scientific inquiry. It also offers pointers to a transdisciplinary and multidimensional, as well as a transformative scholarship of globalization, a concept that has resonated across the social sciences for the past few decades. When I first began to think about the book, colleagues advised me of the need for a comprehensive and critical treatment of the ways in which globalization has been theorized across disciplines and sub-fields, and to what effect. But on the face of it nothing could be further from the truth. There are many volumes that offer both exegesis and critical commentary on globalization, and even more that have tried to fashion *a* theory *of* globalization, or treat it as a prime, if inchoate, causal factor when explaining long-term, large-scale social change. Sometimes these offerings are not so much theory as hortatory remarks and either ideological or polemical in tone.

None of this is surprising. Globalization is a compelling idea that arouses strong feelings even among researchers who caution only that the concept needs more careful specification to be useful. There is also a wealth of more impassioned commentary from those exercised by the perceived benefits or ills of globalization. Globalization sceptics in the academy and beyond remain thick on the ground and, if anything, their complaints have been intensified by the faltering of the global economy since 2007. And even though much criticism points to under-specification of the concept, the fact is that there are many definitions of globalization clustered around common indicators and themes. So, if there is a problem, it lies elsewhere, perhaps in the curiously elliptical treatment of the concept. Thus globalization understood as 'space-time compression' is a notion that is wonderfully plausible, yet rarely grounded, or only vaguely construed, in empirical research. Conceivably, the problem resides in the blanket application of the term – globalization translated as interconnectivity leaves almost nothing outside its remit. Even 'difference' has been subsumed under the rubric, for diversity is not only seen as an enduring feature of a globalized world but often deemed integral to its constitution. Globalization as the process through which the world is being made into a single place has an intuitive appeal, until one begins to unpack precisely what is meant by that strong attribution. Finally, there is the matter of normative and ideological engagement. In some tracts the temper of commentary has an almost Orwellian gloss, where globalization is cast as good or bad by definition.

While this makes for compelling reading, it is not always good social science. Arguably, and despite its appeal as a 'must-have' concept, there is still a relative dearth of empirical-analytic investigation, especially at the micro and meso levels of experience and enactment and on the 'softer' aspects of globalization. Most notably, there is little work that connects individual lives and global constraints. At the same time, the scholarship is littered with work on globalization *and* the environment, security, gender and so on, or else with research on vicissitudes in the globalization *of* such issue areas. In short this is a field seemingly without boundaries and promiscuous in its appeal to many researchers and disciplines. So what am I trying to achieve in this book?

The first thing to say is that I am not trying to construct *a* new theory *of* globalization; still less elevate the concept into the sole explanation of recent or long-term social change. Such debates are important because they highlight the extent to which globalization and globalization research are challenging, if not transforming, social theory. For the study of globalization has yet to effect a paradigm change in the social sciences, though it may well constitute a 'positive problem shift' in how knowledge about the social is constituted (Lakatos, 1970). Here I have something of a normative as well as a scholarly intent to declare, at least where the future of globalization scholarship is concerned. I endorse treating globalization as more than a scholarly zeitgeist; seeing it as the catalyst for significant change in the focus and conduct of the social sciences. To achieve this end involves recognizing and, more to the point, operationalizing and implementing the transformative potential carried in the very idea of globalization, but only sometimes realized through its scholarship. The disciplinary and cross-disciplinary scholarship discussed in this book is interrogated with regard to whether it underwrites usual science or contributes to its transformation.

So, this is resolutely a book about how the global is theorized and how the idea of transformation appears positively in the work of some scholars and is derided by their opponents. As well as analysing the ways in which the transformative motif has been couched, in chapter 9 I offer pointers to how it might be realized through a scholarship not in thrall to disciplinary regimes and social-scientific givens. Throughout the book I canvass and critique different ways of theorizing globalization from across the social sciences. I also explore different academic traditions and reflect on how particular schools of thought have framing effects on debate that are often left unexamined. The continued imprint of methodological and theoretical nationalism on global theory provides a narrative thread through chapters 1–3 and particularly so where political science and sociology are concerned. Even the stuttering evolution of critical thinking from hyper-globalists, through sceptics to transformationalists, from so-called first to third wave theory, often fails to shake off these trammels.

Yet globalization is a concept that, in principle, forbids compartmentalization in any one area of social science. And indeed, though many disciplines have engaged with the idea, none has embraced it fully. But, as we shall see, strict allegiance to disciplinary traditions and ontological givens vitiate the possibility of a social science of the global and often trivialize contemplation of it. In this book I try to draw out commonalities and differences in focus and approach, the better to understand the provenance and findings of a diverse scholarship, and to look for pointers to a non- or trans-disciplinary approach to globalization research and theory. The remit of globalization scholarship is very wide, taking in both hard issues (patterns of economic globalization) and tantalizingly soft features (what is global consciousness?). To do justice to all this is a monumental task and I have had to simplify it for purposes of analysis and presentation. In chapter 1, I justify my decision to keep the remit of the book to scholarship that emerged across the social sciences from the 1980s onwards, when a body of literature specifically about globalization was first published. In the event, this restriction is not observed fully, since one has to acknowledge the influence of earlier social theory on contemporary scholarship.

Throughout, I prefer the term 'scholarship' to 'theory' because the second is subsumed under the first, and because not all of what we will canvass can be understood as theory. The Ancient Greek word for theory, 'theoria', had objective and subjective connotations; the first suggests seeing and observing 'outside' the self, and the second refers to one's own emotions and needs. This is a necessary tension in good social science.

The main task was to decide how to organize the material. I had three main presentational tasks in mind to embed my substantive goals. The first was to identify and evaluate the work of important authors in the broad field of globalization studies and cognate areas of the social sciences. While globalization appears as an integrating or a divisive topic in many disciplines and sub-disciplines, it is only recently that one can talk with any validity about a field of globalization studies, and more often than not that is just an amalgam of scholars from different disciplines who see some common ground under the globalization umbrella.

But I did not want to write a book so reliant on specific authors and particular texts that the broader warp of globalization theory gets lost in an exegesis of their work. At the same time I have tried not to undervalue the contribution of individual scholars by limiting their contribution to one area of globalization theory. So it is that Saskia Sassen, Anthony Giddens and Roland Robertson, to name but three, weave in and out of the narrative. The upshot is that there is, necessarily, a cumulative feel to chapters 1–3, where the same concepts and issues are inflected differently through the work of diverse authors and the framing of the subject by different disciplines.

This seems apposite, allowing me to develop my second concern, which is to examine some of the key themes that have emerged in attempts to theorize globalization. Five such themes are central to the scholarship on globalization as it has emerged since the early 1980s, and they can be used to assess its quality and impact. Obviously, there are other areas of concentration that could have done service here. The themes are organized as chapters 4–8. They include globalization as a spatial and temporal phenomenon (chapter 4), the eminently normative theme of globalization and governance (chapter 7) and what many commentators take as the valence issue for contemporary globalization: the relationship between it and capitalism (chapter 8). Two other thematic or conceptual-thematic chapters are deployed. The first (chapter 5) fills what is still something of a lacuna in globalization research by examining culture and the treatment of globalization as a socio-cultural phenomenon. The second (chapter 6) addresses how globalization is theorized as a historical process and how such theorization is informed by and impacts on modernization theory and theories of modernity; both intimately linked with treatments of globalization.

My third concern was to delineate the main strands in globalization research and to identify disciplinary contributions to it. Thus, I reserve the first part of the book for a review of the main currents in globalization scholarship and for definitional matters. Chapter 1 develops some important themes in globalization research and offers a critical unpacking of global concepts that share the same root – global – but inflect it differently, resorting to quite different, and sometimes incompatible, approaches to its study. It is followed by two chapters of disciplinary contributions to research on globalization. These chapters are succeeded by the five themes outlined above. Chapter 9 looks at globalization research less in thrall to *usual* science, and at the possibility for a social science of the global being made out of the wrack or transcendence of discipline-based social research. In this chapter I explore the promise of a paradigm shift and a two-way transformation – in how the world is ordered and in the social science of globalization.

When thinking about which disciplines to examine, my choices were directed by the significance of the concept in the field concerned. I advert political science, especially international studies, sociology, anthropology, geography and cultural and communication studies. Economics appears, but hardly from the mainstream of the discipline, which has largely eschewed globalization research; except, of course, in the work of apostates who have come over from the dark side of positivist theory and neo-liberal economics in search of a normative critique of globalization. Law too is deemed to show limited engagement as a discipline. I fear as well that I have been somewhat cavalier in my direct treatment of some cross- or non-disciplinary areas of research as these have inflected globalization scholarship in particular and often beneficial ways. Feminist theory is a major contender here. Also, despite my protestations that research on globalization has tended to marginalize some voices, especially where these spring from activist accounts, as well as from those outside Anglophone academic exchanges, I must confess that the coming pages are dominated by research from the Western academy. I can only plead the magnitude of the task and the need to treat main currents and modal concepts – themselves globalized – in detail to retain coherence and allow the book to flow.

CHAPTER 1

What's in a Name? Themes, Concepts and Obfuscations

Introduction

Although the genealogy of the term 'globalization' reaches back to the 1920s, it is possible to identify the precursors of contemporary global theory in the writing of luminaries such as Immanuel Kant, G.W.F. Hegel, Karl Marx and Georg Simmel; while the study of global history has its roots in the historiography of civilizations with considerably less than planetary extent (Spengler, 1918; Toynbee, 1934–61; Robertson and Inglis, 2004; Browning, 2011). Writing about the key concept of globality, Jens Bartelson (2009b, 113) refers to a 'medieval cosmology', perhaps even a scholarship, which entertained the idea of what we now call statelessness. We should also remember that any discussion of global change involves both human biological and social change as well as changes in the natural world. So it could be argued that we have chosen an arbitrary starting point from which to launch this analysis, while being unduly limited about its scope.

But as James Mittelman notes, although globalization is a concept whose early study owed much to developed research on social change under modernity, the rise and spread of capitalism and the origins and development of the state system – in other words, to classical social theory – it is really only towards the end of the 1980s that anything resembling a theoretical and empirical literature explicitly about the global begins to emerge (2004; Sklair, 2007). Some early and popular work on globalization tended to abrogate history and the influence of key historiographies in pursuit of the claim that the last decades of the twentieth century constituted a major rupture with preceding modernity. There may be some empirical weight to this view, but as we shall see the idea of the global cannot, or should not, be bracketed within a scholarship that not only claims globalization's novel ontology, but is cavalier in its treatment of earlier readings of world-making practices (Rosow, 2003; Browning, 2011; Featherstone, 2006).

The search for tight conceptualization and analytical rigour has to be uppermost in the minds of those who study globalization, but its popularity and notoriety have meant that almost any discussion of the concept leaves room for obfuscation and ideological special pleading. We will adopt a more forensic and interrogative stance on the ways in which globalization has been theorized during its brief period of intellectual and popular celebrity. In that pursuit, we will canvass the breadth of social-scientific scholarship on the theme of the global, since not all reflection can be understood as theory and not all theory is good scholarship (Shaw, 2000; 2003). Threaded through the critical account is the awkward and, for scholars of globalization, enduringly sensitive question of just how much we have learned about the world and how far the social sciences have developed through employing globalization as a descriptive term and a concept that fosters and perhaps transforms social-scientific explanation (Albert, 2007; Leander, 2009).

Scholarship on globalization is driven by both normative considerations and the pursuit of an empirically rigorous and historically informed social science; not always an easy mix. While it is the product of a number of disciplines it is probably no exaggeration to say that today much of it is located within the, admittedly broad, field of international studies, especially international political economy (IPE) – standing as a feature of that field's continuing search for intellectual identity – and, of course, in sociology (Bruff, 2005; Berry, 2008; Mittelman, 2004; Sassen, 2006). Which is not to claim that contributions from other disciplines have not had a significant, even seminal, influence on the canon, or that there is no developed globalization scholarship outside international studies and sociology (Sassen, 2007; Tomlinson, 1999; 2007; Rossi, 2007; Modelski et al., 2008).

Contributions from geography are among the most ambitious and most cited in globalization studies; while anthropology, cultural and communication studies, history and, in considerably smaller measure, mainstream economics all contribute to a rich weave of research on the complex theme of the global. Cross- or non-disciplinary themes such as gender, health, poverty and war have also inflected their research with a global(ization) dimension. In turn the study of globalization has drawn on these themes to produce more fine-grained accounts of, *inter alia*, migration, pandemics, inequalities and violence in the contemporary world. But in the case of economics a word of caution is necessary. While a good deal of globalization scholarship has addressed the economics *of* globalization, or considered globalization *as* an economic phenomenon or ideology, economics as a discipline has not engaged wholeheartedly with the concept (Stiglitz, 2002; Rodrik et al., 2004). The dominant approach from mainstream economics consists of cost–benefit analysis of globalization effects and, from authors like Joseph Stiglitz and Dani Rodrik, quite impassioned critiques of market economics. In these accounts commentary has passed over from the formal scientism of neo-classical economics to the realm of normative engagement.

In work on globalization from IPE the engagement has been much more wholesale around the interplay of states, non-state actors, markets, commodity chains and networks, as well as around the staple antinomy of agency versus structure as the ontological basis for social inquiry. On some accounts, IPE research, especially in the USA, has been depleted by a desire to ape more scientific, positivist work from mainstream economics at the expense of the investigation of big ideas and grand themes, including globalization (Cohen, 2009; Keohane, 2009; 1986). At the same time, the effects of neo-Gramscian ideas and constructivist thinking on understanding the political economy of the global may have been to soften the analytical cutting edge of mainstream economics unduly. Despite its normative or 'black-letter' approaches to global themes such as human rights and corporate governance, international law has also been less than engaged over globalization, especially from within the academic core of the discipline. Today, synergies between international law and international relations (IR) are receiving much more attention (Cutler, 2005; Noortmann and Ryngaert, 2010). And disciplines aside, there are many authors whose ideas have been extensively borrowed across fields contributing, as Martin Shaw says, to a 'relativisation of . . . historic disciplines' (2003, 42; Giddens, 1990; 1992).

Yet the grail of critical globalization scholarship – *multidimensionality*, by which is meant a systematic account of the analytically separate but interconnected and perhaps mutually constitutive dynamics of economics, politics and culture, delivered through a robust *interdisciplinarity* or *transdisciplinarity* – has proved elusive, approximated only in a small number of studies, achieved in even fewer (Robertson, 1996; Rosenau, 2003; Hay and Marsh, 2000; Appelbaum and Robinson, 2005; Featherstone, 2006; Rosow, 2003; Giulianotti and Robertson, 2009; *International Political Sociology*, 2009). On the face of it this dearth is strange, because as Roland Robertson says (2007a, 406), '[c]ategories for the comprehension of human life are . . . becoming destabilized' mainly as a result of our growing sense of the global. As our consciousness of the world grows, so do our fears about its fate, along with the recognition that we cannot contain many problems and crises at particular scales, or provide understanding of them from within the confines of normal social science (Albert, 2007).

This same awareness conjures its own brands of protectionism, ones not confined to personal and collective coping strategies for a world perceived as unsafe through the threats of planet death, pandemic, global terrorism or economic slump. Within academia the walls between disciplines remain extant to a degree that mocks the ambition to create – Ulrich Beck says 'reframe' – analytical categories for a globalizing world (Beck and Sznaider, 2006; Scholte, 2000; 2005b; Rosenau, 2003; Rosow, 2003; Rosamond, 2006; Robertson, 2007a). Much social science suffers from the propensity to analyse areas of collective life in terms of discrete categories – a besetting weakness – and the study of globalization, a concept that challenges the very idea of boundaries, has not been well served by scholarship largely predicated on their maintenance.

Globalization is no journeyman concept and yet it remains infuriatingly ambiguous and elusive. While sceptical commentary suggests that this is a necessary consequence of an unworkable, perhaps unteachable, idea, in no small part ambiguity results from a recurring failure to separate 'global' concepts – globalization (process), globalism (ideology) and globality, a notion which musters as consciousness, condition, framework, even system – which share the same root but often reflect different discourses about, and sometimes cleave to diverse theoretical positions on, the 'global' (Harvey, 2000; Shaw, 2003; Caselli, 2008; Meyer, 2007). We will examine these consequential differences later in the chapter.

The study of globalization also triggers powerful normative and ideological sentiments. At their most stark or most facile, these turn on the question of whether globalization is a good or a bad thing. Such accounts sometimes rehearse the case for alternative forms of globalization to subvent progressive and humanitarian goals or else offer prescriptions for different kinds of universality. This empirical-normative agenda has spawned a number of key research questions. First, what is globalization and what is not? Second, does globalization deliver massive and disjunctive social change? Third, are apparently dramatic changes in world politics and economics merely an unfolding of world history as universalizing modernity achieves its denouement? Fourth, can the idea of the world being made into a single place, demonstrating a systematic rather than a jobbing unicity, be taken seriously? Other important questions address the provenance of globalization, asking whether it is a purely contemporary or a historical phenomenon; whether it musters as a progressive or a regressive force (Wallace-Brown, 2008); whose interests are best served (Woods, 2006; Abdelal, 2007); and finally, whether the idea of the world's unity also requires what Jean-François Bayart (2007, 31) rather inelegantly calls its 'uniformization' (see also Guillen, 2001).

Undoubtedly these are important issues, but more challenging for the social sciences is the claim that globalization confounds conventional thinking about the organization and conduct of social life and thus requires a transformation of social scientific knowledge (Scholte, 2000; 2005b; Cameron and Palan, 2004; Rosow, 2003; Shaw, 2003; Bartelson, 2009b). For as Saskia Sassen notes, when discussing globalization, the issues are rarely confinable to the perspectives of one branch of knowledge, even though the tradition in the parvenu fields of social science has been to organize knowledge about different spheres of social life under specific disciplines, each with its preferred epistemologies and methodologies. Instead, good scholarship on globalization requires, at the least, 'operating at the intersection of multiple disciplinary forms of knowledge and techniques for research and interpretation' (Sassen, 2007, 11).

Much scholarship on globalization engages with the concept forearmed by established (Western) intellectual and disciplinary traditions, which can make it hard for scholars to speak to each other across disciplinary boundaries (Cameron and Palan, 2004; Rosamond, 2006; Mittelman, 2010). As a result, the study of globalization occupies a rather uneasy space between disciplines and paradigms; which is a weakness, because its study is often seen as in some way inauthentic, or merely diversionary; and a strength, because it might hold out the prospect of a social science more in tune with twenty-first-century social and political realities.

Theory and the Scholarship of Globalization

Early claims that globalization had achieved the status of an 'ascendant paradigm' were manifestly overblown (Mittelman, 2004). Yet disputes about globalization's theoretical status are productive because they highlight particular moments of intellectual doubt and excitement as well as reflecting the turbulence and enduring complexity of the real world. Indeed, Martin Shaw has argued that the emergence of globalization scholarship itself reflected the crisis and demise of the old Cold-War system and gave a decidedly geo-political twist to an already advanced crisis of modernity (2000).

When ideas about postmodernity 'first emerged in the 1980s, predominantly in the cultural sciences, they reflected a general sense of [an] emergent crisis that had not yet reached the stage of decisive political change' (Shaw, 2003, 35). Prescriptions for a new 'post-Cold-War' world appeared at the beginning of the 1990s as the Soviet world-empire broke up and a prevailing sense of epochal change also shaped emerging trends in social theory. The idea of 'globalization' became dominant in the mid-1990s, just as that turbulence was partly resolved and new world power relations – driven by liberal economics and new communication technologies – became modal (2003, 35). In Shaw's estimation, our obsession with globalization and our attempts to gloss it as a new theory of the present and paradigm for the future are part of a wider crisis or transformation of world order yet to be resolved fully.

All theories simplify social complexity; while social life is rarely 'cut from whole cloth' (Giddens, 1990, 27). To be convincing, theory – other than normative theory, which expresses values and cannot be disproved by pointing to actual features of the world around us – should permit some existential reference and thus afford a purchase on what is happening in the world. Theory should also be clear about its explanatory limits, and in this respect, as Shaw also reminds us, since the mid-1990s 'the decline in the fashion for naïve globalization-thought enables us to see what is more fundamental and durable in global development' (2003, 35).

Globalization scholarship: Globalization as a proto-paradigm

The scholarship of globalization is riven with disputes, many of them reflecting quarrels within and between disciplines. Within international studies James Mittelman (2004) identifies a robust and continuing battle between those he labels 'para-keepers' and 'para-makers'. The former are protectors of existing paradigms who resist the claim that globalization offers a new way of organizing social life and constituting knowledge about it. Para-keepers, says Mittelman, are found among realists, including Marxist realists, inter-dependence theorists, world-systems analysts, some social democrats (often under the anti- or alter-globalization banner and in certain brands of con-structivism) and new institutionalists (Wallerstein, 1974; Keohane and Nye, 2000; Hirst et al., 2009). Para-makers claim to have 'shifted to an innovatory paradigm' (Mittelman, 2004, 21) wherein globalization reveals deep flaws in modernist social science. Recent work by sociologists Ulrich Beck, John Urry and Martin Albrow are avatars of such radical approaches (Beck, 2006; Urry, 2003; Albrow, 1996).

The ranks of para-makers include a tranche of theorists conveniently mus-tered as 'de-territorialists', some apostate or post-Marxist treatments of empire, complexity theorists and a smattering of writers who see modernity as giving way to globality (Scholte, 2005a; Cerny, 1999; Hardt and Negri, 2000; Rosenau, 1997; Albrow, 2007a). What divides proponents within and between camps are mainly questions of epistemology and methodology (what globali-zation means for our understanding of the world around us and how it should be studied). These intellectual differences have translated into an increasingly dynamic scholarship of globalization where the temper of com-mentary and the objects of research have changed since the early 1980s. Beck and Sznaider opine that as the distinctions between national and interna-tional and local and global have become blurred or dissolve, so have the 'premises and boundaries that define the units of empirical research and theory' (2006, 13).

Robert Holton (2005) suggests that over this period globalization research has come in three overlapping but recognizable waves – hyper-globalist, sceptical and post-sceptical or, as some would have it, 'transformationalist' – each more self-conscious and cautious than its predecessor (Hay and Marsh, 2000; Martell, 2007;Bruff, 2005; Berry, 2008; Rosamond, 2006; Bartelson, 2009a). The wave motif also receives endorsement from Held and McGrew (2007), who identify four such waves: theoretical, historical, institutional and deconstructive. The waves are by no means discrete, but taken together, they describe a shift to a more textured, historical, agent-aware, multi-layered, culturally informed and, arguably, undogmatic scholarship of globalization. Oblique or sweeping statements about global issues give way to 'more middle-range explanations [which] account for the complex manifestation of global processes within particular social realms', including religion, sport, health and sexuality as well as the staples of economics and politics (Giulianotti and Robertson, 2009, xiii; Maliniak and Tierney, 2009; Keohane, 2009).

First wave *globalist* or *hyper-globalist* positions are associated with early glo-balization theory from the 1980s to the mid-1990s when, often in neo-liberal guise, they enjoyed a vogue far beyond the academy. Post-Washington-consensus and in the wash from the global economic crisis which began in 2007, their appeal in some business and policy-making circles is diminished but not extinguished. Although the gist of such interventions was to treat globalization primarily as an economic phenomenon, in fact there are important differences of emphasis and diverse normative prescriptions in globalist accounts. Berry (2008) distinguishes between neo-classical and Marxist globalists, who share the view that globalization is a material reality centred on economic processes and the completion of a global economy, but differ in their approbation of such developments. True to their epistemological roots, neo-classical arguments (Ohmae, 1990; 2001; Wolf, 2004) explain global markets as the expression of rational behaviour by individual actors, an assumption at one with the tenets of economic neo-liberalism. Such positions also adopt a realist stance on agency, such that the assumed rationality (self-interest) of all actors is held to engender both dynamic and stabilizing effects in much the same way as the imputed behaviour of states in realist models of the international system, or consumers in the market place.

Marxist globalists treat the making of a global, market-driven economy as the latest twist in the development of capitalism as an exploitative system of wealth creation and uneven development (Callinicos, 2009; 2002; Harris, 2006; McMichael, 2001). In these accounts agents are more red-blooded and certainly more reflective than in neo-classical theory, but still severely constrained by their structural location in the social division of labour in class-divided societies. But eminently materialist and usually structuralist positions are themselves challenged, or perhaps just glossed differently, in work influenced by the Italian Marxist Antonio Gramsci (1971; Robinson, 2006), which gives more credence to the role of ideas, to contingency, and to agents being active in reproducing or transforming the conditions of their existence.

Gramsci's work has had a considerable influence on some brands of theory, particularly in 'critical' IPE and 'open Marxism' (Cox, 1987; Gill, 2000; Rupert, 1998; Drainville, 1994), where the focus has been on the role of ideas in shaping perceptions of and accommodations to globalization. Critical theory, as it is often labelled, is generally offered as a useful step away from the brute materialism of mainstream Marxist arguments and the simple ontology of realism. But it may do no more than muddy the water around the issue of the dominance of either agency or structure, by seeming to flirt with a more voluntaristic and action-centred interpretation of globalization while still clinging to an implicit theoretical essentialism which privileges capitalist production forces and material factors as (ultimately) determining (Cox, 1987; 1989; Bruff, 2005; Guzzini and Leander, 2006).

This gloss on their arguments will be anathema to neo-Gramscians, but Gramsci himself noted that social theory must always be sensitive to the 'decisive nucleus of economic activity' (1971, 161). In a useful exegesis on this conundrum in IPE literature, Ian Bruff (2005) has recourse to the sophisticated neo-Gramscian arguments of Stuart Hall, doyen of cultural studies in the UK (1996; Hall and Soskice, 2001). Hall paints globalization as a complex, contradictory and above all negotiated process and this, on the face of it, gets him off the hook of economic determinism. In the event the same obfuscations around the interplay of agency and structures are apparent in his account. In Hall's work, how globalization appears to us is shaped by interpretation, which is socially constructed. But any indeterminacy in outcomes implied by such a view is offset by the sense that material considerations are key to the maintenance and reproduction of the capitalist system. As we shall see, what are often called 'third wave' positions on globalization do battle on the same ground as Hall, and their reliance on the socially constructed or discursive nature of globalization leaves them with unanswered questions.

Second wave or *sceptical* accounts of globalization have little time for any of this. They hold that anything resembling a globalist thesis rests on very thin evidence and that such evidence as exists actually reveals globalization as neither new nor particularly global (Hirst and Thompson, 1996; 2000; Hirst et al., 2009; Krugman, 1996). Moreover, there is little good data to support the claim that the world (economy) is becoming or has become globalized. Unsurprisingly, sceptics retain states and national economies as the key players in what they depict as an inter-national rather than a global system and, on first reading, their views too have a decidedly realist flavour. But neo-institutionalist variants on the sceptical theme are more inclined to see states as institutions with variable power, so that the effects of globalization are not the same on all states and in all parts of the world. Instead of the realist stance that all states are grey in the dark, regardless of circumstance and history, institutionalists prefer to see them as distinct entities, each with its own traditions, cultural practices, policy preferences, legitimacy and capacities (Weiss, 1998; Mann, 1997; Mosley, 2005; Rodrik, 2000). Because of this variability, globalization too is better seen as an uneven process, less inclusive than globalists suggest and contingently detrimental or galvanizing in its impacts on states, economies and cultures (Martell, 2007).

Sceptical positions on globalization are a necessary antidote to zealous hyper-globalism and are capable of generating useful hypotheses about the dynamics of the global economy (Berry, 2008). But they smack too much of unreconstructed realism and are often remiss in their neglect of agency and the importance of ideas in shaping the world and consciousness of it. Because they are troubled by the very idea of globalization as an empirical reality, there is usually very little attempt to accommodate, let alone subscribe to, the globalization hypothesis. But some forms of sceptical thinking do venture beyond a largely economic focus to offer a critique of the hyper-globalist claim that economic globalization is being accompanied and accelerated by the growing cultural homogeneity or cultural hybridization of the world (Barber, 2007). For example, research on the role of new media in trans-nationalizing communication and facilitating the creation of a global civil society or a global public sphere is frequently sceptical of globalist claims to have compressed time and space, thus eliminating what Kai Hafez calls 'the fundamental character of "ego-centric" national media systems' (2007, 3; Inglehart and Norris, 2009; Chandler, 2007).

And in works which achieved recognition well beyond the academy both Benjamin Barber (1995; 2007) and Samuel Huntington (1996) do not so much reject the idea of globalization as point to the vitality of its antithesis in the shape of alternative or anti-globalization ideologies and movements, whose very existence suggests greater cultural fragmentation and political polarization rather than homogeneity or hybridization. Whatever their faults, the real value of positions which stress the contested nature of globalization against bland claims of global convergence is that they qualify the totalizing and probably unsustainable claims of hyper-globalists, without rejecting all evidence of growing interconnection and interdependency. In this respect they are hardly pure globalization sceptics but remain agnostic and/or ambivalent about its progressive nature and possible outcomes.

In this brand of commentary, the set of papers edited by Hay and Marsh, which looks to 'demystify' globalization (2000), serves as a conceptual taster for the shift away from zealous hyper-globalism and the more curmudgeonly treatments of the sceptics, to what is generally understood as the third, post-sceptical or transformative wave of theorizing. At first glance their position is self-consciously sceptical, but it intimates a new wave of thinking determined to rescue globalization scholarship from the excesses of and gaps in the first two waves. In these authors' view, globalization is a discourse which is not itself material in the way hyper-globalists insist, but which has profound material effects when realized through the actions of agents who either subscribe to the discourse or are affected by its adoption in, for example, government policy on regulation of labour conditions. These material effects make globalization 'real' in ways airbrushed out of most sceptical accounts.

Hay and Marsh's volume appeared in 2000 and by the noughties the research emphasis begins to reflect a greater variety of influences, including – *inter alia* – post-Marxist structuralism and constructivism and forms of 'critical scholarship' (Held and McGrew, 2007). These accounts all emphasize the discursive and contingent construction of global social 'reality' while, at least in some versions, looking to retain the idea that globalization is transformative of social relations (Held and McGrew, 2007; Hay and Rosamond, 2002; 2004; Callinicos, 2003; Risse, 2007; Rosamond, 2006). In such interpretations, globalization ceases to be 'out there' in the sense rightly dismissed by Anthony Giddens (1990; 1992) or imposed by dint of irrepressible world-historical forces. Instead, it is what actors perceive it to be and there are no givens, no structural necessities, no historical inevitabilities and no unfolding teleology of human progress or decay (Fukuyama, 1992; 1996). Expressions like 'globalization as discourse', 'tendency' or 'cognitive structure' begin to dominate the literature and, on the face of it, agency and ideas are back in fashion. Arguably, the most significant contribution of such scholarship is that it charts a course between the two poles of globalization theory: the sceptics' insistence that the concept provides no real 'guide to the interpretation of empirical events' and the catch-all claims of hyper-globalists that signs of globalization are everywhere and that it is unstoppable (Hay and Rosamond, 2002; Risse, 2007; Rosenberg, 2005, 1).

The almost common-sense quality of much third wave theorizing relies on the notion derived from interpretative sociology that all meaning is socially constructed and reproduced through social learning and forms of discourse (ideologies and texts of various sorts, including symbols) rather than through material factors. Of course, the intellectual provenance of social construction-ism is pretty mixed. It takes in the 'new science' of Vico in the eighteenth century, some humanistic Marxism, phenomenology, ethnomethodology and linguistic insights into relational practices, as well as the contributions from both micro and macro sociology (Lock and Strong, 2010). Out of such a rich intellectual context, globalization emerges as an (ideological) discourse that frames thought and actions by setting limits for what is desirable and even possible. In other words, the discourses allow actors to simplify and manage the environments within which they act (Hay and Rosamond, 2002; Cameron and Palan, 2004).

The approach is a refreshing contrast to all 'inevitabilist' and many struc-turalist positions on globalization because it underlines not only the contin-gent quality of what is often presented as given or else immanent in the 'deep structures' of social formations, but the capacity of agents to reproduce and alter the terms and conditions of their own existence (Chase-Dunn, 1989; 1992; Chase-Dunn and Gills, 2005). Framing globalization in this way is, or ought to be, an important advance in scholarship (Hay and Smith, 2008). Indeed, unless you are a dyed-in-the-wool structuralist, there is at least an intuitive plausibility about constructivist accounts of globalization and about the idea of globalization as a discourse which possesses almost mythological qualities – a conjured 'reality' narrated through the rhetoric of political elites, corporate public relations and even the musings of 'first wave' academ-ics and publicists. Discussion of the international economic order from a purely sceptical and largely material perspective usefully counters the exag-gerated claims about globalization as inexorable (Friedman, 1999), but con-structivist political economy raises the analytical stakes by pointing out the ideological, political and highly contingent character of that process (Hay and Rosamond, 2002; Woods, 2006; Abdelal, 2007; Cameron and Palan, 2004).

Yet questions about the explanatory value of constructivist accounts remain and they qualify the plausibility of the arguments. First, although not debil-itating in itself, as Thomas Risse states, we should be aware that constructiv-ism is not a theory of globalization, more a 'meta theory of social action' (2007, 132). Second (and constructivists understand this), if globalization is a construct, then so is all social life. The logic of the thesis should then dictate that there can be no master or authentic discourse which can 'objectively' construct the best of all possible worlds (Wiener, 2008). The difficulty is that while the research offers useful insights into the workings of social relation-ships where hegemony is assured through non-material forms and some controlling interests are well served, even on its own terms much of the literature looks like an apology for a particular normative/ideological position on globalization in which some narratives are infinitely preferable to others. Here, an emergent and at one time almost hegemonic social-democratic or even a modified Marxist discourse is deemed capable of conjuring (and is applauded for prescribing) a more benign world than hyper-globalist or neo-liberal ideology translated into policy. All of which gives a conspiratorial gloss to some third wave positions on globalization that is rather at odds with the expressed concern to contribute to a more rigorous empirical science of globality. It is also evident that the emphasis on discourse sometimes masks a conviction that structure is dominant, albeit in the last instance (Hay and Coates, 2002; Berry, 2008).

Third, while it is significant to know that globalization is a discourse, the research task must always be to discern why and how dominance was achieved and with what consequences. Colin Hay, among others, has conducted empirical work on the processes by which globalization discourse becomes dominant, and then reflects on the fallout from that dominance. This is good social science, but from the standpoint of trying to understand the dynamics of power relationships and the process of social change, it triggers the niggling thought that if the social world is being made and reproduced solely through dominant narratives, how does change occur? What are the mechanisms through which marginal discourse becomes dominant and dominant discourses are undone? The danger with constructivist accounts is that if narrative is the one 'reality', change can take place only through the superseding of one dominant narrative by another, with each laying claims to veracity. So the key factor may not be discourse at all, but some other constraint or resource. For constructivist globalization research the main issue is not only whether, or how, such competing claims can be verified empirically (presumably they cannot, despite attempts to uncover the 'facts' about globalization), but how discourses frame and sustain a contested and contestable 'reality'.

Finally, although it appears as a critique of constructivist IPE in general, rather than a counterweight to constructivist treatments of globalization in particular, we should advert the room for confounding purely subjectivist accounts provided by critical realism (Archer, 1988; Bhaskar, 1998; Patomäki, 2010a; 2010b). Critical realists argue that there is a social reality independent of any human conception, and its proponents suggest that there are unobservable events that cause all observable ones. Because of this, the social world can be understood only if analysts identify and understand the structures that generate such unobservable events. Critical realism has some merit as a critique of neo-Gramscian IPE, but we should caution that applying such insights to globalization must not revert to the simple empiricism favoured by sceptics, but afford a middle way between the naive phenomenology of some constructivist accounts and forms of brute structuralism. Of course, it may be that all it achieves is a further dose of theoretical equivocation.

Curiously, third wave commentators on globalization remain sceptics in their depiction of the discourse of (hyper-)globalization as no more than ideological smoke and mirrors, and yet transformationalist in their understanding that a dominant discourse may indeed shape the world and the destinies of those who inhabit it (Berry, 2008; Martell, 2007). This is social theory tailored to our hyper-reflexive times and yet still nostalgic for a particular 'imagined' economy or society. Perhaps justifiably, it is suspicious of grand narratives and sceptical of the universalist claims of early globalism, especially where these can be seen as offshoots of (neo-)liberal theory. As we shall see in later chapters, the upshot is both gain and loss.

What's in a Name?

To reiterate, good social-scientific inquiry relies upon conceptual rigour to produce sound theory. At the same time, all theory must recognize its limitations. By treating globalization as a temporary, derivative and entirely conjunctural phenomenon, Justin Rosenberg challenges globalization theorists to situate the undoubtedly huge changes which occurred globally at the end of the last millennium in a more encompassing theory of social change, the better to weigh their explanatory value (2000; 2005; 2007; Albert, 2009; Axford, 2007a). Because his criticisms of globalization theory have considerable relevance for our discussion to date, and for how the root concept *global* is construed in different branches of theory, they are worth further consideration (Axford, 2007a).

Globalization as a conjuncture: History and happenstance

Rosenberg wants to situate the study of international relations within the broader warp of classical, especially Marxist, social theory. He finds contemporary globalization theory wanting in its duty of care to good social science. Within the genre, attempts to address the core project of how to explain long-term, large-scale social change have been hijacked by the polemical debate between hyper-globalizers and transformationalists; which debate is largely rhetorical since, for him, transformationalists are a sub-set of hyper-globalizers, often devoid of literary panache. Rosenberg also questions the wisdom of taking the 1990s as a seminal decade in the transformation of world politics and in the putative (global) transformation of the social sciences (Shaw, 2003).

Rosenberg's gloss is that observed changes were wrongly interpreted by students of globalization, who mistakenly abstracted the decade from the historical record to concoct an intuitively plausible, but largely unsubstantiated, body of thought called globalization theory. These theorists (Held and his co-authors, Giddens, Scholte and a bevy of neo-liberal hyper-globalizers) allegedly show scant regard for important questions about the nature and rigour of social scientific inquiry – conceptualization and operationalization – and rely on assertion and ideology to justify their eclectic arguments. Rosenberg offers a way out of this condition, and for him it spells the end of 'globalization theory' as a way of explaining social change.

Rosenberg counsels a historical reinterpretation of the 1990s based on three main tenets. *First*, that the dramatic concentration of 'spatio-temporal dislocations and compressions' in the decade (the end of Fordism as a system of mass production, new digital communications technologies, the erosion of national systems of production and the breakdown of traditional identities linked to territory, along with the particular tensions created by the fall of state socialism and the rise of neo-liberalism) were produced by a process of social change already in train and not vice versa. Thus globalization (if such it is) has to be seen as a dependent variable. *Second*, what might otherwise be taken as a high point in the transformation of social relations and institutions was driven largely by temporary pressures created by a historical 'vacuum' – a unique set of circumstances culminating in the 1990s – rather than reflecting (or being caused by) the epochal emergence of a new form of human society – globality. *Finally*, in order for the real nature of social change in this period to be understood, the 'vacuum' must be reinterpreted as a 'conjunctural' moment in a longer socio-historical process of uneven and combined development set in train by the emergence and continued expansion of capitalist society. Changes attributed by others to contemporary globalization are better understood by reference to pre-existing forces and events that are explainable by the mainstream of existing social theory, especially that of Marx and Trotsky.

This is good polemic and provocative social science. However, the constituency Rosenberg brackets as globalization theorists – those who wish to treat globalization as the *explanans* of social change – is of an altogether more cautious frame of mind than he suggests, although he treats their caution as mere obfuscation. These writers are not only more cautious in their support of a historical, multi-layered and multidimensional process but more agnostic on causality than he allows. Such caution should be applauded. Unless we are willing to specify invariant relationships between notionally independent and notionally dependent variables (and Rosenberg is not), the course of social change is the outcome of reflexive and sometimes recursive relationships between agents and the conditions for action; in other words, agents are influenced by the conditions in which they act. In turn, their actions either reproduce or modify those conditions. Possible outcomes of such relationships include unintended as well as intended consequences. Uncovering complex relationality, not invariant relationships between agents and structures, should be the guiding principle of all social research. The idea of globalization simply being either a cause or an effect is severely qualified by this insight.

Rosenberg's argument tries to rule out the idea of globalization as a structural phenomenon in its own right and treats it more as a contingent feature of the emergence and contested expansion of capitalist society on a world scale. Writing in 2007, some two years after this argument was published, he opined that while it is entirely permissible to use globalization as a descriptive category which catalogues variable, even intensifying, processes of interconnection, its would-be theorists have failed to meet the three basic intellectual requirements needed to confirm it as an explanatory concept. The first is that, for all the sound and fury around the idea, it lacks clear definition (2007, 417). The second is that any such definition must be able to yield a plausible hypothesis about the causal significance of the empirical phenomena used to 'identify' globalization (for example, the undoing of sovereignty as the organizational principle of the modern world order). Finally, the hypothesis must be tested in actual circumstances and provide 'concrete historical explanation' when set against rival explanations of the same phenomena (Axford, 2007a).

Rosenberg's critique amounts to more than just taking a side-swipe at hyper-globalizers and transformationalists on the way to a Marxist theory of social change. By lambasting globalization theory for being much too ambiguous or elliptical he opens up a proper debate about its definitional status, about what exactly is to be studied and to what ends. Well and good; as John Ruggie notes (1998, 2), what we cannot describe, we cannot hope to explain. And there is no doubt that some globalization scholarship has subsisted on casual definitions of globalization as a process, principally by relying on what Rosenberg calls 'the usual associations' (2007, 417) – interconnectedness, supra-territoriality, space-time compression and, of course, their presumed consequence, the demise or 'transformation' of the territorial state.

Now, imperfect or underspecified concepts are not uncommon in a good deal of social science, so why should this be important? Rosenberg links definitional weakness to what he sees as the major failing of globalization scholarship, namely its inability to generate an 'intelligible hypothesis' (2007, 418) that permits concrete historical examination of the facts. He also claims that if there is a globalization hypothesis that follows from plausible, but loose, conceptualization, it is precisely the one which has caused the most problem for globalization scholarship; namely, the future of the state and state system in the current era. So the problem with globalization theory is that, because of the failure to define the concept more precisely and then operationalize it, pretty much anything can be described *as* globalization or ascribed *to* it.

A Rose by Any Other Name?

For students of globalization Rosenberg's critique is a salutary intervention, but it reduces manifest complexity to something more formulaic. For one thing, it is inappropriate to define a phenomenon in terms of its (presumed) effects rather than its properties; and to say that globalization *is* the demise of the state does mistake cause for effect. In addition, a focus on the state and its future still reflects the concerns of traditional realist and neo-realist theory. While this focus is echoed in other scholarship and remains crucial to any considered examination of global trends, it is essential to question whether studying globalization need be quite so state-centric. There are many ways to analyse the relationships between states and globalization and only one of these assumes that globalization theory *needs*, indeed has to be defined *as*, the disappearance of the national scale in general and the state in particular (Brenner, 2004, 61; Beck and Sznaider, 2006). But does conceptual permissiveness aid or detract from scholarship on the global? In what follows we will examine the ways in which actual usage even approximates Rosenberg's three requirements for good globalization research.

Globalization, globalism or globality: One out of three or three in one?

If globalization is a 'keyword' (Williams, 1978) then it is one with different connotations for different theorists and activists. So far, so obvious; but the ramifications of this point are important because, as Rosenberg says, if we cannot identify and define what we are studying how can we lay claims to knowledge, let alone construct good theory? A sensible caution; but in one key respect it is not one that informs his own analysis.

At least part of the problem with Rosenberg's critique of globalization theory is that he fails to distinguish between, or else is happy to conflate, three global concepts: *globalization*, *globalism* and *globality*. We have to separate these uses the better to understand the differences between *normative/ideological* engagements with globalization – often through issues such as global justice, global governance and cosmopolitanism, or else as an apology for particular kinds of globalization – and *empirical/analytic* applications, which either use the concept as a simple, geographical term denoting 'world-wide' connection, or cleave to a more systemic and systematic understanding of the global as an 'orienting reference point for the social scientific observer'(Beck and Sznaider, 2006, 4). Too often there is not enough reflection on the tensions between normative and explanatory accounts (Browning, 2005). To guard against any conflation we must elaborate the conceptual terminology in which *globalization* is taken *as* process, *globalism as* ideology and *globality as* state of affairs, condition, consciousness or frame of reference (Keohane and Nye, 2000). Each of the terms has semantic and methodological implications (Schafer, 2007).

Globalization as process

Words ending in the suffix 'ization' denote a process; that is, change over time; but what sort of process? Even an informal conspectus reveals that 'globalization' is employed in different ways. These range from a sense of epochal change in train (Albrow, 1996) or the unfolding of a teleology (Fukuyama, 1992; 1996), through description of a 'series of connected developments unfolding in programmatic coordination' (Modelski et al., 2008, 13), to more middle-range usage on the 'complex manifestation of global processes within particular social realms', including religion, health, sexuality and sport (Giulianotti and Roberston, 2009, xiii).

Wolf Schafer helpfully identifies uses of the concept in which it is either transitive, that is, describing a relation between a subject and an object, or intransitive, where no such relation or action is implied (2007). In globalization research both uses are apparent, particularly the first. Thus globalization can be taken as a process which imposes itself on, or affects, an object; as in 'globalization compresses the world', where globalization is the agent or cause of change; and as a process without a subject or agent, as in 'the world globalized intensively in the 1990s'. It is clear that while both uses require empirical referents, the former implies a causal or at least a subject–object relationship, while the latter does not make globalization the agent of change.

In fact, as Schafer also points out, globalization is ambi-transitive, in that globalization processes, or at least the actors and institutions driving them, possess agency, and can also occur without a subject imposing them (2007, 5). But the second usage gives us no real sense of agency, context or history and its only value may be to defuse ideological or polemical claims about the provenance and effects of globalizing processes, but at the cost of having to rely on an anodyne and agent-less account of social change. Such positions have to be set aside to understand ways in which different forms of globality may, or may not, be linked directly to, or caused by, globalization processes.

But is globalization as process just another, more intense form of internationalization or transnationalization, or can it be subsumed under what George Ritzer calls 'related processes' (2010, 64–106)? If it can, does taking the concept to mean no more than, say, liberalization or Westernization – typically Americanization – dilute or negate its analytical novelty and its explanatory worth (Scholte, 2008)? Certainly the willingness to subsume the concept in, or else conflate it with, cognate processes is a feature of much writing on globalization. Ritzer (2010) identifies six 'related processes' and their seeming antitheses: imperialism, colonialism (and post-colonialism), development (and dependency), Westernization (plus post-Westernization), Easternization and Americanization (along with anti-Americanization). His conclusion is that it is important to distinguish globalization from any and all of these look-alikes, but adds that it remains a messy truth that there are 'strong overlaps among and between them' (2010, 79). Elements of previous periods of imperialism and colonialism survive into the current era of globalization, most obviously in the guise of liberal economic thinking and practices, while Americanization remains a global cultural force for all the talk of hegemonic decline.

At the same time Ritzer talks about getting to grips with the 'fundamental nature of globalization' (2010, 80), which suggests a definitional core. Thus all related processes are deemed part of a larger process of globalization, and being able to subsume them under it turns on the notion that, when compared with any of these other processes, globalization 'consists of multi-directional flows, with no single point of geographic origin' (82). In other words it is a decentred process, not reliant or less 'focused' on the territorial state and transplanetary in scope (Sassen, 2006; 2007; Appadurai, 2006; Scholte, 2005b).

Ritzer's main body of work is hardly a celebration of globalization (2004; 2012) but it adheres to the intuitively plausible, yet allusive definition which critics find so frustrating (Rosenberg, 2000; 2005). With some approbation Ritzer quotes John Tomlinson's statement that globalization is a 'complex, accelerating, integrating process of global connectivity . . . [a] rapidly developing and ever densening network of interconnections and interdependencies' (Tomlinson, 2007, 352). The sense of globalization as intensive and extensive connectivity is widespread and can be found in work with quite different theoretical and ideological pretensions. Scholte's account of globalization as supra-territoriality is a prominent example (2005a; Held et al., 1999), while Hardt and Negri's treatise on 'Empire' (2000) and Manuel Castells' epic trilogy on 'The Information Age' (2000a; 2000b; 2004a) both offer the image of a networked, decentred and de-territorialized world of capitalism as a rejection of orthodox Marxism and state-centric models of IPE.

All these models rely heavily on the notions of connectivity or institution-alization as key processes, depicting globalization as a form of intensified and increasingly extensive exchange and/or a process involving the diffusion of world-wide institutional rules and standards or cultural scripts. In their examination of globalization as an evolutionary process of global change, George Modelski and his colleagues (2008) also trade on the idea that globalization implies the emergence of institutions and networks of planetary scope and which is multidimensional in character. In their scholarship, evolutionary processes take humanity as a whole as the unit of analysis, rather than societies, and social evolution is not a 'unitary phenomenon' but a 'cascade of processes' – economic, political, cultural and so on – which are 'closely and systematically related' (2008, 421).

The same volume draws on scholarship from the social and natural sciences, as well as history as a discipline and in Modelski's own contribution there is a strong flavour of world-systems analysis and Darwinism (2008, ch. 2). He sees globalization as an evolutionary process of the world-system driven by 'Darwinian-type' mechanisms of search and selection that act on all humankind and produce institutional change of global reach. These processes are periodic and not cyclical as is the case in Wallerstein's world-systems analysis, and each period delivers its own social dynamics and trajectories. Because of the variable nature and impact of different kinds of social and technical innovation, these are not always predicated closely on what happened previously.

The virtue in this still rather abstract account is that it offers a diachronic view of globalization; seeing it as a process in time, a historical process; one which draws on the history of humanity and tries to identify the key factors contributing to change of global proportions, whether via urbanization, technical innovation or political reform. Against it is a formidable array of scholarship which supports the prescription for diachronic analysis and the idea of globalization as a set of processes rather than a singular process, but objects either that globalization does not conform to the requisites of evolutionary theory (Giddens, 1984, 238–9; 1999; by inference, Popper, 2002) or that the whole thing smacks too much of functionalist reasoning applied to the emergence and survival of social systems of global scope (Axford, 1995). In fact, Modelski is critical of older and more ideological theories of modernization as a form of social evolution because they impart a peculiarly functionalist and Western feel to the idea of societal development (see Parsons, 1966; Eisenstadt, 1987; Fukuyama, 1992; 1996). Both modernization theory and Marxism share a theoretical commitment to social and societal evolution (Gouldner, 1978).

But all evolutionary theory, even strong teleology, accommodates some contingency. Francis Fukuyama's (1992) version of Hegelian universal history, mediated through the writings of Alexandre Kojève and Friedrich Nietzsche, is clearly a directional theory of social change. But here too the teleological burden of the argument is moderated, because the march of history displays not smooth, but punctuated evolution. Even when the denouement is the prescribed triumph of liberal democracy on a world scale, progress towards it remains contingent (Gouldner, 1978; Fukuyama, 2011; Wendt, 2003). Fukuyama's picture of the 'end of History' has it as no more than a prolonged interlude that may carry with it the seeds of further change, even degeneration. Meanwhile, complexity models of globalization as process are quite happy to talk about it as being irreversible, but also unpredictable and chaotic (Urry, 2003, 138).

Anthony Giddens' disjunctive theory of global change, which is aggressively non-functionalist, is also very condemnatory of evolutionary theory. In evolutionist accounts, says Giddens, complex histories become simplified stories that can be told only through a grand narrative of historical change (1990, 5; Wright, 1989). Instead, he draws a sharp distinction between traditional and modern societies. This turns, in large measure, on his depiction of modernity as a period of extreme contingency and doubt, the nemesis of pre-existing world-views and social practice. Indeed, a sense of species insecurity stands as the most prominent marker between pre-modern and non-global globality and modern globality.

For Giddens, globalization is a modern phenomenon, producing a 'history [with] a quite different stamp from anything that has gone before' (1984,

238–9). In his account, two key dimensions of modernity appear as synonyms for globalization. The first is the idea of 'space-time distanciation', which refers to the complex relations between embodied co-presence and interactions across distance (the connection of presence and absence) in which immediacy and the conditions for intimacy are transformed. In the modern era, the degree of time-space distanciation is much greater than in any previous period, to the point of extreme disjunction. Accordingly, the relations between local and distant social forms, actors and events become stretched, producing social relationships 'disembedded' from particular contexts, his second feature (Giddens, 1990). The 'stepping out' of time characteristic of space-time distanciation uncouples social relations from local contexts of interaction and 'stretches' them across much larger spans of time and space. The internet and its increasingly routine use in everyday life are a seminal illustration of these features of modernity, even though, as Saskia Sassen has pointed out, digital connectivity also facilitates the reinvention of locality and local or particular identities (2008).

Giddens would strongly disavow that his theory of social change bears any of the hallmarks of evolutionary theory. Unlike the work of Karl Marx, where evolutionary change is always driven by a trans-historical dialectic – the immanent contradiction between forces and relations of production in class-divided societies – the shift from societies characterized by low space-time distanciation to ones displaying a high incidence obeys no general principle of historical change (Wright, 1989). Instead, Giddens insists that the movement from one social form to another is based on factors specific to the transition in question (Wellman, 2008; Axford and Huggins, 2010; Tomlinson, 2007). But the dynamics of change, what others might call the motors of social evolution can manifest in any sphere of life – material, cultural, political – because each is autonomous. As Erik Olin Wright notes of Giddens' argument, ' [w]hile in specific historical cases one might be justified in saying that one or other of these constitutes the central locus of impulses for social change, there is no general priority of one over the other and their interconnection is best characterized as historically specific and contingent' (1989, 98).

Modelski's depiction of globalization as an evolutionary process further distinguishes between institutional and connectivist processes. Institutional processes point up the organizational dynamics of change, while connectivist ones privilege spatio-temporal factors. Modelski favours an institutionalist analysis of evolutionary change and identifies four institutional processes – the evolution of the global economy, global political evolution, the rise of a global community and, somewhat confusingly, globalization itself – whose interaction permits institutional innovation and thus change (2008, 20–8). Connectivist positions could be mistaken for purely descriptive statements about links between actors previously separated and insulated by space and time. But such a disarmingly simple treatment is often just the starting point for empirical investigations that explore the impact of connectivity on social relations and social forms and thus offer (the beginnings of) a theory of social change.

Of the two approaches, it is connectivist accounts which most inform the treatment of globalization as process, although we can point to evolutionary models of global institutionalization and, of course, world polity models of global cultural structures (Harvey, 1989; Dicken et al., 2001; Wallerstein, 1979; Sassen, 2007; Tomlinson, 2006; Hardt and Negri, 2004; Castells, 2000a). For John Tomlinson globalization is 'quite simply' a description of networks and flows and their implications for social ontology. These implications reside in the various flows of capital, people, images, knowledge, crime, disease, fashions and beliefs that traverse national boundaries. For all its apparent descriptive breadth, this is a quite modest claim, although any explanatory clout is couched in the detail of just how significant such 'implications' can be.

In fact, institutionalization and connectivism are not mutually exclusive. In the sophisticated transformationalist argument deployed by David Held and his colleagues (1999; Held and McGrew, 2007), globalization is revealed as a set of processes that extend, intensify and speed up flows and connections. But to avoid any sense that process somehow floats free of structures and of context, these authors also describe connectivity as grounded in organizational and institutional arrangements – global norms, epistemic communities and governance regimes – which monitor, regulate and otherwise manage the connections, movements and flows. And hard indicators that identify and codify trends and processes are crucial to the social science of globalization as an empirical-analytical enterprise. At the same time, if the science of globalization stops at description it remains a workaday concept, hardly fitted for Rosenberg's explanatory task.

Axial features and types of globalization process   The idea of globalization as process usually decants into a consideration of its axial features that, in turn, permits examination of types of globalization. Modelski gives us a glimpse of some of these axial features. He describes a multidimensional process involving the expansion of world commerce and capital movements; political globalization ranging over institutional innovations, from imperial forms of rule to democratic national and inter-/supra-national institutions; the rise of transnational social and political movements; world-wide cultural trends; and the emergence of a sense of world-wide community and public opinion. These processes have not played out over the same historical time span, nor do they move along identical trajectories, but together they provide what Modelski calls a 'process structure' (1990, 14) which is leading to a new 'level' of world organization. With some variations in the sort of timescales envisaged, the same features are rehearsed in most literatures on globalization, so that in principle it should be possible to map historically the emerging characteristics of a globalized world and to examine its relational, even its systemic qualities (Axford, 1995).

Typologies of globalization are usually attempts to offer a more descriptively fine-grained account of axial features in what might otherwise appear as an amorphous, even a monolithic, process. Leslie Sklair differentiates between three competing approaches to globalization as an intellectual and a strategic project (2007): internationalist, transnationalist and globalist perspectives, with the second preferred both on theoretical/methodological grounds and – because it depicts a contested and pluralistic world-historical project – as a normative position. He further distinguishes between generic globalization, capitalist globalization and alternative globalizations, and these categories display different forms of *transnational practice*, which, for him, is the definitive global process.

Generic globalization should not be conflated with or definitionally subsumed under capitalist globalization. Undoubtedly, says Sklair, capitalist globalization is the 'dominant global system at the start of the 21st century', but generic globalization processes – the revolution in electronic communication, what he calls the 'post-colonial moment', the emergence of transnational social spaces and the beginning of new forms of cosmopolitan practice – have much greater emancipatory potential for excluded or marginalized groups. These generic elements are producing irreversible dynamics that may be a facet of capitalist expansion, but also move to autonomous logics and are susceptible to intervention by counter-cultural and counter-hegemonic forces. The final category of 'alternative globalizations' is a derivative and/or normative trope allowing the author to introduce the possibility of anti- or non-capitalist paths to globality, especially that of socialism (2007). Bearing in mind that it is often hard to separate social-scientific endeavour from the ways in which ideology frames scholarship, it is to the latter accounts that we now turn.

Globalism as ideology

Rosenberg casts most globalization theory as either ideological or normative. While this claim can be challenged, there is no doubt that some of those he brackets as 'globalists' do traffic an ideological/normative stance or worldview which justifies or seeks to undermine the existing world order (Mittelman, 2004; Browning, 2005). Ideology is a type of normative statement, in that norms as prescribed rules can be given focus and direction through an ideology that expresses a coherent vision for how things should be organized (Browning, 2005, 196). Ideologies may claim to be forensic as well as programmatic: the new order will replace the disreputable old order and be measurably better, more efficient, and so on. According to Manfred Steger (2002; 2005a; 2007) globalism is a new ideological configuration, challenging the main categories of thought in use for the past two centuries, including statism and the organizational principle of territoriality.

The truth is that much criticism of contemporary globalism, as well as a modicum of praise, follows from its ideological provenance in the doctrine of economic liberalism and its quotidian successes in the late twentieth century. Some of the most popular globalist beliefs of the twentieth century can be seen in the vibrant apologies for free market capitalism found, for example, in the work of Thomas Friedman (1999; 2005; Ohmae, 1990; 2001; Bhagwati, 2005; Wolf, 2004), of which more later. But globalist views are not confined to the ranks of market liberalizers (including neo-liberals) and neo-conservative libertarians.

In addition to market globalism there is also *justice globalism*, based on egalitarian ideals, global solidarity and distributive justice, and *jihadist globalism*, mobilized in defence of allegedly Islamic virtues seen as under threat from the first two variants (Steger, 2009, 30). Particular values and meanings, as well as prescriptions for different global futures, appear too in the self-styled post-Marxist treatment of empire (globalization) elaborated by Hardt and Negri (2000; 2004; 2009), in Manuel Castells' general approbation of information capitalism (2000a; 2000b; 2008) and in a tranche of writing which musters under the global governance or cosmopolitan motif, including some dalliance with the prospects for and desirability of global society (Beck, 2006; 2005; Held, 2010; Keane, 2003; Falk, 2002; 2005).

These ideologies embrace quite different 'truths' about globalization. James Mittelman notes that, depending where you stand in the hierarchies of power and privilege, 'globalization is ([either] an ideology of freedom for expanding not only the world's bounty, but also human potential', or an ideology of domination (2004, 47), and this is a recurring antinomy in scholarship. Both Hardt and Negri and Castells can be seen as celebrants of globalization. Each account has different theoretical and ideological projects in mind but they share a concern to move beyond orthodox Marxism, without fully jettisoning Marx.

In Hardt and Negri's earliest formulation, empire constitutes a potentially liberating force because it de-territorializes the 'previous structures of exploitation and power' (2000, 52). The rise of a world market and the diffusion of economic and political power into myriad networks also make it easier to mobilize and express the oppositional and emancipatory energy of the 'multitude', which is a look-alike for global civil society. Inevitably, some critics see the idea of a global 'multitude' as a lamentably under-specified concept, a utopian solution to the regressive features of globalization, or just a prime example of wishful thinking. In a review of the third volume in the empire trilogy, entitled *Commonwealth* (2009), John Gray dismisses their intervention as 'radical theory in the idiom of Monty Python' (Gray, 2009; Munck, 2007). But for all their faults, Hardt and Negri offer an intriguing picture of a post-national, post-imperialist and postmodern empire – a smooth, networked world of diffuse power – which is at some conceptual distance from more conventional treatments of imperial power, even though the coherence of their empire is guaranteed by the continued hegemony of the USA (Gill, 2009; Ferguson, 2004). The theme of hegemonic shift and predictions of new constellations of financial, economic, military and cultural power inform both empirical and ideological accounts of contemporary globalization. The influence of the latter, as Mittelman says, stands as an important register of the still contested agendas of globalization (2004, 48).

At the heart of these contested agendas lie the ideology and practices of neo-liberalism, for some synonymous with late twentieth-century globalization (Mittelman, 2004). Manfred Steger writes that when coupled with markets, neo-liberalism stands as the core ideological concept of globalization (2005a, 16; 2007; Klein, 2007; Callinicos, 2010). And in a critical paper, David Harvey labels neo-liberalism a 'grand narrative', with its intellectual provenance in the doctrines of classical liberalism and writers such as John Locke and Adam Smith (Harvey, 2005a; 2005b) and its practice exemplified by what Naomi Klein calls the 'shock doctrine' (2007) of market economics visited on some African, South American and Asian economies, and on newly independent states spilled from the Soviet world-empire after 1989. Echoes of this shock doctrine can be heard in the rescue package for the Greek, Irish and Portuguese economies put together by Eurozone countries and the International Monetary Fund (IMF) in 2010, 2011 and 2012, although this pattern of intervention is also held up as the end of pristine neo-liberalism (Callinicos, 2010).

The main tenets of the faith combine liberalism's championing of individual liberty with the ideals of free market philosophy and economics. Neo-liberalism, often cast as the libertarian version of liberalism, has its immediate intellectual roots in the work of Austrian School theorists such as Friedrich von Hayek (1944) and Ludwig von Mises (1963 [1919]) and North American intellectuals such as James Buchanan (1969) and Robert Nozick (1974). It owed its popularity to the development of this corpus by Chicago School economists such as Milton Friedman. Both Hayek and Friedman looked to free economic theory and policy delivery from what they saw as the stifling impact of Keynesian thought translated into public policy. Following the Great Depression of the 1930s, liberal ideas were deemed in need of resuscitation to combat what was seen as an excessive and stultifying pattern of state interventionism in domestic economies, and to refute the ideology of collectivism that had not only compromised market relations but eroded the boundaries between private and public domains.

By the 1980s, free market principles were being endorsed by such as Margaret Thatcher and Ronald Reagan, whose conservative administrations applied neo-liberal tenets – open markets, deregulation of economic activity and faith in the self-regulating market – to many aspects of policy in the core states of Britain and the USA. Economic theory and principle soon became the established political creed and its supporters notable for their proselytizing zeal. The institutionalization of neo-liberal doctrine as a world economic script then proceeded through the agency of 'global' bodies such as the World Bank and the IMF. Along with the USA, these organizations touted neo-liberalism as the exemplary route to modernization for other countries, particularly those deemed to be in a 'transitional' condition. What emerged was generally bruited as the 'Washington Consensus', a belief in 'unimpeded private market forces [as] the driving engines of growth' (Williamson, 1989, 1243). Thus was fashioned the most controversial globalist dogma, namely that 'there is no alternative' to liberal globalization.

In a rather downbeat classification Mittelman labels these positions as 'centrist neo-liberal thinking' (2004, 50), but the ideological orthodoxy they espoused has been subject to increasing challenge intellectually and, both metaphorically and physically, on the streets. From within the liberal canon, reformist globalizers such as Joseph Stiglitz (2002; 2006), Dani Rodrik (1997), Paul Krugman (2007; 1996) and Jeffrey Sachs (1997) have all pointed to its failures and debilitating impact on those whose economic performance it was meant to burnish. But, while reformist globalizers are acerbic critics of neo-liberal globalization, their concern is often couched in a basically sympathetic critique, counselling less dogmatism, more attention to local conditions and some adjustment of policies – more debt relief, less structural adjustment or conditionality – rather than a wholesale abandonment of the idea of global economic integration through markets. Even quite radical positions sometimes do little more than prescribe humanizing or democratizing economic governance as a way of 'taming' neo-liberal globalization (Khor, 2001). Of course, other critical positions are more inclined to uncouple, rather than just loosen, the path of globalization, even capitalist globalization per se, from the particular engines of neo-liberal ideology and policy. Until recently, these have tended to inhabit activist discourses and inform more strategic interventions (Marcos, 2009).

The neo-liberal heyday, from the early 1980s through the 1990s, represented 'a remarkable ideological achievement' (Steger, 2005b, 41) in that its proponents were able to marry an ostensibly new and progressive idea – globalization – to older prescriptions about free markets and limited states, and have the latter taken as the apogee of the former. For example, in *The Lexus and the Olive Tree* (1999) and *The World Is Flat* (2005), journalist Thomas Friedman set out what 'may be the most comprehensive, widely read defence of neo-liberal globalization' (Antonio, 2007, 67). In summary, he charts and applauds the emergence of a 'flat world', that is, one in which there are fewer and fewer barriers to free trade, communication and pretty much everything else associated with economic exchange across borders, as well as with a good many social and cultural transactions.

Some critics see an ideological continuity rather than a rupture between Friedman's market (neo-liberal) globalization and a new form of 'imperial globalization' that emerged in the early 2000s (Steger, 2005b, 41; see also

Callinicos, 2009). And it is possible to accommodate this view under a broadly functionalist view of social change, whereby American neo-conservatism in foreign policy introduced a more obviously geo-political edge to global liberalism, but still parades as its functional equivalent in the playing out of the basically ideological agenda of capitalist globalization. The neo-conservative moment in US economic and security governance and the fallout from the 2008 financial crisis perhaps muster as increments in the demise, or possibly the transformation, of global neo-liberalism. They certainly underline the increasing importance of military-security, as opposed to purely economic, factors in the debates on globalization. Alternative globalist ideologies out of Marxism or ethical cosmopolitanism attest to the sporadic vitality of different genres, but, arguably, fail to find any real purchase outside the academy.

In the pantheon of globalisms, market liberalism begets imperial globalism, which begets either the trope of empire, some form of countervailing transnationalism or maybe even cosmopolis (Gills, 2005). Admittedly this is a very schematic way to compress the complex processes of globalization and the ideological agendas of globalism referred to above, but it does have the merit of drawing attention to the resilience of ideas and normative prescription as sources of physical and intellectual conflict. As James Mittelman notes: these days as ideological consensus is everywhere contested and weakening, the room for conflict about the ends of all ideological discourse continues to expand (2004, 54).

Globality as consciousness or system

Globalisms tend to utopias by default, and while rival claims may contest whether globalization is progressive or regressive, the denouement is always prefigured either in the dogma itself, or in the implied logic of various empirical processes. Herein lies the difficulty for attempts to build explanatory accounts of global change. By and large, critical globalization scholarship has been trying to disengage from the idea of globalism as teleology, or globality as simply the outcome of one or many linear processes of globalization. Critical treatments of globalization focus instead on the socially constructed nature of globalization and of globality (Bartelson, 2009a) and such an approach certainly avoids the mistake of signalling or prescribing a determinate outcome, but at what analytical cost? At the same time, constructivist research tells us that social constructions can appear immutable and have powerful effects on consciousness and behaviour. But should a theory of globality produce a more robust ontology, one less reliant on the forces of contingency and subjectivity?

This is a pertinent question, since the social ontology of globality is still a relatively uncharted domain. Because of this, various questions arise: is it (or are they, if one concedes the possibility of multiple globalities) *sui generis*, not only distinct, but unencumbered by or ontologically separate from the state system and territoriality, as well as from modernity (Albrow, 1996)? Does globality reveal systemic qualities, and if so, in what ways do these modify a constructionist stance? Is globality really *glocality*, an imbrication of scales and a negotiated or enacted condition? Finally, does globality subsist only as consciousness or are there harder material indicators?

Words that end in 'ity' refer to a condition, a distinctive mode of existence or state of being. The concept of globality today is commonly used to denote the emergence of a single socio-political space on a planetary scale. While this sounds monolithic, implying universality, systematic integration and world-wide reach, it could be viewed in a more permissive light, with globality seen as a possible outcome, an immanent potential, or just reflecting a less demanding definition of global systemness (Axford, 1995, 86–93). To make empirical sense of the concept, much scholarship on contemporary globaliza-tion depicts globality as the outcome of processes that effectively transcend the international system, thus making it ontologically distinct.

Jan Aart Scholte, (2000; 2005a; 2005b) falls into this camp, of course, and offers a strong position on the ontological distinctiveness of globalization, but more 'middle-range' positions have become increasingly popular as the force of grander narratives of globalization decline. For example, John Ruggie (2004) sees the new global public domain not as coterminous with the inter-national system, but existing in 'transnational, non-territorial, spatial forma-tions and anchored in norms and expectations as well as institutional networks and circuits within, across and beyond states' (2004, 519). Similar treatments on the interaction of local and global can be found in the work of Sassen (2006; 2008) and Robertson (1992; 2009) although these accounts, and especially that of Sassen, actually qualify the idea of globality as *sui generis* without ever reducing it to a condition which originates just in the interna-tional system.

All this still seems quite elliptical, so what are we talking about? Let's return to what seem to be the key features of globality, which reside in both practices and consciousness (Shaw, 2000) before examining whether it is helpful to talk about it as a system (Bartelson, 2009a). What are the referents? The idea that globality resides in 'thick economic, political and cultural interconnections and global flows that make currently existing political borders and economic barriers irrelevant' is entirely plausible (though why not 'thin' too?) (Steger, 2005a, 13). But that definition seems merely to reprise common descriptors of globalization processes, albeit with the 'social condition(s)' they prefigure being legion. Moreover, Steger wants to eschew any sense that these 'thick' interconnections are precipitating a determinate outcome. Rather, there are many possible outcomes, presumably many poten-tial globalities, which might, for example, secure the completion of global capitalism or a world order built around alternative ideals.

Now, process and change are indelibly linked even if we reject determin-ism, and, this far into our study, there is less reason to quibble about the analytical usefulness of some built-in contingency that allows for the possibility of different worlds. However, the emphasis on process and potential variety still does not allow us to distinguish globalization from globality. Scholte essays a distinction when he declares the definitive features of globality to be 'transworld simultaneity and instantaneity' (2003, 88) – in other words the realization of a single world space, by way of supra-territoriality. As he opines, there can be no doubt that this is, or would be, a new 'social geography', most obviously when set against the resolute ontology of the international system.

Martin Shaw (2000; 2003) provides more than just a spatial definition for globality. For him it comprises a 'transformation of the spatial content of social relations'. In other words, global clearly means 'worldwide' and thus is 'primarily a spatial reference to the world as a whole and social processes which intensify worldwide linkages' (2000, 62). But it is more than a simple spatial referent or one entirely reliant on 'mechanical interconnectedness'. Rather, globality has social as well as spatial meaning. Above all, it is a matter of consciousness and constitutes a 'self-consciously common framework of human society worldwide' (2000, 62). As Shaw notes, such views are not unique to his conception of globality. They are prefigured to some extent in the universalist claims of both religious and, in the case of cosmopolitanism, secular world-views. The idea of a 'common framework' is given substance in, for example, the cooperative responses of political elites to the threats of planetary destruction, while a more 'practical consciousness' also resides in the existence of the widespread perception that we are all subject to global constraints as a matter of routine. Of course, for Shaw, military and geopolitical considerations rather than, or as well as, economic factors contributed to a more systematic global consciousness by the end of the twentieth century, and this shift in consciousness has been profound enough to constitute a global social revolution, even if it is unfinished.

Should this increasingly modal global consciousness be seen as a purely contemporary phenomenon? Shaw's idea of a social revolution privileges globality as a break with the immediate past – with modernity – although he is at pains to point out that the 'rupture' still leaves globality 'enmeshed' in older social forms and practices; which may be equivocation. At the same time, Robertson and Inglis argue that notions of globality – 'where the world is taken as a whole, where all parts of the global are seen as increasingly interconnected and where individual experience is connected to worldwide forces and circumstances' (2004, 173) – were extant in the Graeco-Roman world, some two millennia ago, even if the sense of 'worldwide' then did not mean planetary, as it does today. These positions may not be as incompatible as they seem. What they underscore is that different conceptualizations of the global are tied to particular historical moments or periods, so that while the character of *global* as denoting 'worldwide' consciousness and practices remains the same, particular conceptions and configurations of it, as well as the forces driving them, can change. Thus, global mentality – a sense of the global, if you will – as well as structures, might actually pre-date and even prefigure modernity, while the 'unfinished revolution' bruited by Shaw could still deliver further transformation.

In a sense this is an empirical argument: how much and how fast are things changing, in what direction(s) and with what consequences? But it is also a matter of conceptualization and the inferences that may be drawn from particular conceptualizations. Take the idea of globality as global consciousness. Is this primarily a kind of empathy, whereby all members of the human race have a built-in capacity and predilection for social cooperation, or does it simply refer to an awareness of global constraints, which may trigger quite different sentiments and mobilize very different politics? There is also the core ontology of the concept to consider.

Shaw defines the global as a 'common consciousness of human society on a world scale: an increasing awareness of the totality of human social relations as the largest constitutive framework of all relations' (2003, 146). He argues that society is now constituted by this inclusive human framework, rather than by distinct tribes, civilizations, nations or religious communities, although none of these are (yet) precluded as features of the human social condition. Taken at face value this is clearly a new structure of social relations, and this sense emerges too from studies such as *Global Transformations* (Held et al., 1999) that reveal a tension between an essentialized, one-dimensional notion of globalization and the idea of globality as systematic, perhaps systemic. Of course, one might question any conceit that defines a modal condition (globality) as entirely or largely subjective (a matter of consciousness) – and, in doing so, also query the nature and extent of global systemness – by posing the money question: how is a global system possible?

In any social system it is the relationships between social forces (actors) and systemic properties that express the extent and intensity of systemness, and the way they are linked also provides clues to the dynamics of social change. But specifying exactly what is involved here, at least in the sort of detail that would satisfy Justin Rosenberg, remains highly problematic. At the same time it is clearly possible to specify some content, albeit with a degree of abstraction. Echoing structurationist thinking (Axford, 1995), we might understand the constitution of the global system as follows: global structural rules and resources provide an enabling and constraining framework for action. Under global rules the scope for agency is, or may be, enlarged because of the growing complexity of modern life, in which agents are faced not just with a dominant set of structural properties, but with intersecting, overlapping and sometimes contradictory sets, where institutional scripts (national, local, etc.) cross-cut. While this sometimes leads to a sense of powerlessness or triggers profoundly negative sentiments about globalization, often it will result in actors choosing to engage with contested rules to try to fashion alternative outcomes. Global systemness now appears less as a neat functional accommodation between parts of a system and between the system and its environment and more as a negotiated and contingent condition. At the same time, what might otherwise appear simply as the conjunctural impact of, say, market rules, cultural trends and geo-strategic factors, on the consciousness and behaviour of actors, is better understood as a form of mutual constitution. The contexts in which consciousness is generated and the intensity of consciousness vary, but the outcomes underscore what are basically integrative tendencies (globalities) in and across politics, economics and culture.

What are the analytical advantages that follow from distinguishing process from ideology and both from globality as condition or system? In much early and especially hyper-globalist discourse on globalization, the global 'level' was taken for granted and globalization depicted as the force through which non- or sub-global actors accommodate or identify with the global (Urry, 2003). The ideological discourses that often accompany such accounts express powerful, if sometimes naive, support for determinate models of globalization. By contrast, as Jonathan Friedman says, an analytical focus on globality or global systems as a constitutive framework for consciousness and action entails 'a theoretical framework within which the institutional structures of the world are themselves generated and reproduced through global processes' (2006, 138). These institutional structures and processes, as well as the consciousness with which they are linked reflexively, possess qualities of systemness because the totality of global flows, networks, interactions and connections triggers a shift in the organization of human affairs and in ways of thinking about, as well as enacting, social relationships. Of course, for students of globalization, precisely when this shift is held to have taken place, why, and with what effects remain the crucial issues.

Rather confusingly, Friedman also says that global processes are structural (immanent) aspects of all social dynamics, which implies that they have been 'operative throughout history' regardless of any 'shifts', as Justin Rosenberg notes (2007, 418). But the difference between studying globality or global systems and globalization processes seems to be that the former are not the result of a few (recent) decades of intense change, a contemporary and largely economic phenomenon, but the outcomes of historical processes of variable intensity and extensivity, moving to economic, cultural and political forces and their imbrication. As Shaw says (2003), globalization is a necessary but not sufficient condition for globality, and one cannot comprehend the latter by paying attention solely to indicators of the former. He goes on, 'the term globalization carries with it connotations of the inexorable, mechanical spread of market relations' (2003, 176). Globality, on the other hand, is all about 'conscious global-oriented action' in all spheres of life, which makes it the biggest constitutive framework within which social relations takes place, but a framework that is mutable.

Conclusion

Would any of this satisfy Justin Rosenberg and answer his three questions about the intellectual authority or unwitting mendacity of globalization theory? One might argue that there is still too much definitional obfuscation around the concept, despite its alluring and enduring plausibility, and that rigorous methodological globalization still needs clearer specification and operationalization. In particular, work on the complex intermingling and dissolution of geographical scales requires attention to the key concepts of connection and consciousness, their intensity and their extensiveness.

For Rosenberg, this would be just a starting point, since the complex intermingling and dissolution of scales is 'actually a feature of all social formations throughout history', not 'the result of any particular substantive process of globalization' (2007, 419). So, establishing 'methodological globalization' is one thing; generating and demonstrating a 'globalization hypothesis' may be quite another, especially where it implies and sometimes demands that globalization is treated as a causal factor. Rosenberg says that if a globalization hypothesis means anything, it must 'entail the end of bounded entities and therefore must fundamentally qualify sovereignty' (2007, 419). If one accepts at least the first part of that limiting claim, the future for globalization scholarship is quite bleak.

But our discussions to date suggest that tying the authority of globalization scholarship solely to the demise of the state is either too parsimonious or too skewed an enterprise. Similarly, recognizing that intermingling and dissolving geographical scales is a feature of all social formations across time should not assume isomorphism of either process or outcomes – how could it? As such, generating a plausible globalization hypothesis does not turn just on the ontological centrality of the state or on the certainty of its demise. While such a strong hypothesis at least has the merit of being unambiguous, it is a straw man. But we are still left with Rosenberg's final caution on the need to find concrete evidence with which to corroborate any globalization hypothesis when set against rival claims. This caution still makes sound analytical and empirical sense. So his concerns have not been dispatched entirely and are still very useful cautions with which to interrogate globalization scholarship. The playing out of these themes and issues in the context of discipline-based research informs the two chapters to follow.

CHAPTER 2

Theorizing Globalization: Political Science and Sociology

Introduction

We should bear in mind that it is not easy – and may be unhelpful – to differentiate contributions to knowledge precisely on the basis of their disciplinary roots, because the fact is that disciplinary categories are often blurred. At the same time we must be careful not to suborn theoretical diversity either within or between disciplines by insisting that there is a natural or immanent coherence waiting to be discovered. In what follows and in chapter 3, for each discipline and sub-field it will be useful to bear in mind (1) the extent to which the argument is oriented to the global rather than, or as well as, the international or national; (2) the particular qualities of globalization being emphasized; (3) whether it offers a historical approach to the study of globalization; (4) the extent to which globalization is seen as transformative rather than just affirmative of existing social relations and forms; and (5) what it brings to the perennial debates about agency and structure.

Political Science: International Relations and its Variants

In political science and especially in IR the 'strong canonical framing of the international' through the lens of territorial states and bounded societies still makes it difficult to entertain the agency of 'global formations with their multi-scalar character' (Sassen, 2007, 7) and even more so to fashion globalization theory that is not predicated upon the national state and society. Of course, within the discipline there is work that challenges the ontological statism of IR, but far stronger, until recently, has been the largely uncritical acceptance of the centrality of the state, even if we exclude unreconstructed realism (Hay, 2007). In the main this is because territorialist and rationalist explanations remain at the heart of the discipline's attempts to explain world order. But much of the current interest in the prospects for global governance ranges over both territorial and statutory forms and the spread of 'private' institutions of governance, where these comprise a growing number of civil society and corporate actors (Hall, 1999; Cutler, 2003; Bartelson, 2009a; Noortmann and Ryngaert, 2010).

So a more permissive notion of governance also informs IR interpretations of world politics, especially those with a normative agenda. But within the discipline, permissive approaches to forms of non-territorial and non-state governance are of quite recent vintage. In realist guise, state-centred treatments of world politics reify the state as the main actor and the state system as the context for action (Guilhot, 2008; Hay, 2007). In such accounts the core value and enduring dynamic of the international system are the passionately egoistic behaviour of states, whose utilitarian cast largely precludes 'significant cooperation' between them (Wendt, 1994, 384; 2006). At the same time, in neo-realist interpretations of international politics unambiguous lust for power is mitigated by the demands of rational behaviour imposed by the military and economic constraints of the international system of states (Waltz, 1979; Krasner, 1983; Mearsheimer, 1994). In turn, liberal and liberal-institutionalist variants on what makes states cooperate (Haas, 1958; Keohane, 1986) offer more optimistic prognoses on the systemic likelihood of cooperation. But, at root, all varieties of realism and liberalism remain wedded to a neo-utilitarian model of the forces that enable and sustain world order (Ruggie, 1998).

These days, very little survives of the sort of theoretical essentialism that informed early accounts of state behaviour and the dynamics of the international system (Krasner, 1994). The main change has been to challenge the neo-utilitarian canon through recourse to different versions of social constructivism and, in particular, to problematize and 'account for what neo-utilitarianism assumes: the identity and/or interests of actors' (Ruggie, 1998, 4; Katzenstein, 1996). In realist positions, the ontology of the state is taken for granted, but in social constructivist arguments and those influenced by sociological (often neo-Weberian) modifications to Marxist realism during the 1980s, the very concept of the state is deconstructed. Here it appears less as a 'unitary' actor with given preferences, more as an amalgam of interests and identities, a social force whose behaviour owes more to historical and to genetic-cultural factors and managing contingency than its status as an assumed rational actor (Miliband, 1985; Skocpol, 1979; Evans et al., 1985; Mann, 1986; 1996). In IR and, more notably, in IPE, these revisionist tendencies appear under the label of institutionalism or neo-institutionalism. The burgeoning interest in developing a truly historical sociology of international relations also offers modifications to the 'enduring sameness' of realist depictions of international relations (Waltz, 1979).

There are a number of institutionalist positions which all start from the basic assumption that actors follow and are to that extent conditioned by institutions (Hall and Taylor, 1996). Unlike realist accounts of international order, this is quite a systemic formulation, but critically one in which the ontology of actors as purely self-interested is not assumed and where the notion that institutions shape behaviour implies that rules constrain actors, but are capable of being changed by them. This is an altogether more action-centred position and one that also recognizes the power of contingency. Of course, from the standpoint of globalization theory, it is precisely the ways actors engage with institutions and to what effect that remains highly contested. For now, the significance of institutionalist arguments for the study of globalization is that they seem to challenge the aforementioned 'canonical status' of the national by focusing on the changing nature and dynamics of the international system and the part played in it by states and by a more diverse range of actors. Three broad themes are apparent.

The first, commonly known as 'complex interdependence' or increasingly 'IPE', depicts a more complex world order and milieu for resolving conflicts than is countenanced in realist and neo-realist theory (Woods, 2006; Bruff, 2005; *Review of International Political Economy*, 1994; Bruff and Tepe, 2011). International and some transnational processes are identified in which the key actors are not just states but, *inter alia*, non-state actors such as banks, multinational corporations and even markets, at least where the last are institutionalized. John Ruggie's accounts of 'embedded liberalism' (1982; 1993; 1998; 2008) sought to explain the functioning and relative efficiency of markets in terms of the ways those institutions were rooted in social expectations, norms and economic ideas, thereby introducing constructivist tenets to the study of IPE. So, the dynamics of the international system and the international political economy are provided by the interaction of security processes still structured at the level of the state or state alliances, and global or proto-global structures exemplified by the IMF, commodities markets and cross-border networks of political activists. Constructivist political economy departs from purely material (economic) interpretations of global process to privilege ideational, political and, sometimes, cultural factors.

The second strand, which builds on the theme of complex interdependence, develops the concept of international regimes, where this refers to different kinds of institutionalized systems of cooperation in more-or-less specific issue areas. These include climate change, commercial fishing rights in international waters and the assignment of internet domain names. Activity is deemed to be regime governed to the extent that the behaviour of actors conforms to the rules laid down by, or the expectations implicit in, the regime, even where these are not explicitly legally binding. Regime theory also draws attention to the ways in which interdependence, or mutually accepted constraints on action, can arise from market failure, or the threat of it (Keohane, 1986). Certainly this sort of stimulus to cooperative behaviour was apparent (if not fully realized) in the response of the G20 countries to the international banking crisis during 2008–9. Of course, any such cooperation might be seen as no more than an instrumental response to systemic crisis tendencies or pressing contingencies. More expressive solutions to the problems of world order are visible in the 'pooling' of sovereignty characteristic of the European Union (EU) that, in its early days, drew on strands of idealist thinking to justify and prescribe cooperation between nations. They are apparent too in the moral universalism that infuses some brands of cosmopolitan thought.

The question of world order also informs the third strand of institutionalist scholarship. In realist thinking, the threat of domination or hegemonic power on the part of one state and the fear of unbridled anarchy are the engines of cooperative and competitive behaviour between states. By contrast, some institutionalists saw hegemonic power as a source of system stability and a stimulus to cooperation in the shape of international regimes, and here the focus was, and remains, the position of the USA as hegemon. Of course, accounts of the USA as a benign hegemon and facilitator of liberal globalization now look more in tune with the world *c.*1987 than with post-9/11 sensibilities and trends, when America's hard and soft powers seem vitiated (Gilpin, 1987; Cox and Quinn, 2008). While the validity of such claims is open to argument, the point to note is that regardless of actual conditions or ideological slogans, an analytical focus on cyclical, rampant or weakened hegemony is still only a variant of state-centred IR. Exploring the capacity of states – even hegemonic states – to adapt to changes in the circumstances in which they operate still imparts an almost Darwinian and realist feel to discussions about a world where fitness to survive and prosper is held to supply the basic evolutionary logic (Gullick, 2004; Gowan, 2003; 2004). Although the clarion call from IPE during the 1990s was to engineer a new approach and reject old orthodoxies, as students of globalization we might question just how far the debate has moved in terms of the ontological centrality of the state.

Other institutionalist writers are more exercised by the extent to which hegemonies are confirmed or transformed under conditions of globalization (Rupert, 1998; Drainville, 2004; Robinson, 2002). What distinguishes this body of mainly IPE thought is its apparent devotion to the ideological character of globalization as a factor in securing the domination of class-based hegemonies or 'hegemonic blocs' (following Gramsci, 1971; Cox, 1987; Gill, 1995; 2000; Hoogvelt, 1998) whose remit and interests are seen as increasingly transnational rather than just national or local. Of course, the presumption of a dominant or hegemonic capitalist class is a feature of all Marxist writing on class-divided societies. The difference here is that class formation and class structures are global rather than national, and the transnational capitalist class (TNCC) is its expression.

The TNCC is an amorphous category, comprising those who own and control large transnational corporations (TNCs), various professionals (for example, in law, accounting, computing and transport logistics), marketing and media interests and, last but not least, those Sklair calls 'globalizing state or inter-state bureaucrats' (2007, 98; Harris, 2009; van der Pijl, 1984; 1998; Robinson, 2006), a class of officials who, in the cant expression, 'think globally'. This kind of argument also figures in work influenced by sociological research on elites, where the theoretical assumptions and research methods are much less indebted to the tenets of historical materialism (Mills, 2000;

Dahl, 1963; Sklair, 2007; 2002; 2001; 1991). Not only is the TNCC a potent collective agent for enacting various kinds of transnational capitalist practice, but its presumed existence admits the possibility of oppositional, if usually subaltern, agencies in the guise of an emergent global proletariat (Callinicos, 2002) or a global civil society 'multitude' (Hardt and Negri, 2004), whose collective agency intimates a more pluralistic and multi-centric world order.

More sociological reflections on the notion of hegemony, especially when derived from the work of neo-institutionalists such as the Stanford Group (Meyer and Schofer, 2005; Meyer and Jepperson, 2000), point up the continuing significance of powerful states or major corporations in promulgating 'global' liberal rules – world models – such as human rights conventions and rational-legal forms of governance. They also note the influence of international non-governmental organizations (INGOs) (Boli and Thomas, 1999), networks of professionals and scientists, and a host of other non-state actors in creating and sustaining global practices (Ruggie, 2005).

To reiterate; what distinguishes IR approaches to globalization, and what in many respects still defines this field of inquiry, is the continued centrality of the state as an actor in world affairs. The persistence of the international order of sovereign states gives credence to this world-view, so that it remains the elephant in the room in all discussions about the nature and extent of global integration and about the significance of non-state agency. For all that, the main burden of the critiques and modifications canvassed above has been to interrogate the canonical status of state-centrism, and to recognize that state societies always exist within a field of other actors with whom they are in persistent exchange and interaction (Albrow, 1996, 6).

Two broad conclusions are possible; three if one admits the hyper-globalist thesis that the state is in terminal decay. The first is that, for all the wary or committed engagement with institutionalism and forms of constructivism, there has been only limited theoretical advance on neo-realism. What others present as globalization, in IR is always likely to remain a form of internationalization or, in more recently fashionable variants, a peculiarly 'millennial' version of hegemony or imperialism (Hardt and Negri, 2000; *Globalizations*, 2005). The second is to understand that while political science may engage with the notion of transformative change through globalization, it may be that only by drawing on definitional and theoretical insights from other disciplines can its sub-fields really embrace methodological globalization.

Of course, embrace may mean not abjuring the state or the analytical trinity of identities, borders and institutional orders which is the basis of territorial definitions of world order, but contextualizing them in terms of their historicity and exploring the complex intermingling and dissolution of geographical scales. These are features of all social formations throughout history and may be particularly intense and of a particular cast today (Axford, 2007b; Albert et al., 2001; Rosenberg, 2007; Rosenau, 2003; Der Derian and

Shapiro, 1989; Walker, 1992). Embrace may also require what Andrew Linklater identified as the crucial task for critical international theory, namely, 'the practical project of extending community beyond the nation-state' (1999, 171; Edkins and Vaughn-Williams, 2009); which is both a criticism of the limited horizons of conventional IR theory and a normative call to arms (Bartelson, 2009b).

Sociology

Some of the issues that attend a political science of globalization apply to sociology. This discipline too has been wedded to what Sassen describes as the 'closure represented by the nation-state', largely through its own canonical point of reference or object of study: national society (2007, 7). National concepts and national data sets still provide the basis for most sociological research, even where it essays comparative analysis, and the same is true of comparative political science. Social theory derived from the work of Durkheim, Weber, Simmel, Saint-Simon and Comte, as well as Marx, remains the basis for much contemporary sociology and provides ample scope for the study of global relations. But the origin of the crusade against methodological nationalism lies in the more recent perception of sociology as a discipline historically defined and conceptually limited by the idea of national society (Beck, 2006; Chernilo, 2006; Robertson, 2007b; Turner, 2006). What is at issue is the extent to which sociology needs to redefine itself in order to analyse global phenomena. Jens Bartelson says that while sociology might seem well placed to conceptualize society in global rather than national terms, the reality is that it is wrong to assume that national and global society share the same characteristics and – more important – can be examined through the same analytical lens (2009b, 113). This observation resonates throughout what follows.

Critiques of sociology's flaws as regards global theory are themselves contested. The counter-argument is that classical sociology always looked to define 'the social' per se, not just national society. As such, it can address global phenomena without needing to reinvent itself (Turner, 2006). As if to corroborate this argument, in IR there has been a growing engagement with different forms of historical sociology as a self-conscious way of dealing with gaps in conventional theories about the state and the international system. Many students of comparative macro history – that is, the project to create models of social-historical process that will explain change across societies and civilizations (Snyder, 1999) – would call themselves sociologists and be willing to describe their research as a form of historical sociology. With these cautions in mind it is appropriate to identify four main sociological approaches to the study of globalization and an additional, emergent one. Taken together they constitute an attempt to shift the analytical focus of social theory, at least of sociological theory, from the national/societal to a world level of analysis, or else collapse the binary distinction between the two (Boli and Lechner, 2005; Sklair, 1991; Rossi, 2007).

There remain important differences between these approaches which turn on their depiction of the world in its making, on their differing emphasis on agency and structure, and on their understanding of culture as central to the explanatory account. Approximating standard usage (Lechner and Boli, 2005) we can name the approaches as *world-systems analysis*, *world polity theory* and *world culture theory*, sometimes confusingly called *globalization theory*, along with *world society theory* as a fourth category, albeit one rooted in different traditions from, say, the English School of IR theory. The emergent category is Ulrich Beck's *methodological cosmopolitanism*, which, he argues, must supersede methodological globalization as the analytical framework for study of an interconnected world (Beck and Grande, 2007). On a cautionary note, it is also worth noting Saskia Sassen's intriguing aside about looking for the building blocks for the sociology of globalization in 'scholarship that did not have this subject in mind' (2007, xiii).

World-systems analysis

World-systems analysis (WSA) is a generic title for a number of highly developed approaches to the explanation of long-term, large-scale social change which share common ground in their treatment of world history as the emergence of a single (world-)system. They differ as to its origins and sometimes over its essential dynamics. They also provide an intellectual counterpoint to modernization theories once much in vogue in the field of comparative politics and development studies, with their reliance on theories of social evolution, historical directionality and convergence to explain development (or lack of it) in different parts of the world (Parsons, 1966; Eisenstadt, 1987; Huntington, 1996; Fukuyama, 1992; 1996). Born out of the traditions of dependency theory, itself a significant contribution to theorizing unequal global political economy (Frank, 1969a; 1969b) WSA also draws on the microhistorical empiricism and methods found in the *Annales* school of historical research, notably in the work of Fernand Braudel (1979; 1981) to contextualize and underpin what might otherwise appear as a very schematic and abstract formulation of world-historical processes (Arrighi, 2005; Wallerstein, 1974; 1979; Chase-Dunn, 1989; 2007; *Protosociology*, 2004). WSA also retains a polemical feel, and this is important for its engagement as an intellectual contribution and a political project aimed at addressing the institutionalized inequalities of the modern world (Wallerstein, 1993).

The key contribution of WSA to social theory is its insistence that national societies can be analysed only through the ways in which they are linked to and influenced by extra- and trans-societal networks of exchange, called world-systems. Historically there have been two categories of world-system: *world-empires* and *world economies*, and this distinction marks off many forms of historical system from the quintessential *modern world-system* of capitalism, which originated around 1500, although this provenance is contested. In WSA, historical (pre-modern) world-systems in the shape of world-empires were not global in their geographic reach and, because of physical and cultural barriers, had limited exchanges with other such systems. Each world-empire, or mini world-system, possessed a unified and overarching system of rule or set of administrative-legal institutions even though it might exhibit a great deal of cultural and economic variety. Often, strong regional powers were able to achieve dominance over lesser entities to establish imperial tutelage of the kinds seen in imperial Egypt, Rome and China as well as in some lesser empires (Colas, 2007).

By contrast the modern world economy of capitalism has resisted all attempts at closure by a succession of hegemonic powers to become the dominant, indeed the only, world-system of the modern era. Unlike world-empires, a world economy can comprise many states and cultures but only one economic division of labour, and to date that is capitalism. Having spread out from its European core between the sixteenth and nineteenth centuries through the agency of strong or core states and markets, in the twentieth century capitalism reached its geographic limit and economic liberalism attained the status of a global 'geo-culture' with evident, if variable and contested, purchase on all states and regions. There is now a single global capitalist mode of production based on networks of unequal exchange between more-or-less developed states and economies (Wallerstein, 1974; 1979; 1983). The premises and detail of this thesis are challenged even from within the world-systems camp (Chase-Dunn, 1989; 1992; 2007; Modelski et al., 2008), by macro sociologists influenced by Max Weber (Skocpol, 1979) and by more orthodox Marxists intent on rejecting exchange as the basis for analysing capitalist economics (Brenner, 1977). But, for the moment, these criticisms need not detain us.

In WSA, the structural components or 'deep structures' of the world economy comprise a world-wide division of labour in the form of core, semi-peripheral and peripheral economies, an interstate system complete with cyclical hegemonies, the internationalization of capital through a process of commodity production, and commodity chains which link producers and consumers in core and periphery (Dicken et al., 2001). The role of states in this world-wide system of exploiting core and exploited periphery is key to the dynamism of the world-system, and a state's strength or capacity is reflected in its position in the global hierarchy of core, semi-peripheral and peripheral economic zones. Hegemonic states (the United Provinces, Britain – twice – and the USA) prosper, but their dominance is transitory, because no one state, no matter how powerful, can prevent competitors from exploiting possibilities for development and innovation which are either not controlled or poorly managed by the hegemon. As a consequence there is a markedly cyclical quality about the structuration of the world-system, expressed in the idea of global cycles, or long waves as these are sometimes called (Kondratieff, 1979 [1935]; Patomäki, 2006). Long waves were originally conceived as periods of sustained economic expansion followed by periods of stagnation and contraction.

In Wallerstein's account of the modern world-system, ascending and declining hegemonies accompany periods of economic expansion and contraction. As the current crisis (starting in 2007) in global finance and world trade unfolds, the absence of a true hegemon and the tarnished condition of neoliberal ideology are seen as factors propelling the system towards collapse. In this 'period of transition', as Wallerstein has it, the USA is the declining hegemon, but the question of whether either China or India has the all-round capacity, let alone the will, to emerge as the new contender and restabilize the capitalist world-system by inaugurating the next hegemonic cycle remains moot (Arrighi, 2007).

Writing in 1998 during the East Asian financial crisis, but before 9/11, the turmoil of the second Gulf War and the sub-prime mortgage debacle, Wallerstein opined that the current 'ideological celebration of so-called globalization is in reality the swansong of our historical system' (1998, 32). As with all Marxist-influenced accounts of historical change, Wallerstein's world-system of capitalism contains built-in crisis tendencies whose impact is only postponed by contingency and the failure of structural weaknesses and conjunctural factors to coincide at critical moments and thus precipitate world revolution.

There is no doubt that WSA has made significant advances in establishing a truly global frame of analysis (Bergesen, 1990; Wallerstein, 1998; Sanderson, 2005; Robinson, 2011; Modelski, 1988; 1990). Its insistence on a historical social science to be achieved through studying the rise and decline of historical systems is, in itself, a transformative prescription, mainly because it cautions against treating national states and societies as the starting point for social analysis. At the same time it is guilty of promulgating an overly systematized and structurally determined view of the world, which is neglectful of agency, including the agency of states. Wallerstein's particular treatment of states is decidedly realist/utilitarian. States are simply functional sub-units of the world-system of capitalism and it is through their variable capacities and behaviour that the core–periphery hierarchy is reproduced. States are clearly vital to the structuration of the capitalist world-system, but they are subaltern actors; in fact they are simply the transactors and enforcers of unequal commodity exchanges between economic zones. By contrast, in other interpretations of the world political economy one of the main effects of contemporary globalization is argued to be the 'decreasing relevance' of the core–periphery structure (Arrighi, 2005, 33; see Robinson and Harris, 2000; Hardt and Negri, 2000).

One of the consequences of this realist-functionalist model of state behaviour is that there is little room for more voluntarist interpretations of how the world-system is produced and reproduced. So the criticism levelled at realist and neo-realist accounts of the international system also plagues WSA: what is the scope for agency in the process of global integration? In Wallerstein's opus, agency does actually appear in the guise of 'anti-systemic' ideologies and movements that contest the global geo-culture of liberalism and are seen as harbingers of a 'world revolution', or players with some clout in unmasking the cultural hegemony of liberalism (1991; 1993). In a more recent exegesis on the contribution of WSA to understanding globalization, Chase-Dunn and Gills argue that latterly there has been a growth in what they call 'global solidarity' or 'the globalization of resistance' (2005, 53; Chase-Dunn and Boswell, 2000) to counter the intensification of corporate-led, neo-liberal globalization and the allegedly imperialist and anti-democratic cast of post-9/11 world politics (Broad, 2002).

Well and good, but there continues to be a tension between a theoretical position in which agency and culture serve only to underpin the capitalist system by supplying the legitimacy needed for social integration and repro-duction, and an apparently voluntarist treatment of collective agency which in times of crisis may act as a counter-cultural rallying point for local and glocal resistance to such a system. Despite the voluntaristic element, this is still a very reductionist and functionalist treatment of agency and culture, in which the latter is subordinate theoretically and strategically to the deep structures of the world-system, and human agency is left as a residual and reactive category, more often than not constrained by a dominant geo-culture or cultural system of ideas (Archer, 1988; 2007; Axford, 1995; Roudometof and Robertson, 2005; see also the discussion of *civilizational anal-ysis* in chapter 6).

World polity theory

World polity theory places culture at the centre of globalization processes (Boli and Lechner, 2005; Held and Moore, 2008; Lechner, 2009). The world polity perspective owes much to the work of John Meyer and the Stanford Comparative Group, which broke new ground in the 1980s by applying insti-tutionalist thought to sociological thinking about globalization. In contrast to the idea of globalization as a form of intensified exchange – particularly economic exchange – world polity theory emphasizes the socio-cultural char-acter of the global system (Meyer, 2007, 262; Krucken and Drori, 2009). The existence of a world polity is premised on evidence of widespread and growing cultural consciousness of what Meyer calls 'civic virtue' on a world scale. This springs from an awareness of interdependence and shared risk, and thus vul-nerability, when faced with the potential for further outbreaks of 'destructive inhumanity' of the kind that disfigured the past century (Meyer, 2007, 268).

By the end of the twentieth century, so runs the argument, this cultural consciousness translated into a rationalized world institutional and cultural order through the diffusion of universally acceptable models or standards of behaviour in fields such as schooling, accounting, population policy and human rights. Adoption by national states has led to global institutional *isomorphism* in a world still characterized by political and cultural *diversity* as well as by material inequalities across states and regions. In other words, world models now greatly influence national and local policies and practices regardless of the type and even the maturity of the regime in which they are adopted. Meyer also says that adoption of these models as features of a global cultural script impels national states and societies to define themselves, and to be seen by others, as 'virtuous' (2007, 264). While this shift in global consciousness has firm roots in Western and particularly Enlightenment traditions, cultural scripts for what define the good or virtuous society are no longer the preserve of the West; they have become institutionalized across the globe. For example, national education systems espouse common models of enrolment, curriculum development and organization, while common notions of citizenship and individual rights also spread across jurisdictional borders and cultural divides.

Taken overall, there are three main consequences of the adoption of global standards: *first*, as we have noted, national states and societies 'define themselves in standardized and virtuous ways' (Meyer, 2007, 264). As a result, *second*, they are constitutionally committed to progress in the name of 'the people' and espouse notions of public, even universal, good and social progress. This is apparent in economic policy and may be seen in the widespread uptake of first Keynesian and then neo-liberal economics, and is also witnessed in social and cultural fields such as the rights of women, gay people and ethnic minorities. *Third* is the spread of the political culture of individuality, most evident in the globalized politics of rights and extended to health, education, work, welfare and nutritional standards as well as to political equality (Barrett and Kurzman, 2004).

It is easy to see this diffusion as part of a cultural colonization of the rest by the West, mainly by dint of core power influence. But Meyer is at pains to point out that core and even hegemonic states have often been curmudgeonly about the spread of liberal values in areas like human rights, where, for example, the 'great powers' – America, Russia and Britain – were initially opposed to embedding rights in the United Nations (UN) mandate (Drori et al., 2003). Far from being the only, or even the prime, movers in the international system, states derive much of their legitimacy from being part of a larger system, a looser structure of governance and shared obligation called a world polity, whose culture is legitimated, implemented and reproduced by more and more organizations, from scientific and professional associations to environmental movements (Drori et al., 2003; 2006).

The work of the Stanford Group and of Meyer in particular broke new ground in sociology, giving it a strongly comparative and revived historical slant. World polity theory also offers a provocative theoretical account of the processes through which world culture is established and a perspective on the sort of culture that results. The process has not yielded and probably cannot produce the same ontological 'thickness' or sense of community and identity ascribed to national varieties of culture, and the adoption of cultural norms by different states and societies is not the familiar story of how 'a people' can be formed out of a common, imagined past. In other words world culture is not the mirror image of national culture.

Rather, the idea of world culture or world society suggests a more fragile or possibly 'thinner', but no less compelling, source of legitimacy and motivation whereby, increasingly, people believe they live in one world under universally valid and applicable standards or norms. The world-wide impact of such norms is contagious, not only in the sense that more and more actors are constrained to acknowledge their force, but because the culture of world polity and society also encourages the discovery of new common issues which, in turn, are deemed solvable only through the adoption and application of global standards. In other words, the culture of the world polity provides common models for thinking about the world and for acting on its problems, whether we are talking about global warming or unprotected labour.

This virtuous circle is perhaps less complete in practice than the theory suggests and because of this the idea of a simple diffusion of the Western cultural account commutes to the notion that there are 'many globalizations' (Berger and Huntington, 2002) or that globalization as a process of growing cultural consciousness is irreducibly variable and often contested. Meyer himself says that 'global commitments . . . vastly transcend the actual global and national achievements in these areas' (2007, 264). Instead there is a good deal of 'loose coupling' whereby idealized commitments or ringing declarations of support do not translate into actual policy and good practice (Hafner-Burton and Tsutsui, 2005). States, even whole regions, differ in how they interpret individual rights, while proclaiming their virtuous status by subscribing to universal declarations on these rights. Manifestly there is no global cultural consensus, or at least none that delivers uniform outcomes, and, in the foreseeable future, there is not likely to be one. How far does this dilute the claim to discern elements of a world culture?

Following Emile Durkheim, Meyer notes that collective norms have an effect upon the practices of those who actively subscribe to them and those who do not. As a case in point, research conducted by Franco Ramirez and others (1996; Ramirez, 2001) suggests that the recent wave of female participation in universities occurs equally in countries that make a policy commitment to that goal and those that have no such policy. It is also true that in a world increasingly subject to global standards, deviation by states invites at least criticism and perhaps sanctions from other states as well as from the international community. Counter-intuitively, the politics of opposition to global standards also contributes a globalizing dynamic because it embodies the extent to which specific issues have risen to world level and are seen as remediable only at that level, as is the case with climate change.

The world polity school, especially in its neo-institutionalist guise (Lechner and Boli, 2005) sees globalization as a 'broad cultural phenomenon' rather than a structural principle (Meyer, 2007, 270; Albert, 2009). But we should note that what is being described is a kind of global *cultural structure* which embraces and subsumes or modifies national practice or national intent. In other words, this is not an actor-centred account of social process, but one in which both agents and rules are culturally enacted and culturally sanctioned (Thomas, 2009). By contrast, in WSA, despite a bow to the anti-systemic clout of cultural forces, actors face and are constrained by the implacable deep structures of the world economy of capitalism, while in some constructivist versions of globalization structures are malleable to the point where they have no substance independent of the constructed world-views of agents. The latter positions sometimes go so far as to embrace the postmodernist conceit that there are no irreducible realities (George, 1994; Derrida, 1976).

Of course, over the years there have been significant attempts to reunite the duality of structure and action. These include work from humanistic Marxism (Hall, 1996; Miliband, 1969) and some strains of social interaction-ism (Archer, 1988; 2007). Neo-institutionalists of Meyer's stamp insist that social action is highly structured by institutionalized rules that give meaning and value to individual and collective behaviour, so that actors themselves have to be seen as socially constructed. But, while institutions provide a framework for action, agents do not simply reproduce these institutions through their day-by-day interaction with various rules (Giddens, 1984). Rules have to be enacted and this process takes place both 'behind the backs' of agents, as Nicos Mouzelis says (1989) – that is, without reflection on what is taking place – and consciously, perhaps as part of a literal endorsement of the rule (Wendt, 1994).

The key point is that structures are not external to actors but built into social practices. As Alexander Wendt famously noted, 'sovereignty is what states make it' (1994, 123). All social systems have structural properties that pre-exist and outlast actors and this means that they function as more than just projections of subjectivity on to the external world. As Wendt also says, worlds that are 'defined intersubjectively' are not always malleable, because 'intersubjective constructions [still] confront actors as obdurate social facts' (1994, 389; 2006). While actors and actions are institutionally anchored, institutional orders are also socially constructed and thus are capable of being changed through strategic interventions by actors, always allowing for contingency and the ability of actors to mobilize appropriate resources. Such insight, by no means unique to discussions of globalization, is perhaps the main strength of neo-institutionalist variants of world polity theory and the structurationism of Giddens, with the emphasis on the mutual constitution of agency and structure (Wendt, 2003; Giddens, 1984; 1990; Bourdieu, 1977).

World culture (globalization) theory

The strength of world polity theory and its variants lies in the wide-ranging interdisciplinary remit and in the historical depth and comparative scope of empirical research which embraces, for example, the global diffusion of science (Ramirez and Riddle, 1991) and the global spread of INGOs (Boli and Thomas, 1999). It is also a signal contribution because '[C]onceptualizing the world as a polity shifts from a state-centred approach and focuses on rules of the game which are global in scope' (Thomas, 2009, 117). This is a notable theoretical innovation because it links the identities and actions of actors to a political-cultural context that, in some respects, is external to, or not reliant on, nation-states (Gulmez, 2010).

Writing in *World Culture: Origins and Consequences* (2005), John Boli and Frank Lechner attempt a synthesis between the neo-institutionalism of the Stanford School and the richer, interpretative sociology of culture found in the work of Roland Robertson and others. The latter group acknowledges the impact of global cultural scripts, but seeks a deeper understanding of world culture as a source of 'ideas and symbols, concepts and models which seep into everyday life and thereby add a layer to people's experience' (Lechner and Boli, 2005, 36; Tomlinson, 1999).

Roland Robertson's extensive body of work on globalization theory and, more recently, on middle-range facets of global processes is perhaps the most developed treatment of the cultural domain of globalization from within sociology. With various co-authors (1985; 1992; 2002; 2006) he sees the structuration of the world proceeding around two main axes: the relationships between the universal and the particular, and the interplay of local and global. Globalization itself refers to 'the compression of the world and the intensification of consciousness of the world as a whole' (1992, 8). Of fundamental importance in Robertson's sociology of globalization is the argument that 'global consciousness is not only an outcome of the [globalization] process . . . . It is also a motor of globalization' (Rumford, 2008, 135). In thought and to some extent in deed, the world is being made into a single place.

We should guard against taking the idea of the world as a single place too literally. Robertson really does not want to suggest that globalization is just a process of cultural or any other sort of homogenization. He is also critical of the tendency in some early globalization research to depict it as playing out a simple domination-resistance motif, with local activists and communities always on the receiving end of cultural hand-me-downs from core or dominant states and societies, or else fabricated by various global culture industries. At the same time he is happy to acknowledge the explanatory worth of world polity treatments of the 'particularization of universalism', which at least approximate global cultural convergence (isomorphism) when national identities, practices and structures are ordered according to global standards (Giulianotti and Robertson, 2009, 41). Actors are embedded in what

Robertson calls 'constitutive contexts' and these are increasingly part of an 'external' global environment, beyond individuals, organizations and nation-states. The result is that the autonomy and identity of actors are relativized because globalization 'challenge[s] . . . the stability of particular (local) perspectives on and collective and individual participation in the overall globalization process' (1992, 29).

But Robertson is at pains to guard against the notion that globalization simply washes unmediated over situated actors and so is exercised as much by the phenomenon of difference or diversity as by integration and homogenization, with both identified as axial problems in the sociology of globalization. One of the seeming paradoxes of a world in which global consciousness has been growing for some decades is that it breeds a heightened sense of difference. In other words, particular self- and collective identities are not simply being diluted or erased by the growing cultural 'oneness' of the globe. Rather, the mobilization of a sense of difference contributes either to a politics of resistance or to a more pluralist accommodation in which recognition of common problems and singular destinies still does not, or need not, produce global consensus or anodyne 'global' identities.

In other literature this theme is also rehearsed, albeit with different inflections. As we have noted, WSA sees the realm of culture and identity as a source of anti-systemic consciousness and action; while in work on cultural hybridity (Bhabha, 1990), global trends in music, the visual arts and cuisine make for increasingly frequent and intense cultural encounters between local and global and between situated and mobile actors. The interplay may well reinforce existing identities and world-views and rally people in defence of tradition, but the possibilities for hybrid identities which are neither new nor traditional, neither local nor global, are also seen as 'typical' of globalization. Overall, Robertson's position remains agnostic on the trajectory on which the process of global compression is moving, and he is at pains to emphasize the tensions that appear in the world cultural space as a result of the interpenetration of universal and particular, local and global.

Key to his thesis and intimately linked to other axes in his site map of globalization – universal/particular and homogenization/heterogenization – is the concept of glocalization (for a more geographical take, see Swyngedouw, 1992; 2004; Brenner, 1998; 2004). Glocalization is used by Robertson as a gloss on the older anthropological concept of cultural diffusion and is meant to capture what he describes as the '"real world" endeavours of individuals and social groups to ground and recontextualize global phenomena or processes with respect to local cultures' (Giulianotti and Robertson, 2009, 46). In other words it comprises individual and collective attempts to make sense of and accommodate a globalized world or, as Robertson puts it, the 'global human condition' (1992, 26).

The core message is that the idea of glocalization better expresses the important truth that 'global forces do not override locality' (Miller et al.,

1999, 19) and that 'cultural homogenization and heterogenization are not alternatives . . . rather they tend to come together' to produce cultures that are 'commonly diverse' (Cowen, 2002, 16, 129; Hannerz, 1992a, on the global 'organization of diversity').

A contrary but still compelling treatment of the homogenization/hetero-genization debate can be found in George Ritzer's work, which spans the highly successful opus on *McDonaldization* (2012 [1993]) and his enigmatic account of *The Globalization of Nothing* (2004). Ritzer echoes theorists who see a divide between local and global or between Westernization and various embattled cultures and civilizations, and builds his argument around the binary tension between glocalization and his preferred concept of *grobaliza-tion*. Grobalization – global homogenization – is described as 'the process in which growth imperatives push organizations and nations to expand globally and to impose themselves on the local' (Ritzer, 2004, xiii). Moreover, grobali-zation privileges the influence of 'Westernization, Americanization and McDonalidization in global processes' (2004, 194).

Use of the concept also serves to redress what Ritzer sees as the unwar-ranted emphasis on social and cultural heterogeneity and cultural hybridiza-tion, which, along with the assumed 'interpenetration of the local and the global', is held to produce 'unique outcomes in different geographical loca-tions' (2003, 73; 2004, ch. 2). In his estimation this view of globalization is altogether too benign, ignoring both the extent to which a sense of difference can spill over into the nastier forms of identity politics and, more signifi-cantly, the enveloping and obliterating force of global consumer culture. *Grobalization* comprises the 'imperialistic ambitions of nations, corporations, organizations and the like and their desire, indeed need, to impose them-selves on various geographic areas' (2003, 73).

The language of domination and resistance found in Ritzer's normatively inflected account is telling; indeed we might say that his position is almost a kind of pessimistic hyper-globalism in that he assumes the transformative impact of grobalization while lamenting it. But his rather gloomy view of the 'globalization of nothing' is a jaundiced interpretation of cultural globaliza-tion as a form of commodification and domination. By concentrating on the take-up of global commodities and global brands – McDonald's restaurants or Coca-Cola – which he assumes are empty of local content and meaning, he may well overstate the extent to which the consumption choices made by local subjects must always rehearse a simple divide between cultural annihi-lation on the one hand and a forlorn and romantic quest for cultural auton-omy on the other (Axford, 1995; chapter 5 of this book).

World society theory

It is a considerable leap of conceptualization to imagine a global or world society rather than just the national variant, one that has exercised students of IR, as well as sociologists (Buzan, 2004). In English School writings out of IR, we see two models of world society, notably as it relates to notions of territory and borders: a 'pluralist' vision, in which states remain dominant and state sovereignty retains political and legal primacy, and a 'solidarist' prescription, which sees cosmopolitan values and universal norms predicating a new global order. Buzan (2004) says that these two logics coexist in the contemporary world: the system of states, sovereignty, territory, nationalism and great-power politics, alongside a much less stable and defined system of transnationalism, global markets and universalistic values.

Although bifurcated views of world society are not uncommon, once the observer has sortied beyond the conceptual implausibility of the idea that (the notion of) society is retrievable even in the absence of boundaries, the question then is: what exactly is meant by world society? There are a number of ways to answer this. They comprise definitions whereby first, all the attributes of a national society – a functionally integrated social whole supported by a sense of community – commute to the global level, and the problems with making this leap are made clear in various critiques of the idea of global civil society (Axford, 2004; Chandler, 2009; Chandler and Baker, 2005).

Second is a much looser conception reliant upon various and intensifying forms of connectivity and communication between sub-global actors to produce a society effect, albeit one deemed less 'whole' and therefore less authentic or 'thick' than the national version. A final version has the ontology of global society diverging from the first two models and from claims that 'society' presupposes functional integration and cultural community or that a 'society' is possible through interconnection and flows of information, commodities and people across boundaries (Thomas, 2009; Albert, 2009). In this version the idea of a global social whole or singularity is retained and refers to a willingness to address world problems collectively through norms. Functional integration between parts of a (bounded) society is replaced by cultural enactment of rules by various actors. This rather looser conception of society has strong echoes of world polity theory about it, largely through its emphasis on growing consciousness of world cultural constraints on the behaviour of actors that imagine and enact an increasingly 'stateless society', as George Thomas has it (2009, 118; Shaw, 2000) or a global cultural field (Robertson, 1992).

Despite differences, all the preceding accounts work with the idea that there is, or can be, a world society. In doing so they either endorse a model of society yet to be met outside an ideal-typical version of the territorial state and the bounded society, or prefer definitions that depart from the conventional wisdom about society formation found in classical sociological theory. The question for globalization scholars is whether the social ontology of the global can be grasped through use of a concept so patently tied to national indicators. This is not a trivial question, because it challenges the ability of much social theory to comprehend the global. Its importance lies in high-lighting the acute question for globalization theory: is a global social system or (world) society possible, and what would it hold together?

Mathias Albert draws on systems theory to address precisely this question (2007). His argument is that certain brands of social theory – theories of society – are applicable to the global condition, particularly the social systems theory of Niklas Luhmann (1981; 1983; 1997). The core of his argument *pace* Luhmann is that while it is possible to conceive of a world society, its exist-ence and survival are not predicated on the same attributes of stability, consensus and cultural wholeness found in functionalist treatments of social order and seen in models of state and nation-building. Instead the global system is characterized as 'differentiated and polycentric' (Jessop, 1990, 320).

Classical theories of society stress the importance of normative integration to explain why societies cohere despite their heterogeneity. But is this dynamic actually available beyond the nation-state, where the modal social form either is network based or comprises only sporadic outbursts of solidar-ity expressed through world public opinion on issues of pressing concern? Some research on the ethnography of social networks in general and transna-tional networks in particular suggests that they may well be contexts in which strong and enduring identities can be formed (Axford, 2006; 2007a; Keck and Sikkink, 1998). Moreover, the idea of attentive, if not enduring, global publics is increasingly canvassed in literature on global civil society and cosmopolitanism (Thomas, 2009; Fossum and Schlesinger, 2007; Ruggie, 2005; Keane, 2003; Castells, 2008). Albert's position is that if it is possible to conceive of society at a world scale using existing social theory, then we must employ an analytical framework that does not rely heavily on the notion of normative integration, and this is where Luhmann comes in (1997; 2000).

Luhmann develops the ideas of previous theorists of society, notably Comte, Durkheim, Spencer and Talcott Parsons, through the core sociological notion of social differentiation. But he departs from received wisdom about the need for normative integration to ensure social cohesion. Most theorists of (national) society assume that functional differentiation is the form of social differentiation that dominates modern society. All functions within a system become assigned to a particular sub-sector or sub-system of society and these 'sites' fulfil specific and necessary tasks for society as a whole (Albert, 2009, 175). The idea of functional differentiation applies to broad functional catego-ries such as the political system or the economy as well as to the bespoke division of labour found in many formal organizations. While these sub-sys-tems are in many ways autonomous, from a systemic (societal) standpoint they display a good deal of the functional interdependence necessary for the survival of the system.

Used to comprehend national societies as social systems such functionalism is hardly novel, if somewhat frowned upon these days. Moreover, it is sig-nificant that functional differentiation is usually seen to require a socially integrative mechanism to bind diverse functions together, not least in times of crisis. Parsons referred to this as the sense of 'societal community', another form of normative integration (1969, 2). So, in terms of identifying the building blocks of world society, we have gone full circle.

Luhmann tries to break out of this circularity by insisting that the structuration of world society relies on two related processes. The first is functional differentiation both within and between social systems. This process involves interactions and exchanges between systems, sub-systems and their complex environments. For example, nation-states have other nation-states, international organizations and civil society groups in their environment, with which they must interact. Similarly, producers and consumers in any market negotiate transactions to produce effective demand. Second, there is intensive and extensive communication between social systems and the sub-units of social systems, which all 'use communication to constitute and interconnect the events [actions] which build up the systems' (Luhmann, 1981, 48). Society is constituted through the key reference points of functional differentiation and communication and, according to Luhmann, is now resolutely global (Luhmann, 1981, 42; Maturana and Varela, 1980). In fact, communication is the vital ingredient of structural coupling, linking actors across multiple social systems regardless of space and time.

When set against received models of society formation and reproduction, can world society produce anything like functional interdependence and functional integration, and if not, is that significant? If the aim is for global theory to eschew received versions of society then the answer may be that it does not matter; but even in its own radical terms the formulation requires justification and invites criticism. Most telling is the complaint mounted by critics of systems analysis applied to the study of globalization: definitions of any system have one enduring feature, namely that the concept implies closure. Systems are contained and delimited; they interact with their environments in limited and manageable ways, enacting a social universe that is ordered and in which boundaries are maintained (Albrow, 1996).

But globalization is much less tameable and better seen as 'boundary effacing' (Beck and Sznaider, 2006, 18), and the global condition – globality – is composed of more complex and unpredictable relational ties. Nonetheless, Luhmann and Albert argue that world society is possible on the basis of networks of communication and through interconnectedness understood more generally. Certainly this syncs with some revisionist treatments of global civil society where ideas about the possibilities of 'network society' are entertained (Axford, 2004; Axford and Huggins, 2007; Castells, 2000a; 2000b), but it generates opposition from many quarters. One critic argues that 'compared to the strong social embeddedness of formal organizations and markets and their institutional and legal ties, networks emerge as nearly devoid of institutional anchoring and social implications' (Kallinikos, 2004, 1). Critically, in terms of polity or state building, network structures and network identities are often cast as too fluid – on the cusp between dynamism and decay – to support stable infrastructures of meaning and sustainable rules of resource allocation.

In much the same vein, complexity theorist Karin Knorr-Cetina opines that because of this weakness, 'relational connectivity may not be enough to effectively organize complex systems' (2007, 68). In other words, connectivity may not be sufficient to get over the major problem for Luhmann's thesis, which is how to explain social order (society) in situations where this seems possible only through the unlikely convergence of autonomous systems by way of structural coupling – communication (Jessop, 1990). So we may still need a conceptual understanding of world society that looks beyond communication and interconnection. If that is the case, must we reintroduce the idea of functional integration? George Thomas, a proponent of world polity analysis, tries to solve this difficulty by stressing that communication and exchange obviously 'carry content', that is, provide for both interdiscursivity and shared meanings, but critically, remain embedded in wider cultural contexts (2009, 116). He says that to comprehend the idea of world society we have to move 'beyond the interconnections of actors' – their actions – and address 'the consciousness, cultural context and social forms that encompass them' (2009, 116).

Does any of this do service as a way to describe and understand the social ontology of the global, and does it make sociological sense? As a minimum, systems-inflected world society theory is just another, potentially fruitful, way of getting social theory beyond the nation-state. More forcefully we might argue that it 'help[s] us to conceptualize global society as a larger social whole, rather than the total sum of individual human beings or particular societies' (Bartelson, 2009b, 113). In this view the nationalization of social scientific concepts and principles, summarized as methodological nationalism, makes it difficult to entertain the concept of global or world society and thus to imagine a universal and boundary-less society. This despite evidence that such imaginings have intellectual roots in the writings of mostly pre-disciplinary social theorists such as Dante, Kant and Herder, and are also rehearsed in contemporary normative treatments of cosmopolitanism and in debates on the prospects for post-territorial political community (Chandler, 2009).

Methodological cosmopolitanism

Attempts to link theories of the global to classical social theory also inform this, the final sociological category. The project here is crystallized in, although not completely exhausted by, debates over cosmopolitanism and the prospects for a cosmopolitan social science (Rumford, 2008; Beck and Sznaider, 2006; Martell, 2007). As David Chandler says, the 'aspiration to engage in, construct or recognize the existence of a post-territorial political community, a community of broader humanity, has been articulated in liberal terms as cosmopolitanism' (2009, 53; Cheah, 2006), and this aspiration has firm roots in classical social theory as well as informing the work of contemporary theorists. The idea even engages those critics of liberal and so-called 'new' cosmopolitanism, whose ranks include a tranche of 'post'-Marxist, poststructuralist and even post-global theorists including Michael Hardt and Antonio Negri (2000; 2004), Michel Foucault (1970; 1977) and Giorgio Agamben (1998; 2005).

The palpable normative content of these debates also appears in much work on global governance, global civil society, transnational public spheres and democratization (Cheah, 2006; Fine, 2007). For now, we will abstract this 'methodological universalism' (Chernilo, 2006, 32) from the universalistic normative core of cosmopolitan thinking. Our focus will be on the stated prospects for a cosmopolitan social science. Of course, the case for this cannot be separated entirely from the altogether more strategic and ideological goals of liberal or 'new' cosmopolitanism. This is especially obvious in the writing of Ulrich Beck, where there are strong normative prescriptions for cosmopolitan democracy, global justice and citizenship, as well as a focus on more mundane and 'unintended and lived' forms of cosmopolitanism (Rumford, 2008, 9; Beck and Sznaider, 2006, 7; Fine, 2007; Held, 2003; Archibugi, 2008a).

Beck and a coterie of co-authors offer methodological cosmopolitanism as the approach which will 'bring sociology back to its subject matter' (Beck and Sznaider, 2006, 22; Beck and Grande, 2007; Beck and Lau, 2005; Delanty, 2006), and this is presented as an empirical and analytical as well as a normative objective. At the heart of Beck's normative and analytical intent is the case against methodological nationalism, although he is also concerned to inter systems theory and poststructuralism, which, he argues, have robbed social science of agency. Most theories of international relations assume that their field of inquiry is 'delimited to the interaction between bounded political societies in a context defined by the absence of centralized authority' (Bartelson, 2009b, 113), and this is a besetting weakness when attempting to theorize globalization.

Beck insists that we are experiencing a 'cosmopolitanization of reality' (Beck and Sznaider, 2006, 2), which is the scourge of conventional international theory but does not dispense with the state; envisaging not the latter's demise but, once again, its transformation. This cosmopolitan realism decants into a seemingly empirical notion, 'cosmopolitanization', which identifies the 'really existing processes of cosmopolitanization of the world' (Beck and Sznaider, 2006, 7). Apparently, processes of cosmopolitanization are all around us, whether in the grand experiment of supranational governance seen in the EU or in unlooked-for and unintended aspects of everyday life, where there are many instances of day-to-day or 'banal cosmopolitanism' (Beck and Sznaider, 2006, 8).

Beck distinguishes between what he calls the 'cosmopolitan condition', which corresponds to the normative-philosophical dimension, and the 'cosmopolitan moment', which expresses the empirical-analytic component of his thesis (2006, 6; 2008). This is a distinction between a set of normative principles intended to elevate humankind and a process which often moves to the more routine attitudes, choices and behaviour of actors – Beck mentions stateless persons and populations made mobile by war or famine – who become cosmopolitan through happenstance or coercion, rather than by adopting or living out high-flown ideals.

So the *cosmopolitanization of reality* is a beast with much less pedigree than the purely normative strain, but one that corresponds to contemporary conditions which, taken together, comprise a *cosmopolitan moment*. This world is characterized by high risk and four kinds of global 'interdependency crises': ecological, economic, terrorist and moral, where the last refers to the global politics of human rights. When we look at the cosmopolitanism 'for another age' advocated by David Held (2003, 12), the appeal to a more informal and evidently cultural version is also intended to modify or even free the idea from the conceptual strait-jacket cut from ethical universalism. In turn the cosmopolitan moment fosters a shared 'cosmopolitan outlook' whereby 'people view themselves as part of a threatened world and as part of their local histories and situations' (Beck, 2006, 11).

Up to this point Beck's argument looks like previous interventions on the nature and ubiquity of world cultural scripts or global consciousness as defining elements of globalization. But he insists that cosmopolitanization is not just another word for globalization. Globalization is 'something taking place "out there"' (2006, 9) while cosmopolitanization happens 'from within'. The former 'presupposes' an onion-ring model of the world, with local and national as the core and inner layer and the international and global as the outer. By contrast, cosmopolitanization describes those 'really existing relations of interdependence' which follow from the day-by-day practices of people as they live out their lives; so globalization is really 'internalized cosmopolitanism'.

While Beck's interpretation of globalization is something of a straw man and seems to ignore a raft of globalization scholarship disparaging the very model of globalization he takes as modal, more intriguing and somewhat confusing is his apparent take on cosmopolitanization, which is breathtakingly inclusive. A cosmopolitan outlook takes in any perception of living in the world and being subject to global constraints. As he says, issues of global concern are 'becoming part of people's moral life-worlds, no matter whether they are for or against cosmopolitanism' (2006, 11). *Internalized cosmopolitanism*, whereby individuals and groups share the same definition of risk, in turn generates *institutionalized cosmopolitanism* when translated into political forms and organized struggle.

These conceptual nuances are designed to overcome what Beck sees as the 'naïve universalism' of early Western sociology, and there is little doubt that this body of work is a full-blown attempt to reconfigure the rules of socio-logical inquiry even if it sometimes appears as a highly eclectic mix (Rumford, 2008, 11). Cosmopolitanism departs from idealistic universalism because it is 'multi-perspectival' (Beck and Sznaider, 2006, 18) and does not presuppose the national/international dualism found in both WSA and world polity theory. At the same time it does presuppose 'a universalistic minimum' expressed in 'a number of substantive norms which must be upheld at all costs' (2006, 19). These include religious freedoms, freedom from torture and the right to criticize and oppose governments.

Conclusion

The burden of much theorizing out of political science and sociology still has the nation-state and national societies at its ontological core. There are impor-tant variations in this focus, so that the intersocietal and world-level contexts in which national societies are set are sometimes entertained, but nowhere is it relegated entirely, and perhaps that is not possible. By contrast, Beck thinks that only when we have learned to do without methodological nation-alism can we hope to discover ways to study transnational reality and offer a multidimensional and cross-disciplinary approach to globalization. Unlike methodological universalism, transnational reality is full of variety, a post-universalistic construct and certainly not one of those 'zombie' concepts designed to comprehend only national societies (Beck and Sznaider, 2006). Methodological cosmopolitanism addresses the vagaries of denationalization and transnationalization in a world that is globalized, but not singular (Delanty, 2005). At the heart of this discussion and of many of the previous debates is the matter of the relationships between actors, space and territory, and to explore this relationship we need to examine the contribution of geography to the scholarship of globalization before dealing with contribu-tions from anthropology and cultural and communication studies.

CHAPTER 3

Theorizing Globalization: Geography, Anthropology and Cultural and Communication Studies

Globalizing Space: Geography and Globalization

The concerns raised by students of political science and sociology come together in the 'geographer's metric for representing social relationships', the map (Fraser, 2009, 1; Cox et al., 2008). As Nancy Fraser says, the 'problematic of the map can lie dormant for long historical stretches, when a hegemonic frame is naturalized and taken for granted' (2009, 2). The hegemonic frame is the territorial state and the bounded society, along with the Westphalian system of sovereign states. These days the mapping of political space is contested and the frame an object of struggle. Fraser's own interests lie in the framing of social justice, where the issue of which mapping of political space is truly just and who counts as a bona fide subject of justice – citizens of territories or transnational 'communities of risk' – are the key questions for analysts (Fraser, 2009, 4).

The matter of spatial and temporal change is an integral part of globalization scholarship (Oke, 2009; Rosenberg, 2005; 2007). Analysing spatiality is geography's distinctive contribution to the study of 'a single and interdependent world' (Amin, 2002, 62), although not one unique to that discipline. Political geography in particular has a robust history of research with a global remit, and this is seen most clearly in the classic work of Halford Mackinder and others on geo-politics (1907; O'Tuathail, 1996).

Since the revival of political geography in the late 1970s this engagement has been rekindled, so that when geographers today address the global a number of themes are extant and a variety of influences apparent. First is the very impulse to think globally. In a more recent review of state-of-the-art political geography, Kevin Cox and his co-authors (2008) refer to the ways in which the work of Fernand Braudel and Immanuel Wallerstein has influenced the writing of political geographers such as Peter Taylor (1994; Flint and Taylor, 2007; Dicken et al., 2001). For Taylor, relations between cities and localities, the state system and the global economy, reveal how the modern world works. The theme of complex relationality between actors and institutions situated at different spatial scales is central to the geography of globalization and constitutes the second emergent theme in current research. Perhaps the main problematic in such work is the 'decoupling of power and the state' (Helmig and Kessler, 2007, 240). When 'political spaces no longer match geographical spaces', the 'banal statism' of conventional IR theory and international law is more difficult to sustain (Kuus and Agnew, 2008, 98). The ramifications of this insight resonate through the work of many international or transnational economic and political geographers (Sassen, 2006; Agnew, 1994; 2005; O'Tuathail, 2003), and research in political geography converges markedly with findings from work in other disciplines.

Third, and as a case in point, Low draws attention to the impact of a different kind of critical geo-politics heavily influenced by political theory, continental philosophy and especially critical theory, not least in the variants used by some IR theorists like R.J.B. Walker (1992), Hardt and Negri (2000; 2004; 2009), James Der Derian and Michael Shapiro (1989). In these accounts and in others with a more obviously geographical provenance (Massey, 2005; Amin and Thrift, 1997; Blaut, 1993; Harvey, 2003), the theme of irreducible global complexity is rehearsed at length and further complicates the understanding of state territoriality and its canonical status in defining world order.

In 1994, John Agnew enjoined all the social sciences to transcend the 'territorial trap' which contained three problematic assumptions (see also Lefebvre, 1974): first, that the state exercises sovereignty over its demarcated territorial jurisdiction; second, that the realms of politics and economics are divided naturally into domestic and foreign (international); and finally, that state boundaries define and contain the realms commonly known as economy and society. Since then, and to some extent even prior to Agnew's intervention, more nuanced spatial analyses have grappled with the problem of state-centrism and provided a more textured understanding of territory as a factor in political and social organization (Brenner and Elden, 2009; Massey, 1991; Harvey, 2005a; 2003; 2000; Castells, 2000a; Thrift, 2006). Two concepts, *borders* and *networks*, are central to this challenge, and their imbrication produces a dialectic which has profound implications for theorizing globalization, while still not predicating a completely de-territorialized world. In this dialectic, borders betoken territoriality, fixity and ontological thickness, while networks speak of fluidity and enable social relations that cross space at all scales (Axford, 2007b; Dicken et al., 2001; Castells, 2000a).

Much recent research into the relationships between borders and networks underlines their mutual constitution (Rumford, 2008; Sassen, 2006; Walters and Haahr, 2005). This is an intuitively plausible thesis but needs elaboration. While it remains true that processes of 'embodied integration' (face-to-face relationships) tend to tie people to localities, and disembodied, or more abstract, processes (movement of, for example, electronic images and other texts, or forms of capital) are associated with crossing and even erasing spatial and temporal boundaries, the distinction is seldom that neat (James, 2006). So a world made up of whole spatio-temporal units (nation-states) and the more-or-less discrete (national) societies associated with them is unlikely to be completely nullified by the activities of networks. Rather, network links across borders may create 'qualitative disjunctures' between different regulatory and socio-cultural environments that are primarily national (Dicken et al., 2001, 96). Even now, when mobile commodities such as finance capital flow through and around places, states still supply key infrastructures for inter- and trans-national agents and practices. According to Saskia Sassen, the result is a welter of 'mixed spatio-temporal assemblages of territoriality', produced through the overlapping and intersecting spaces and times of the national and the global (2006, 397).

As part of this dynamic tension, the national scale may lose specific components of the state's formal authority, while other scales – both sub- and supra-national – gain strategic weight. All this is quite tortuous science, but may allow a more accurate mapping of the emerging political, economic and even cultural geographies of the world. Earlier we cited Sassen's plea to treat such forms and connections not as just maverick or hybrid variants of either local or global, but as something new. This line of thinking is nourished by some quite abstract philosophy on the theme of 'inside/outside' international relations (Der Derian and Shapiro, 1989; George, 1994), on identity and difference and on the relations between self and other. There is also a developing sub-field of empirical investigation on actual manifestations of the phenomenon that crosses a number of disciplinary divides in sociology, anthropology and geography to identify emerging *micro structures* of networked globality (Knorr-Cetina, 2007, 2012; Knorr-Cetina and Bruegger, 2002), whether in global financial markets or terrorist networks. Micro structures are often cohered by information technologies, which are the arteries of global and transnational connectedness through which interactions flow.

So the 'reassertion of space' in social theory (Soja, 1989; Harvey, 2005b) helps in the task of 'unthinking' state-centred models of social inquiry (Wallerstein, 1991). In the main this involves rethinking space as a timeless and static container of social action (Lefebvre, 1974; Brenner and Elden, 2009). That said, for students of globalization some caution is still necessary. Attempts to escape the territorial trap can result in the abandonment of geography altogether in pursuit of some vision of a completely de-territorialized world (Scholte, 2000; Brenner and Elden, 2009). As Grahame Thompson says, there is still a case for taking borders seriously (2000; Rumford, 2008; Newman, 2005). In more extreme form and seeking to counter the intuitive appeal of the spatial metaphor, some critics actually reject the over-spatialization of social theory. They see it as a dereliction of sound scholarship

produced by over-reliance on what is really no more than a descriptive category (Rosenberg, 2005).

   Such complaints might just conjure a straw man, since recent studies of
globalization are unquestionably wary of any simplistic 'abstraction of spatiality' where this means treating space as entirely constitutive of the social
– 'represented as having effects', in Corbridge and Agnew's modest phrase –
or as a way of explaining globalization (1995, 79; James, 2006, 274). Rather,
they interpret space as just one attribute of the social and treat the signature
property of de-territorialization as counterbalanced by both older and newer
versions of territoriality (Axford, 2006; 2007b; Sassen, 2006) and, of course,
by temporal processes. But in accounts of globalization in which spatiality is
dominant there is often an a-historical narrative of social change that emphasizes the 'powers of spatiality but not the processes that have caused them'
(Oke, 2009, 317).

Space and time

Many disciplines explore the ways in which different kinds of society have
'constructed' space and time. But there are problems with the elegant notion
of globalization as 'space-time compression'. As Oke suggests, most treatments of globalization afford 'primacy to one axis, which results in subordination of the other, or a process of conflation' (2009, 310). Spatial change is
part and parcel of globalization, but the narrative of change occurring
through time is also central to how globalization is theorized, or should be,
even allowing for different conceptualizations of time (Adam, 1994; Urry,
2003). The problem lies in how such theorization integrates or fails to inte-
grate these discourses.

   Most accounts approach globalization as a temporal phenomenon through
its relationship with modernity, while those with a stronger spatial inflection
explore the relationships between bounded nation-states and borderless capitalism. In the former there is no single treatment of the provenance of globalization, which is variously taken to pre-date modernity (Frank, 1998;
Therborn, 2000; Gills and Thompson, 2006), intensify modernity (Giddens,
1990; Scholte, 2005a) or transcend modernity (Albrow, 1996; Hardt and
Negri, 2000; see also Robertson, 1992; Sassen, 2006). Accounts with a stronger
spatial inflection sometimes treat space as constitutive of the social, and focus
on the playing out of two generally acknowledged dynamics of globalization:
changes to the nation-state and changes in the scale of social processes.
Corbridge and Agnew (1995) and Kuus and Agnew (2008) suggest that purely
spatial narratives of globalization de-historicize space and the nation-state,
reducing the latter to a static, essentialized concept not a million miles from
the realist model. More historically informed accounts of globalization and
of changes in the state system and in capitalist modernity are, in part,
attempts to redress this failing.

Thus 'critical' globalizers such as Michael Mann (1993; 1997; 2006) and Goran Therborn (1995; 2000), both historical sociologists, try to reassess the interplay of temporal and spatial dimensions of social change in the light of these failings, while historical institutionalists (Hall and Taylor, 1996), sometimes accused of simplifying historical complexity in their pursuit of 'path-dependent' explanation, are at least examining the ways in which the present repertoire of opportunities available to actors is shaped by former events. If 'history matters' in explaining social phenomena, as we are endlessly told, that requires more than providing a chronological narrative by letting us identify some important, not to say fundamental, social mechanisms and processes and some 'plausible, frequently observed ways in which things happen', as Jon Elster rather disarmingly put it (1989, viii).

Global Anthropology and the Anthropology of Globalization

For students of anthropology, '[g]lobalization represents a significant break with anthropology as traditionally practised, partially because the primary empirical technique of participant observation fieldwork tended to bring the bounded community to the front and center' (Lewellen, 2002, 29; O'Hearn, 2009). In other words, the stock in trade of anthropological research has been 'the local', though not entirely. There is also the high level of structural-functionalist abstraction seen in development studies and, more pertinently, the global perspectives on offer in the important work of Edmund Leach (1954), Eric Wolf (1982; 1999) and Peter Worsley (1984). But there can be no presumption that anthropology has been transformed by such interventions. Rather, as Lewellen suggests, growing awareness of a global dimension to the study of locality has seen a shift in the constituency of groups and communities studied and growing interest in ways to connect micro to macro and local to global. Traditional anthropology looked at bounded communities and cultures but global anthropology – not an uncontested expression – is more interested in transnationals, diasporas, 'deterritorialized ethnicities' and themes such as migration or, more generally, mobility, whether of cosmopolitan professionals or refugees (Lewellen, 2002, 30; Baba and Hill, 2006).

This shift in focus occurred in the wash created by the end of the Cold War, the demise of the Soviet Union and the blurring and partial dissolution of economic boundaries attendant on the spread of neo-liberal capitalism. As Marietta Baba and Carole Hill opine, '[s]uch processes link[ed] peoples, nations and regions together across the globe and create[d] compelling foci for anthropological practice in the world today' (2006, 19). In fact, the global phase in anthropology post-1990 was itself preceded by a raft of scholarship much influenced by those intellectual currents – critical theory, postmodernism and poststructuralism – which fed off the perceived crisis of modernity during the 1970s and 1980s (Clifford, 1988; Geertz, 1973; Lewellen, 2002).

Jonathan Friedman argues that the emergence of global anthropology had its roots in the 1970s, when the key intellectual shift was to recognize the importance of social reproduction as *the* framework for analysis in place of the 'assumed nature of society as a closed entity' which could be studied in isolation (2007, 109; Ong and Collier, 2005). Social reproduction refers to the self-constitution of a social form over time, and for anthropologists the issue was and remains whether the people in question reproduce themselves socially out of their own resources, as Friedman has it, or are reliant on extra-, even trans-societal referents and resources. Many societies previously assumed to be 'totalities' in fact turn out to be 'loci within larger processes' (Friedman, 2007, 110; Eckholm and Friedman, 2008), and this is in line with what students of world-systems were beginning to say at much the same time.

Interestingly, postmodernist ideas too are attractive for those students of anthropology concerned to reject the scientism of earlier social inquiry, with its focus on modernist givens such as the national, the societal and the endogenous as the start and end points of social investigation. Postmodernist writings mirror the disorderliness and fragmentation that are characteristic of a world in flux. In anthropology this sense of dislocation was fuelled by a number of factors. First was the spread of market-oriented practices into the former bastions of revolutionary state socialism. Second are the cultures and technologies of speed that have transformed consumption habits and cultural practices (Tomlinson, 2007; Axford and Huggins, 2010). Third are the liminal conditions that characterized many post-colonial states in Africa. Finally, there are internecine conflicts that have created a raft of humanitarian crises and forced migrations (Baba and Hill, 2006; Friedman and Randeira, 2004; Clifford, 1988). Global anthropology has responded to these issues in two main ways. At its weakest, the global dimension impinges through recognition that no culture or community is completely isolated. Stronger is the sense that, when examining globalization, everything 'overlaps with, flows into and blends with everything else' (Lewellen, 2002, 34).

A number of research themes are apparent. The first draws on the field of critical development studies and involves a more systematic treatment of the idea of complex cycles of social reproduction (Eckholm and Friedman, 2008). Much in line with the treatment of cyclical hegemonies found in WSA, Friedman sees contemporary globalization as the latest cycle in the historical process of capital accumulation (2007). Key to the dynamism of this long-term process is the rise and fall of different geographic centres of economic and political power, which cycles can be traced from the Arab empires of the Middle East in the high Middle Ages down to the latest iteration in the shape of the proto-hegemonic economies of China and India. In Friedman's work the focus is not so much on the empirical detail of globalization as process – movement of peoples across borders, diaspora formation and the global span of digital media – but on the 'underlying structures that generate their appearance, and even their disappearance' (2007, 111). He is primarily interested in the systemic processes that connect the world's localities to create and sustain global systems of interaction and identity. Global systems are not purely global but the result of the articulation of local lives and global processes.

Second is the focus on questions of identity, especially hybridity (Pieterse, 2003; 2007; Bhabha, 1989). This focus has expanded the horizons of anthropological study to embrace such relatively under-studied processes as creolization and the transformation of gender identities as factors in cultural globalization (Cohen, 2007). On creolization Robin Cohen points to the 'universal applicability' of a term that describes a position 'between two or more cultures, selectively appropriating some elements, rejecting others and creating new possibilities that transgress and supersede parent cultures' (2007, 381). He adds, '[a]ccepting the force of hybridity and creolization is also to accept that humankind is refashioning the basic building blocks of organized cultures and societies in a fundamental and wide-ranging way'. Ulf Hannerz endorses this view, saying that in a 'creolizing world' cultures are no longer bounded and autonomous, because they have been reshaped by increasingly complex and asymmetrical flows of people, ideas, things, images and, of course, capital (1992a; 1996).

Many globalizing processes are reciprocal. While local consumption of global products may produce a degree of homogenization – for example, when natives buy the branded icons of the fashion and entertainment industries – the particular form of the transaction should be seen as the 'assimilation of some Western artifact to the particular expression of a process that is entirely' African, Asian, Muslim and so on (Friedman, 1993, 206). At the same time, and this is where analytical reciprocity has to kick in, what is going on is only imaginable when set in a global context. These outcomes constitute neither a sell-out to global culture industries nor, interestingly enough, an obvious form of hybridization. Of course, the latter remains the default position of globalization optimists and those who want to use the concept of hybridity to address the complex and contradictory facets of cultural globalization, as well as a means of rejecting any sort of essentialism and claims to exclusiveness or exceptionalism.

In this regard the work of Jan Pieterse is instructive (2003; 2005; 2007; see also Kraidy, 2005). Pieterse, strongly influenced by development studies research, IPE and WSA, is of the view that as a historical force hybridization challenges both Westernization and homogenization. He argues that 'the importance of hybridity is that it problematizes boundaries' (2003, 14). In his eyes globalization *is* hybridization – 'structural hybridization or the emergence of new, mixed forms of social cooperation, and cultural hybridization, or the development of translocal mélange cultures' (2003, 18; Bhaba, 1989). Boundary maintenance and transcendence are key to these discourses.

Here the pioneering work of Arjun Appadurai (1990) on the coexistence of 'vertebrate' and 'cellular' global systems (2006) resonates with research on global systems found in other disciplines. In *Fear of Small Numbers: An Essay on the Geography of Anger* he offers a dark reappraisal of his previously optimistic interpretation of translocal processes, although the book shares with the earlier studies the sense that the dynamics of the global order still reside in various *disjunctures* and *scapes*. Writing in the 1990s, Appadurai points to the creation of a non-spatial global order being fashioned at the intersection of various 'scapes' – *ethnoscapes* (migration), *finanscapes* (flows of money), *mediascapes* (flows of information and images), *ideoscapes* (the movement of ideas) and *technoscapes* (technological innovation and knowledge transfer). He notes that 'even an elementary model of global political economy must take into account the deeply disjunctive relationships among human movement, technological flow, and financial transfer' (1990, 35). These relationships produce a 'complex transnational construction of imaginary landscapes' (1990, 35) and this construction, whose morphology and stability are unpredictable, augurs a post-national world.

The idea of critical disjunctures is by no means novel in globalization scholarship and can be seen, for example, in Samuel Huntington's 'clash of civilizations' (1996) and in the depiction of globalization as an elemental and continuing tension between boundaries and networks (Dicken et al., 2001; Axford, 2007a). Huntington's thesis has been read as entirely stark in its depiction of the ways in which civilizational disjunctures are shaping world order, but Appadurai's original vision of disjunctive global scapes, while edgily postmodern, is far from negative, emphasizing the liberating qualities of the 'global flow of images, news, and opinion' and the need for a social science more in tune with global realities (1990, xii).

By 2006 Appadurai is more troubled by those 'geographies of anger' which were brought into being by economic and cultural globalization and crystallized post-9/11. Current expressions of ethnic and religious anger and hatred are in large measure a response to the pressures and uncertainties created by globalization and further exacerbate the tensions between the vertebrate and cellular models of world order. As national, local and tribal autonomies are challenged by globalization and familiar cultural structures and practices are eroded, the purchase of a politics driven by appeals to 'blood and belonging', or entailing a search for ontological security, becomes stronger. In this environment, different forms of fundamentalism are really attempts to refurbish certainties of identity, whether local, national or religious. Violence, including terrorist violence, genocide and ethnic wars, may be seen as a particular way of achieving that end. In such a milieu, hybrid identities too can be treated as a threat to the integrity of any authentic cultural space rather than a celebration of fluid global processes.

Cultural and Communication Studies

The work of Appadurai (2006) and Homi Bhabha (1989; 2005) fits well with the burgeoning interest in cultural globalization. It is also closely linked with similar shifts in cultural studies, especially where these are influenced by a post-colonial motif or problematic (Krishnaswamy and Hawley, 2008). As Jonathan Friedman notes, post-colonial world culture 'flows, mixes, hybridizes and does things it didn't use to when it was more bounded in an imaginary past when the world was still a cultural "mosaic"' (2007, 114). The themes of cultural globalization and the idea of global culture(s) resonate throughout these debates, so that one might be forgiven for thinking that the analysis of culture now sits easily at the heart of globalization studies and that culture is recognized as a major force in economic, social and political transformations. But that would be premature (Held and Moore, 2008; Tomlinson, 1999; 2007).

True, the study of culture now informs all but the most steadfastly realist and structuralist accounts of globalization. Issues of cultural identity, cultural production and consumption, and cultural convergence and hybridization are central to the ways in which the burgeoning field of *culture and communication studies* addresses globalization. As Jan Servaes notes 'Viewing a television program or listening to the radio . . . cannot be seen as a simple act of consumption; these acts involve a rather complex process of decoding or appropriating cultural meanings' (2008, 42). He argues that as a result the idea of globalization as cultural homogenization or a process of domination by Western and mainly American media is too simplistic. He prefers a model of production, dissemination and consumption of media outputs whose axis is 'globalized diffusion and localized appropriation' of cultural product (2008, 42). The 'myth' of media globalization as a form of straightforward cultural convergence or cultural imperialism is further challenged by the growing body of comparative empirical work on communication and cultural convergence and diversity (Inglehart and Norris, 2009).

Most commentators acknowledge the profound changes set in train by the shift from the 'old' order of national and local print and broadcast media catering for domestic audiences to a system characterized by what Inglehart and Norris, perhaps tongue in cheek, call 'cosmopolitan communications' (2009, 1; Axford, 2001; Hafez, 2007).

Inglehart and Norris identify three broad scenarios for the cultural implications of cosmopolitan communications. These are *convergence, polarization* and *fusion*, where the first suggests that global communication has contributed to the standardization of cultures around the world and the loss of national autonomy; the second posits that exposure to global media and Western lifestyles generates a backlash, especially from more conservative or traditional societies and cultures in the global South; while the third bears all the hallmarks of the hybridization thesis, a benign multiculturalism or the kind of freewheeling, informal cosmopolitanism envisaged by Held and Beck (McChesney, 2006; Ritzer and Liska, 1997; Adorno et al., 1976 [1969]). The idea of multicultural fusion or hybridization suggests widespread intermingling across geographical scales and across cultures. In one guise this involves the usual array of cosmopolitan mixes – fusion food, ethnicizing of fashion and so-called world music – while in another it discerns and may applaud the 'repertoires of possibility' available to people through routine use of Web technologies and formats to promote social interaction and bespoke identities (Bourdieu, 1991, 26; Axford and Huggins, 2010).

Inglehart and Norris are suitably cautious about the effects of global communications and about media effects more generally, while suggesting that as interconnection between societies becomes more extensive and intensive its cultural impact is very likely to grow. Mainly, they are wary of attributing too many cultural consequences to cosmopolitan media because cultural *firewalls* (their term) exist which 'preserve the imprint of distinctive national cultures, especially in poorer societies' (2009, 147). In their estimation, the enduring weight of distinctive historical conditions and traditions vitiates the power of border-crossing technologies and media formats, even where, as in the case of Google, they can appear as modal.

This judgement may be affected by the authors' apparent willingness to endorse the old antinomies of local/global and homogeneity/heterogeneity which reinforce an either/or view of the world, rather than entertain the possibility of 'many globalizations' (Berger and Huntington, 2002), 'third cultures' which are neither local nor global (Featherstone, 1990), the idea of a heterogeneous yet singular world culture, and the 'complex relationalities' revealed in the study of what John Urry labels 'global fluids' like the internet (2003; 2005; see also Ong and Collier, 2005). As elusive as this formulation may appear, it is one more indication that, when discussing globalization, we may have to think outside normal social science and employ new kinds of imagery and new rules of intellectual engagement.

Conclusion

Not surprisingly, some disciplines and sub-fields covered in the last two chapters are more open to cross-disciplinary currents, while others have a much more developed and extensive scholarship from within, as it were. Borrowing themes, ideas and concepts across disciplines and sub-disciplines is fruitful but often exasperating since, for disciplinary 'sceptics' and 'para-keepers', it points up all the dangers and intellectual sloppiness of a 'pick-and-mix' approach to knowledge production, which is rarely followed through into rigorous theory building and empirical research. In these two chapters we have revealed both the steadfastness of disciplinary traditions as these bear on global scholarship and intimations of a much more open scholarship. A rather downbeat, but realistic, conclusion would be that trans- or inter-disciplinarity still has some way to travel. Is this because the aspiration for an interdisciplinary and multidimensional approach to the study of globalization is impossible or simply because we have yet to try hard enough (Rosamond, 2006; Rosow, 2003; Leander, 2009)?

CHAPTER 4

Theories of Globalization and Space

Introduction

The social science of globalization invests a wealth of theoretical ambition around the concepts of space and re-spatialization. This focus has its detractors, although not because critics always object to the idea of a 'spatial turn' as such. As we know, Justin Rosenberg, a trenchant critic, acknowledges the need for scholars to study the 'changing, multiple, layered forms in which territorialities are imbricated in social reproduction and change' (2007, 419). His concerns are that spatial and temporal factors are no more than contexts for action and/or that globalization theory has not offered a plausible, let alone convincing, explanation of how these factors might play a constitutive part in processes of social change and in the structuration of globality. In this chapter we will examine a number of important themes that exemplify the 'spatial turn' in the social sciences and in the scholarship of globalization.

Previously informed by a simple division of the world into national redoubts and global processes, nowadays more cautious, but also more innovative research on globalization examines the ways in which the social ontology of the world is ordered by different, sometimes overlapping, sometimes competing, configurations of space and time and the institutions and identities tied to them (Axford, 2007a). In this chapter we will privilege three analytically separate themes, although it is their imbrication that actually reveals the 'totality of spatial organization' (Jessop et al., 2008, 391). The first theme is the globalization–territory debate and the concepts of de- and supra-territorialization. In turn, this raises the issue of state–space, of 'stateness' and the changing territorialization of political power. The second, related theme bears on the mutability of geographical scales and of scale as a feature of social processes. The third focuses on the dialectic of networks and borders and provides insights into the tortuous extension of social relations across world space.

Let's rehearse the issues at stake in what follows: globalization is undoubtedly a geographical term that denotes 'a process over time of spatial change – the process of becoming worldwide' (Rosenberg, 2005, 11). While this definition allows Rosenberg to agree that the relational form of any society is 'inseparable' from particular constellations of space and time, he is dismissive of the idea that the 'spatio-temporal dimension of human social reproduction is in some way ontologically prior to other dimensions' and of the abstraction of spatial and temporal dimensions of social life from their 'human, relational dynamics' in actual societies (2005, 13). Thinking about spatial patterns or topologies is a key part of the shift away from simple Euclidean notions of the ordering of social and political life. For all the talk of a post-Westphalian (post-state/post-territorial) social science, the regional metaphor is routinely used to analyse social wholes, mainly because it is natural seeming (Mol and Law, 1994, 643).

Territory and Territoriality in a Globalizing World

Theories of social space also subsist as theories of territory and of territoriality, especially with regard to the idea of state space or the spatiality of the state (Brenner and Elden, 2009). Brenner and Elden usefully differentiate these two related concepts, such that 'territory' refers to a 'historically and geographically specific form of political organization and political thought' (2009, 355), while 'territoriality' entails spatial enclosure of the kind that others would call 'place'. While predictions of a borderless world have proliferated since the early 1990s or so, state territory and state territoriality remain the most visible and intractable features of the international system (Newman, 2005). This much is hardly controversial, save in the most committed of hyper-globalist accounts. The point is that space as territory and the idea of territoriality entailing spatial enclosure are not just descriptive or inert categories, but dynamic; and while often presented as 'natural', are anything but that.

Rather, each state has its own 'territorial strategies' which appear in loaded constructions such as 'foreign' or 'domestic', 'insider' and 'outsider' (Brenner and Elden, 2009, 354), all of which have telling consequences for rules and social practices. Strategies played out as policy or embedded in myths of national origin or cultural wholeness and integrity have significant effects upon all kinds of socio-spatial relations and have also defined the terms of intellectual inquiry about the relationships between space and political and cultural economy (Axford, 2006).

Recall that in 1994 John Agnew warned of the dangers of the 'territorial trap' and questioned the assumptions found in much scholarship on the state. In so doing he was problematizing 'the territorial extension, constitution and boundedness of state power and political-economic life more generally' in periods of globalization (Brenner and Elden, 2009, 354). Since then a raft of scholarship has endorsed his injunction, which, in part, accounts for the growing emphasis on de-territorialization, scale (Swyngedouw, 2004) and networks in discussions of both state power and global process (Castells, 2000a; Perkmann and Sum, 2002; Rumford, 2008). But in the rush to escape the territorial trap, the issue of territory/territoriality as central to any analysis of state power and global political and cultural economy may have been neglected.

Agnew offers a critique of *methodological territorialism*; that which 'subsumes all aspects of socio-spatial relations under the rubric of territoriality' (Jessop et al., 2008, 391). And the lure of the trap he defined is still apparent in state-centric critiques of globalization practices and theory, which have difficulties comprehending a world made through growing statelessness. Indeed, even to recognize what is happening in such terms requires the analyst to step outside liberal-territorialist discourses on such key concepts as political community and to have set aside assumptions about the natural spaces of civil and civic association (Axford, 2004; Chandler, 2004; 2009). Both Scholte and Sassen exemplify important revisionist (even transformationalist) strands in socio-spatial theory applied to territory and globalization.

Scholte on territory and globalization

Scholte's work (2000; 2003; 2005a; 2005b) is the epitome of what some describe, rather slightingly, as the geographical approach to globalization. But, as he notes in a reply to Rosenberg's criticisms of his 'geographical' reasoning, it is possible to argue that scientific explanation can (must) incorporate a spatial dimension without being 'based' on geography alone (2005a). This is hardly a ringing endorsement of the idea that spatial organization (and spatial consciousness) in and of itself causes change, and it is a rather more qualified take on geography than can be found in his earlier volume on globalization (2000). In the second edition of *Globalization: A Critical Introduction* (2005a), anxious to avoid any sense that de-territorialization simply means the demise of place and the end of borders, Scholte uses the concept 'supraterritoriality' to capture the more inchoate spatial configurations and material/ideational structures of globalization.

And yet the concept remains quite radical in its implications. Supraterritoriality refers to a form of (re-)spatialization in which social space is not confined by territory or by distance. The idea also implies that social, political, cultural and economic practices and forms may themselves be patterned by the fact they take place in supraterritorial rather than territorial space and that practitioners recognize and are influenced by this distinction. This strong interpretation of what is entailed by supraterritoriality is further underwritten by the idea that the concept not only transcends territory; it transcends time and space as well. Because of this, Scholte is right to distinguish between the idea of supraterritoriality and that of *transplanetary* connections that simply augment links across borders and are not a novel feature of a globalized world.

Like Bauman's geometry of liquid modernity (2000; 2005; 1998), supraterritorial phenomena may have no shape and are not fixed in either time or space (Ritzer, 2010; Urry, 2003). Examples abound and Scholte illustrates his argument with references to the porosity, and sometimes the irrelevance, of borders to global financial transactions, migration and the internet (Castells, 2000a; Urry, 2003). Of course, none of the authors cited here assume that liquidity is total or that flows are unhindered, and this is an important qualification in what follows (Ritzer, 2010). Moreover, in Scholte's thesis, it is at least implicit that territory and territoriality remain important to the explanatory account, in areas such as production, governance, ecology and, of course, allegiance.

Now, there is no doubt that supraterritoriality has all the attributes of the late/postmodern zeitgeist pilloried by Rosenberg, because it exemplifies social process at odds with the organizational practices of boundary maintenance and the hierarchical decision rules through which such practices have been sustained. But such recognition need not prescribe an either/or model in which territory and scale no longer matter. Rather, it involves 'rejecting the notion of scale as a bounded, territorially complete concept and of any notion that social relations are, or have to be, contained at particular scales' (Bulkeley, 2005: 884).

As Neil Brenner argues: 'scales evolve relationally within tangled hierarchies and dispersed inter-scalar networks' and 'the very intelligibility of each scalar articulation of a social process hinges crucially upon its embeddedness within dense webs of relations to other scales and spaces' (2001: 605, 606). Thus it is possible to think of networks – in trade, finance, diaspora, terrorism and so on – as 'significantly de-territorialized' (Urry, 2003: 58) but also inserted into territories at, as well as across, all scales (Axford, 2006). Peter Dicken talks about a world still made up of unified spatio-temporal units (nation-states and societies) that is unlikely to be undone entirely by the activities of transnational networks. Rather, network links and global fluids (Urry, 2003), where they cross borders, are more likely to create 'qualitative disjunctures' between different regulatory, socio-cultural and political environments, at the same time as they enable routine connection between actors separated across time and space (Dicken et al., 2001: 96; Axford, 2009).

All this sounds perfectly reasonable on Scholte's part and is a necessary distancing of his work from the contagion of hyper-globalism. But one interesting, perhaps important, question and a further subsidiary query are thereby posed. The important question is this: does Scholte's more cautious take on supraterritoriality dilute the transformative intent of his thesis? The second-order question concerns his ability to identify truly supraterritorial (as opposed to transplanetary, or merely international) processes and forms (Martell, 2007). First then: Scholte's transformationalism starts from the position that the construction of social space has effects that are not reducible to any mode of production. By 2005 he still offers the robust claim that it is reasonable to suppose 'space carries some relatively autonomous significance in social relations' (2005b, 393). His more cautious take on the idea of 'relatively autonomous' – a phrase from the lexicon of weasel words in any theoretical discourse – is to argue that 'history flows from a confluence of inter-related spatial, cultural, economic, political and psychological forces' (2005b, 394–5), which is multidimensionality in spades.

Globalization (as re-spatialization) now appears less as an 'autonomous' force and merely 'promotes, encourages and advances concurrent other shifts in social structure' (395). This qualified account goes some way to defray criticism that proponents of globalization as geography do little more than substitute one form of constitution for another, so that space performs the same explanatory function for Scholte as mode of production does for Rosenberg, or market structures for neo-liberal hyper-globalists. However, the cost of revisionism is (always?) some theoretical equivocation, and Martell (2007) takes Scholte to task for shifting his position so much that he has now occupied ground better suited to a sceptical account of globalization, where the potency of globalizing (re-spatializing) processes is actually called into doubt.

As to the second-order question, there are two strictures. The first is that many of Scholte's examples of supraterritoriality pre-date what most people see as the key pre-millennial decades after 1960 and thus anticipate, rather than constitute, globalization. But this may be less daunting for Scholte than it first appears, since it is hard, and usually wrong, to locate the precise origins of all recent globalizing forces solely in post-1960s trends, except possibly for the internet. Even if one were to treat the final decades of the twentieth century as a period when the concatenation of Soviet collapse and Western (economic) restructuring created conditions in which globalization flourished, some of these trends were apparent prior to that time; indeed were immanent in the changing process of capitalist reproduction and expansion. These trends include the end of Fordism and the rise of a new international division of labour (NIDL), new communications technologies, the erosion of national systems of production and the breakdown of habitual solidarities in many societies, with the consequent spread of mutable identities.

More telling perhaps is that many of the illustrations used by Scholte are of transplanetary connectivity rather than of a supraterritoriality that dispenses with territory entirely, although the latter category is hard to define. In the next section we consider how Saskia Sassen deals with similar concerns as she examines globalization through the analytical lenses of both spatial theory and political economy.

Sassen: territory, scale and globalization

Sassen 'is most concerned with the spatial, or scalar, realities of globalization as a process that restructures space and place' (Robinson, 2009, 1). Her ambition to contribute to the sociology of globalization is evident in three main areas. The first is her pioneering and highly influential global cities thesis;

the second her work on transnational migration; the third features research on the state, global digital networks and emergent global formations (1988; 1991; 2011 [1994]; 2008 [2006]; 2007). Much of this corpus is distilled in her 2007 work, *A Sociology of Globalization*. Unlike Scholte, she has no overarching view of globalization processes and only a jobbing, or implied, sense of globality. For all that, hers is a major contribution to the understanding of globalization as a socio-spatial phenomenon, although it is curiously neglectful of the process as discursive or subjective, and thus finds few points of contact with constructivist thinking (Albrow, 2007a). Yet her thesis is clearly one of epochal transformation in train, albeit that the transformative potential is being realized through the ways in which globalizing dynamics are taking place 'inside the national' (2006, 1). First we will examine her discussion of territory, authority and globalization, before using her treatment of scale and networks to inform the subsequent parts of this chapter.

Sassen writes about the state and territory out of the same sociological tradition as Henri Lefebvre, Georg Simmel and Karl Marx, but applied to the global age (Albrow, 2007a). Like many other students of globalization, Sassen wants to abandon a framework for analysis that relies on the simple dualism of national and global. Instead she focuses on the interplay and tensions between two main concepts and processes: *denationalization*, which involves playing down the national frame of reference in all its guises, and *embeddedness*, which holds that global processes are located in particular times, material places and social conditions. These ideas are by no means unique to Sassen's work and can be found, for example, in Giddens' pioneering use of *embedding* as a feature of space-time distanciation (1984; 1990; 1992).

Sassen uses this conceptual scheme in pursuit of a better understanding of globalization as a complex and variable process. She notes the existence of 'self-evidently global institutions' (2007, 5) exemplified by the World Trade Organization (WTO), global financial markets and the International War Crimes Tribunal. But her attempt to map an analytic terrain for the study of globalization requires more than this, and so she invokes a second set of dynamics which are not 'global' in the same way as the WTO, but 'take place deep inside territories and institutional domains' that are usually designated as national (2007, 6).

These dynamics – including cross-border networks of activists fighting eminently local struggles and the use made by national courts of international law and conventions – demonstrate that as a process, globalization 'inhabits' and relies on the national and yet challenges the received wisdom that the nation-state is the natural container of all social process. Indeed, the overall aim of this conceptual strategy is to escape what Martin Albrow calls 'the intellectual *cul-de-sac* that equated the nation-state with society *tout court* and inferred that globalization, in challenging nation-state control, also meant the disembedding of society from any kind of material foundations' (2007a, 6; see also Robinson, 2009; Albert, 2009; Thomas, 2009; Robertson, 2009). This prescription is not without difficulties and sometimes produces even more obfuscation. The key point in Sassen's schema is that a good deal of globalization consists of what she calls 'micro-processes' which serve to 'denationalize' 'what had been constructed as national' (2006, 1; see also Sassen, 1990). Let's look at this in more detail.

Denationalization is key to Sassen's attempt to map new 'geographies of power', which challenge, but by no means overturn, the two signature features of the modern state: political sovereignty and territorial exclusivity. The nub of her argument is that the modern doctrine of state sovereignty, which was constructed historically through a process of 'nationalizing territories', is being transformed by globalization. But this radical premise leads to a somewhat unsatisfactory, though hardly unexpected, conclusion, which is that state sovereignty and territoriality are thereby only relatively transformed. For Sassen, globalization brings about new spatial economies beyond the regulatory capacity of any one state. Because of this, it is truly reconfiguring the territorial exclusivity of sovereign states; but the key question is, to what extent? The idea of new geographies of power is an attempt to ground the argument that while states are being transformed, they remain potent in, or at least integral to, the political economy of a globalized world; which thesis could be a re-jigged form of vulgar Marxist functionalism, at least in less practised hands.

Four components make up her new geographies of power. The first is the 'footloose' nature of both contemporary capital and business. This rootlessness takes the form of, for example, collaborative business models in activities such as trans-border outsourcing and global supply chains, while new digital architectures affect the very geography of capital accumulation, so that 'many of the newer objects of capital accumulation flow through spaces' (Scholte, 2005b, 398). The second component is a novel kind of territoriality best described as 'extra-territoriality', which affects a state's sovereignty by diluting, and sometimes abrogating, its capacity to regulate various institutions and activities. Free trade zones are an obvious example because many of their activities are not subject to local rules. But the clearest illustration is the phenomenon of global cities, which are the territorial embodiment of global processes. As Robinson has it, '[t]he global financial, stock, foreign exchange and other markets in these cities constitute de-territorialized activities that do not fall under the regulatory umbrella of the states in which such cities are located' (2009, 20).

The third component is the emergence of a new legal regime for governing mainly economic relations and transactions, which bypasses national legal systems. International credit rating agencies that adjudicate on the debt security and creditworthiness of national governments fall into this category, and their power to parlay investment into or away from particular countries renders them a crucial element in the growth of (private) global economic governance (Cutler, 1999; Ruggie, 2004). Finally, Sassen refers to the

'virtualization of economic activity' (1996, 22) and cites the instance of currency markets which trade without much let or hindrance from national
regulators, including central banks. In later work, she also discusses the part
being played by the internet and mobile telephony in the creation of networks of political activists who are players in a novel kind of transnational
politics and are contributing to new forms of citizenship (2008 [2006]).

Taken together, these are powerful instrumentalities in the making of a
de-territorialized global political and cultural economy. Yet the state is very
much at the heart of Sassen's thesis, both facilitating a new system of transnational governance and being instrumental in its own transformation. For
critics such as Robinson this still leaves Sassen clinging to a re-jigged form of
state-centrism (2009; see also 2004). Robinson's own position derives from a
neo-Marxist analysis of the class composition of states and economic groups,
which he says is lacking in Sassen's account. And it is true that the latter has
a curiously realist feel to it, in that states are not analysed in terms of their
genetic-cultural qualities of 'stateness', or as arenas in and through which
social forces compete. Instead they are assumed to present a uniform face to
an external economic reality – in this case, globalization. States 'confront'
economic forces in the shape of 'footloose' capital and flexible labour markets,
as well as having to negotiate the meaning of citizenship because of the
growing salience of human rights regimes that ascribe membership on the
basis of shared humanity and not national legal status.

The upshot is an emergent and powerful tension, even a dialectic, which
is still being played out. On the one hand, economic globalization de-
nationalizes domestic economies and economic governance, while on the
other, states struggle to re-nationalize aspects of, for example, immigration
policy, either under the guise of controlling labour market supply or as a
component of enhanced and politically charged policy on homeland security.
Of course, the existence and visibility of a global human rights regime further
complicates matters where the management of immigration is concerned,
because it reveals that what is often presented as an administrative/rational
procedure over allowable numbers is actually a more expressive issue about
the nature of citizenship in a 'borderless' world.

Now, it may be that Sassen is remiss to treat states as though the 'economic
and the political are externally related', separate and even oppositional,
spheres, each with its own independent logic (Robinson, 2009, 22). And certainly her position limits the ambition to effect a multidimensional analysis
of globalization where political, economic and socio-cultural spheres are
mutually constitutive, rather than oppositional. But Sassen's argument, elaborated in *Territory, Authority, Rights* (2008 [2006]) and played out in a more
obvious disciplinary context in *A Sociology of Globalization* (2006), is not simply
that states matter, even if one allows for the fact that economic globalization
seems to entail a set of practices that de-constitute the national frame of
reference. Instead of a tiresome battle around one or more versions of

globalization as dominant and states/territoriality as subordinate, or vice versa, Sassen offers a more textured interpretation of changing practices that affect the spatiality of the state. These practices are visible in urban and especially metropolitan environments, in transnational migration and in the creation of what she calls 'new digital assemblages', which are producing distinctive and complex spatialities that cannot be completely subsumed under the national or the global and thus, as we noted in chapter 1, 'have their own sociological reality' (2006, xiii).

The empirical focus of much of Sassen's work has been on urban and especially metropolitan spaces and on transnational migration as a signature feature of ways in which such spaces work to reproduce, but also restructure, production processes and labour markets. In *The Mobility of Labor and Capital* (1988) she first articulates the idea of 'global cities' as economic hubs from which the global economy is managed and serviced and through which migrants, as labour market factors, flow.

Of course, actual status varies with the demand for different types of labour and technical skills, the category of worker and the (still mainly national) rules governing both mobility and settlement. Under globalization, patterns of labour migration mirror changes in the world economy so that core economies make increasing use of such labour in the service sector, where migrants occupy either relatively unskilled jobs not exportable to less costly labour markets, or those skilled posts that cannot be filled solely from domestic sources. At the same time as these labour types are drawn to big cities, mainly in the global North, other migrant labour is attracted to export processing zones largely in the periphery of the world economy. Sassen says that the 'growing concentration of immigrant labor in service jobs in developed countries can be viewed as the correlate of the export of jobs to the Third World' (1988, 53); they are the 'systematic equivalent of [an] offshore proletariat.'

Other scholarship has also underlined the extent to which 'world-cities' are not just located in discrete national territories, but have to be conceived as important sites of production, finance and business intelligence which provide the coordinating mechanisms of the world economy (Taylor and Knox, 2005). In the *world-cities* hypothesis, such key sites were grouped as to their location in a hierarchical international division of labour, and this corresponds to the findings of some world-systems scholarship, while largely retaining the old national/international distinction (Abu-Lughod, 1971; 1989). Sassen builds on this thesis and uses Manuel Castells' ground-breaking concept of the *informational city* to posit a new transnational and even global order (Castells, 1989; 2000a; 2008). As Robinson notes (2009, 12),

> [s]he theorizes a new global spatial order founded on global flows of money, information, and people through transnational networks of cities, coining the term 'global city' in 1984 . . . in order to move beyond the nation-state/inter-state system as the unit of

analysis and to distinguish the specificity of the global as it gets structured [in cities] in the contemporary period.

Global cities, led by New York, London and Tokyo, now practise a networked global economy, and their strategic interconnectedness engenders a 'transformation in the spatial expression of the logic of accumulation, and in the institutional arrangements through which it takes place' (Sassen, 1991, 20). But in a networked world places still matter, and Sassen identifies four types of places as avatars of the new spatial forms of economic globalization: export-processing zones (for example, maquiladoras along the USA–Mexico border); offshore banking centres (for example, the Cayman Islands, Bahrain); high-tech districts (for example, Silicon Valley); and global cities themselves. In developing this argument, she points to a curious feature of the global economy: it displays 'an ever-more spatially *dispersed* yet globally *integrated* organization of economic activity' (Robinson, 2009, 13). Transnational production involves the diffusion across the globe of functionally integrated economic activities, or chains, and along these chains global cities play crucial roles at the nodes of what it is appropriate to call transnational urban systems linking financial and business centres in the global North and South. Rio, Mumbai, Shanghai and Hong Kong, as well as others, now join London, Tokyo and New York in the pantheon of global cities. To all intents and purposes they now coordinate the global economy.

Sassen's thesis in this regard is powerful and strongly developed, but it is still too state-centric for some critics, even though she is increasingly at pains to identify new spatial and temporal orders which qualify the ontological centrality of the state (2006). Other criticisms focus on her key concept of global cities. These critiques advert the unduly economic focus in Sassen's arguments and the neglect of cultural and political factors (Eade, 1997). In other work she is taken to task for privileging cities in the global North as the key nodes of the world economy when predictions of urban growth all point to surges in population size and economic activity in metropolitan areas in the South, for example in Lagos, Manilla, Mumbai or Cairo. Some critics even question the analytical value of abstracting 'global' cities from the broader economic dynamism found – at least in financial and other service industries – 'much further down the urban hierarchy' (Storper, 1997, 56). All these criticisms may be valid, especially in relation to the global cities hypothesis, but they far from traduce its analytical purchase on the importance of urban spaces as ones through which globalizing processes flow and are (sometimes) embedded.

Of late, Sassen has turned her attention to the ways in which digital architectures – digital assemblages – are modifying, even transforming the routines and structures of governance (2006, 2007). She is concerned, primarily, with the emerging complexity of social practices and authority relations seen in the use of technologies whose key property is a challenge to the very idea of place and of boundaries, but which enable actors to refurbish or reinvent the idea, and perhaps the ideal, of locality or community, sometimes tied to territory (Axford, 2006). The focus of this work is the way new mobile communication technologies and the globalization of production are still rooted in localities (often, though by no means always, in big cities), which themselves become global through their networked connections and their cosmopolitan or multicultural lifestyles. In this account the political and cultural economies that constitute the national subsist in and, at the same time, constitute the global; they are not separate scales in practice, or for purposes of analysis.

In this respect, Sassen's conceptualization of globalization is at one, at least in spirit, with the treatment accorded to *glocal* processes by Roland Robertson. Both authors want to reject the idea of local and global being distinct zones of activity; self-contained or discrete geographical scales. Sassen's intriguing notion of 'analytical borderlands' that subsist between the national and the global (2006) is intended to capture the sense that new spatio-temporal orders constituted by digital networks, or as she has it, 'digital assemblages', work to disrupt the 'national project of containment' (2006, 379). Never immaculate, the national is now routinely disrupted by the speed and density of digital connectivity, but even this does not stand outside the national in the sense of constituting a separate global modality. As Sassen says, '[n]either the national nor the global represents a fully stabilized meaning today' (2006, 379).

Scale and Social Process: Reviewing Topological Presuppositions

The language of levels or scales continues to inform the study of globalization, even though its leitmotif is the 'destabilizing of older hierarchies of scale' (Sassen, 2008, 158; Cox, 1993; Swyngedouw, 1992). Sassen's take on this is to argue that one of the key aspects of the current phase of globalization – what others call the late or post-Westphalian phase of modernity – has territorial states as 'necessary' (her word) participants in the formation of regional and global systems, if only as the 'contexts' for the development of various 'transboundary spatialities' (2008, 158). This is not simple functionalist or vulgar Marxist reasoning used to rationalize the apparent contradiction in the salience of both fixed boundaries and mobile networks or flows, but an attempt to comprehend the multiple scales at which the global is constituted (Bulkeley, 2005). Critically, territory and territoriality are not abrogated, but this involves 'rejecting the notion of scale as a bounded, territorially complete concept, and of any notion that social relations are contained at particular scales' (Bulkeley, 2005, 884). As Neil Brenner argues: 'scales evolve relationally within tangled hierarchies and dispersed interscalar networks' (2001, 605).

David Harvey's 'troubling geographies'

Harvey's corpus spans themes and topics as diverse as urbanism, the environment and postmodernism. For our purposes the key themes are the role of space in capitalist accumulation and the ways in which a contemporary Marxist critique of political economy also accommodates the socially transformative potential of de-spatializing processes. Writing in 1989, Harvey gets to the nub of the matter when he says that de-spatializing processes 'so revolutionize the objective qualities of space and time that we are forced to alter . . . how we represent the world to ourselves' (240). In other words, the modern geo-political imagination, wedded to the isomorphism of people, territory and culture, is now ill equipped to offer a firm analytical purchase on those forces that are altering the frame of agency and rendering conventional territorialities and subjectivities ambiguous, sometimes nugatory. His more recent work on the 'new' imperialism, seen in America's post-9/11 frisson of economic uncertainty and decline linked to geo-political aggressiveness, is also examined through the particular spatial framework developed in his trademark concept of the 'spatial fix' (2001; 2003; 2005b). In this work the so-called 'new' imperialism is a distillation of powerful emergent trends in world capitalism and geo-politics (2003, 26).

In Harvey's work there is both analytical and – to a lesser extent – empirical continuity in his concern to theorize the transformation between one accumulation regime and another, a pursuit which informs not only the discussion of historical transitions in capitalist accumulation, but also the geo-political regime change constituted by the war in Iraq. There is too an enduring commitment to exploring the spatialities and temporalities of capitalism and capitalist social formations (Jessop, 2007). In this endeavour the concept of the spatial fix is central. It is a concept that identifies different forms of spatial reorganization and geographical expansion that help to alleviate and manage the crisis tendencies immanent in all forms of accumulation. The idea is found early in Harvey's work on Marx in the 1970s and develops through reflection on 'temporal fixes' (2001; 2003; also see Smith, 2001) to find its most recent expression, that of the 'spatio-temporal fix', in the critique of the 'new' imperialism extant since the turn of the millennium (2003; 2005a, 2005b; Jessop, 2006). In fact, Harvey maps both historical capitalisms and the contemporary variant found in globalization. He offers a conceptual map of world-capitalist dynamics infused with a powerful normative critique of recent attempts at crisis management or deferral through military intervention by the preponderant power (see also Arrighi, 1994; Silver and Arrighi, 2001).

In *The New Imperialism* (2003) and *A Brief History of Neoliberalism* (2005b), Harvey looks for a connection between processes of capital accumulation and expansionist political-military projects. He sees the American neo-conservative Project for the New American Century (PNAC), which inspired the US-led

War on Terror and the invasion of Iraq, as a clear illustration of such a connection and exemplar of what he calls the 'spatio-temporal fix'. In his conceptual scheme, the term 'fix' has a double meaning, thus:

> [a] certain portion of the total capital is literally fixed in and on the land in some physical form for a relatively long period of time (depending on its economic and physical lifetime). Some social expenditures (such as public education or a health-care system) also become territorialized and rendered geographically immobile through state commitments. The spatio-temporal 'fix', on the other hand, is a metaphor for a particular kind of solution to capitalist crises through temporal deferral and geographical expansion. (2003, 115)

Temporal deferral and geographical expansion 'fix' the over-accumulation crises that arise from the chronic tendency of capital to accumulate over and above what can be reinvested profitably in the production and exchange of commodities. Because of this tendency, surpluses of capital and labour are left either unused or underutilized. But the incorporation of new space into the system of accumulation helps to absorb these surpluses in two ways. First, it promotes activities required to open up the new space and provide the necessary infrastructures for accelerated accumulation. Second, once the new space has been made productive, surpluses of labour and capital can be deployed in innovative and productive ways made profitable by the spatial enlargement of the system of accumulation (Harvey, 2003, 109–12).

But that is not, or may not be, the end of the story. Sometimes, further crisis tendencies arise from the dislocations that occur when moving capital from one place to another. These dislocations Harvey calls 'switching crises', and although the notion is inadequately theorized in terms of its necessary or contingent relationship with more routine crises of accumulation, it clearly has some purchase on the quotidian problems that must arise when such movements are attempted. In other words, the concept usefully qualifies the notion of a seamless and entirely fluid world economy, which has places and events as mere transit points on mobile networks of capital.

The implications of this scenario for current developments in the world economy are obvious, not least with regard to the putative hegemonic shift now taking place. Harvey's argument is that, rather than go quietly into the good night, the USA has resisted, and will continue to resist, the spatial fix implied in the shift of over-accumulated capital from West to East; not only because it presages an acceleration in the transfer of economic hegemony, but because of its political and strategic implications too. The upshot is a classic 'catch-22'. On the one hand any 'unconstrained' transfer of capital to new regions has an adverse impact on the hegemonic centre because of intensified international competition. On the other hand, while constraining development abroad may limit potentially damaging international competition, it also inhibits opportunities for the profitable investment of surplus capital that is required in order to maintain the dynamism and competitive edge of the hegemonic centre (Harvey, 1982, 435). For a hegemonic centre, either outcome threatens to erode not just its assets but its power as well.

Harvey envisages two possible ways out of this catch-22. One is to use purely financial means 'to rid the system of overaccumulation by the visitation of crises of devaluation upon vulnerable territories' (2003, 134; 2005b. Most economists see devaluation as the only effective 'solution' to over-accumulation. It entails scrapping economic dead wood through means as diverse as banking crashes, inflation, plant closure, even depressions or, as Joseph Schumpeter put it (1976 [1942]), through the creative destruction of physical and human capital. Applying these crisis solutions in the domestic setting of a core or hegemonic power is costly and politically dangerous. But the ability to export a crisis of devaluation to another country or countries is also tricky and may not be possible in a strongly interlinked world economy, where it is hardly possible to insulate particular domestic economies (and politics) from world trends. So the other solution is the use of political and military means to turn international competition to the advantage of the more powerful states. Using such means constitutes, says Harvey, the 'sinister and destructive side of spatial-temporal fixes to the overaccumulation problem' (2003, 19).

Notwithstanding the technical complexity of neo-Marxist theories of crisis tendencies and management, Harvey has a quite elemental take on the kind of spatial fix evident in the PNAC and the motives driving it. Of the engagement in Iraq he writes, 'it can be captured in the following proposition: whoever controls the Middle East controls the global oil spigot and whoever controls the global oil spigot can control the global economy, at least for the near future' (2003, 19). In other words, the intervention was 'all about oil', which appears rather simplistic until one locates the sentiment in the theory of capitalist imperialism that he favours and the kind of spatio-temporal fix that it requires.

In brief, Harvey labels the period between about 1970 and 2000 as one of 'neo-liberal hegemony'. But following 9/11 everything changed and confidence and dynamism drained from the capitalist system. As a direct consequence the USA launched a series of imperialist wars and aggressive military engagements to bolster its interests and to offset a potentially devastating global devaluation of capital in the wake of proto-crises such as the failure of the dot.com revolution. In doing so America was seeking to offset further crisis tendencies through what Harvey calls a policy of 'accumulation by dispossession'. This strategy, or crisis response mechanism, aims to release key assets at very low cost but, as we noted above, applied domestically it is likely to be politically costly and socially disruptive. So the obvious solution is to export the misery and to effect fraudulently and, where necessary, by force of arms the expropriation of key assets (in this case, oil). Harvey is at pains to point out that such ventures are by no means unique to US actions since the early 2000s or so, but apply to any number of historical cases where it was more expedient to tackle a crisis of accumulation by this kind of spatio-temporal fix.

As a geographical representation of historical capitalism and an attempt to understand its crisis tendencies, Harvey provides ample evidence that the globalization of historical capitalism entails fundamental structural transformations of the spatial networks in which that system of accumulation is embedded. This view seriously, albeit contentiously, challenges the notion, still dominant in world-system analysis, of a quantitatively expanding but structurally invariant world capitalist system, with Kondratieff cycles, hegemonic cycles and logistics as its empirical manifestations. Instead, the notion of a spatio-temporal fix imparts a much more contingent or expedient feel to such events and suggests that more needs to be understood about the role of 'interstitial' agencies and networks, rather than, or as well as, structural givens, in the playing out of the spatio-temporal fix.

We may still harbour unease about the validity of Harvey's thinking applied to the post-millennium exertions of the USA in the Persian Gulf and elsewhere. If, as Harvey argues, the aggressive expansionism of US imperialism rests on the crisis caused by the over-accumulation of capital, so that profit rates fall, he is mistaken about the motives driving US foreign and military policy at the time of the second Gulf War. During the period in question, there was no over-accumulation crisis; profit rates were rising and there was little in the way of unproductive surplus capital. How then to explain the USA's new unilateralism? If Harvey's theory is tied to the unproductive generation of surplus capital it fails to explain the 'new' imperialism (Arrighi and Silver, 1999; Callinicos, 2010).

What Harvey's work does tell us is that Marxist crisis theory may be less than a perfect analytical template on which to map the spatial-temporal dynamics of historical capitalism and contemporary globalization, and is no guarantee of an appropriately spatialized conception of political economy (or empire). To be sure, this much is also apparent in Hardt and Negri's rather exotic, 'post-Marxist' account of globalization as *Empire*, in which different spheres of power – economic, political and cultural – seem to have no home, but inhabit networks; or more accurately, invest a 'virtual and discontinuous global network' of connections (Smith, 2001, 18; Hardt and Negri, 2000). In *Empire* (2000), although less obviously in both *Multitude* (2004) and *Commonwealth* (2009), Hardt and Negri assume that global power is both anonymous and spaceless, while Harvey, despite his faults, does 'recognize the recasting of scaled geographies – from the scale of the body to the trans-planetary – as an intensely political process' (Smith, 2001, 17). Significantly, he also understands the 'implicit spatiality of political power'. And in what follows the dialectic of space(lessness) and place occupies centre-stage.

The Dialectic of Borders and Networks

Attempts to develop critical accounts of globalization have produced increasingly sophisticated treatments of the interplay of spatial and temporal orders and how these affect the processes of globalization and the constitution of global systems. Indeed, it is not stretching the point too far to say that the dialectic of borders and networks may actually distil the contested ontology of the global. Exploring the imbrication of such apparent antinomies offers profound insights into the extension of social relations across world space and also lets us reconsider the obdurate, though changing nature of the nation-state and the whole idea of the national.

It was once common to treat borders and networks as avatars of quite different and mutually incompatible constructions of time and space. In this crude antinomy, borders speak to territoriality, fixity and ontological thickness; while networks promise interconnection and fluidity, enabling social relations that cross space 'at all scales' (Dicken et al., 2001, 92). Arjun Appadurai's account of the conflict between the 'vertebrate' and 'cellular' geographies of the world after 9/11 has the protagonists as nation-states (though in Huntington's imagery in 1996 they are the 'realist geographies' of ascribed civilizations) and new forms of connection, solidarity and organization (2006, 116). Both orders are global in reach and the encounters between them have the potential to transform the 'morphology of [the] global economy and politics' (Appadurai, 2006, 28).

Borders remain crucial to an understanding of the contemporary world, although the analytical gloss today is on their permeability and socially constructed nature (Newman, 2003; Balibar, 1999; Rumford, 2008; Holton, 2005; Thompson, 2000; 2003). While the concept of 'border' continues to be rich in signification, it is undergoing profound changes in meaning. Because of the changing socio-political and socio-cultural spaces opened up by processes of regionalization and globalization, borders are 'no longer entirely situated at the outer limits of territories; they are dispersed a little everywhere, wherever there is movement of people, information and things' (Balibar, 1999, 1).

Networks constitute a 'relativisation of scale' (Jessop, 2000, 325) and are exemplars of the current global political and cultural economies because they are both mobile and mutable. From a governance standpoint, borders are seen to underwrite formal organization and hierarchy while networks challenge and subvert them. In short, networks offer alternative topologies of the global, characterized not by fixity or closure, but by movement. In practice, networks are various and variable, in both their intensity (of connection) and their extensiveness. Bob Holton says that 'the 'typology of networks now extends to business and trade, policy and advocacy, knowledge and the professions, together with empire and terror, kinship and friendship, religion and migration' (2005, 46; 2009; Taylor, 2004).

Karin Knorr-Cetina portrays the ontology of networks thus:

[a] network is an arrangement of nodes tied together by relationships – some instrumental, some affective – that serve as channels of communication, resources, and other coordinating mechanisms. Cooperation of various kinds, strategic alliances, exchanges, emotional bonds, kinship ties, personal relations, and forms of grouping and entrenchment can all be seen to work through ties and to instantiate sociality in networks of relationships. (2007, 72)

Some networked relationships are relatively contained by geographical and territorial boundaries, others are manifestly trans-boundary or global.

When discussing globalization, the concept 'network' obviously carries a potent analytical charge, whether used as a metaphor or as an analytical or empirical category (Singh Grewal, 2008). Often it appears alongside, or is conflated with, cognate notions such as *chains, flows, liquids* and *hybrids* (Axford, 2009). These terms now inform the conceptual landscape of the social science of globalization, witness to its transformative potential as an analytical and empirical alternative to the standard modern social forms of hierarchy and market (Hannerz, 1996). But it is always wise to temper any 'excessive emphasis on purportedly new features of social life'. Different theorists employ networks to very different ends (Holton, 2005, 210). Let's treat with these issues by examining a full-blown macro-level interpretation of the world as a form of network society.

Manuel Castells: The network state and the network society

Manuel Castells (2000a; 2000b; 2006; 2008; 2009) offers an encompassing theoretical treatise on the emergence of the network society in the information age. His sophisticated arguments rehearse the advantages of a network perspective for a systematic understanding of contemporary social change. Although it trades at the meso level for much of the empirical detail used, this is really a macro-morphological and transformationalist argument. For some critics his quite bullish account of the progressive social impact of communication technologies makes him a techno-apologist for neo-liberal globalization (Jessop, 2003). But this criticism rather underestimates Castells' ambivalence over the social and political consequences of information technologies.

At the heart of Castells' thesis is the idea that network morphologies and network logic overtake other forms of social organization, and this logic invests all social and economic life (Barry, 2001; Axford, 2009). Of course, this is not a theory of globalization per se, and in some respects his body of work on urban spaces actually pre-dates much conventional globalization scholarship. But his output on informational capitalism and the network society resonates strongly with, and also influences, what others would call transformative accounts of globalization. By 2000, when he published the revised first volume of his *Information Age* trilogy, he was engaged directly with arguments about globalization (Jones, 2010).

Castells' global sociology is built around three interrelated concepts and themes that underpin his thesis of the emergence of a global network society. All these flow from the premise, first articulated in *The Informational City* (1991), that 'whilst organisations are located in places and their components are space-dependent, the organizational logic is placeless, being fundamentally dependent on the space of flows that characterize information networks' (1991, 140). The themes are, first, that all social relations are inherently spatial and that the spaces in which people live out their lives 'reflect and shape social life in its totality' (1991, 141). This is a rather more careful formulation than it first appears because Castells wants to hedge his bets. Space is not seen as an independent variable, but neither is it a mere context for action and agency. There is also the temporal dimension to consider. Where once practices were only 'simultaneous in time' if they were conducted in the same (local) place, new types of spaces and thus new forms of social interaction and meaning are opened up when time is compressed or erased through the use of information technologies.

Second is the much-used notion of 'space of flows', which develops from the idea of there being 'placeless' organizational logics. Lest we think of this as a benign construct, pointing to the disappearance of time and space as constraints on social relationships and presaging an anodyne global future, Castells as early as 1991 sounds a warning note: 'the space of flows can be abstract in social, cultural, and historical terms, . . . [but] places are . . . condensations of human history, culture and matter' (1991, 14). In other words, the shift may precipitate a new kind of local-global politics, built around digital inclusion and exclusion and forms of resistance to the obliteration of place, including the identity space of the nation-state.

Sovereignty may be ceded both to the space of flows and to regional and other translocal entities. States are then caught in a dilemma. If they steadfastly represent the interests of their domestic populations, they may isolate themselves from key networks. If they follow the network logic, they may cease to represent these populations, become no more than nodes in such networks, and thus surrender sovereignty: rather portentously, Castells says, '[n]ation states will survive, but not so their sovereignty' (2004b, 8). In even more pessimistic (realistic?) vein, he also writes '[n]etworks lead to the destruction of human experience: power is separated from political representation, production from consumption, information from communication' (2004b, 10).

Castells' third theme is *timeless time*, suggesting that under conditions of globalization there has been a proliferation of social times (see also Holton, 2005; Gurvitch, 2003); 'social' because, over history, different conceptions of time have been dominant depending on prevailing social dynamics. The social character of time is altered markedly under globalization. Both cyclical and linear temporalities (features of the medieval and modern eras respectively) assumed a relatively predictable, sequential unfolding of events mediated by context, conditions and motivation. But 'timeless time' introduces a new kind of temporality. Not only is time stretched and compressed in the ways identified by Giddens and Harvey, but it is 'experienced disjunctively' (Jones, 2010, 60), that is, through events or instances which may not have a sequential structure – or in other words, are unpredictable. And it is clear that processes of globalization are at least closely linked with a 'sense of virtually simultaneous or instantaneous time' (Holton, 2005, 99), especially where they are driven by information technologies. John Tomlinson makes much the same point in his discussion of the 'culture of speed' (2007) and the changing social construction of speed, such that we should distinguish between the 'machine' speed of industrial modernity, the 'unruly' speed of 'living life in the fast lane' and the cultures of immediacy which characterize the new millennium.

Once we introduce such considerations, it becomes necessary to treat time and speed as cultural phenomena, with cultural consequences, rather than just an unfolding sequence of events or a fractal experience. Castells is aware of all this and his work is suffused with concerns about the ways in which technologically driven globalization is altering the relationships between space and time by eroding the physical and psychological boundaries around places, and through either liberating or threatening identities tied to them.

Of course, it should be said that Castells has a greater scheme in mind than the possible angst suffered by agents as they confront or accommodate new technologies. Information technologies exert transformative effects on 'the organizational arrangements of human relationships of production/consumption, experience, and power, as expressed in meaningful interaction framed by culture' (2000a, 5–6). New communication technologies inform the temper of change in societies, and all processes of transformation – in economy, in the reworking of states and state power, and in culture – are implemented through networks, particularly informational networks. This is no simple description of organizational change, because Castells insists that we now live in a network society, with global networks as key factors in social change, in the operation of power – including the nature and functioning of state power – and in configuring relationships between structure and agency (Holton, 2005, 1).

The network society is evident in all areas of life both within and across territorial boundaries. It is particularly visible and important in business networks and in what Castells calls the *network state*. Here is a vision of a networked future that is quite breathtaking when set against received models of social organization. But for all its analytical breadth and theoretical ambition, it has to be said that he has a one-size-fits-all model of social change, in that networks conceived as (information) technologies are seen as the solution to all the problems of communication, empowerment, community and democracy, while networks conceived as social and political relations are portrayed as functional responses to globalization and the economic and social problems of national societies, as well as some forms of supra-national governance too. This line of argument is apparent in his treatment of the EU as a form of network state, where his thesis is a signal – though flawed – contribution to an important debate about the imbrication of networks and borders (Rumford, 2008). This judgement may seem curious given that the EU is 'a political institution in which the model of the network has come to provide a dominant sense of political possibilities' (Barry, 2001, 101).

For Castells, the network state is a product of globalization and, as a consequence, his argument about its emergence in Europe is quite functionalist in tone (Axford, 2009). He says, '[the] core, strategic economic activities are globally integrated in the Information Age through electronically enacted networks of exchange of capital, commodities, and information. It is this global integration that induces and shapes the current process of (among other things), European unification, on the basis of European institutions historically constituted around predominantly political goals' (2001, 2). So the network state is characterized by the sharing of authority along a network, and a network by definition has nodes rather than a centre. Nodes may be of different sizes, producing asymmetrical relationships within the network.

Yet, 'regardless of these asymmetries, the various nodes of the European network are interdependent, so that no node, including the most powerful, can ignore the others in the decision-making process. If some political nodes do so, the whole political system is called into question' (Castells, 2001, 5). This is the crucial difference between a political network and what he calls a 'centred political structure', and it is a difference which suggests to him that what is happening in the EU as a response to the challenges of globalization may be 'the clearest manifestation to date of this emerging form of state, probably characteristic of the Information Age' (2001, 5).

Network forms of governance or state reflect major technological and social changes leading to the information and knowledge society. Indeed, for Castells, networks *become* society, whether in national or transnational guise. This is a remarkably contentious claim, both in terms of the idea that communication networks can provide the necessary functional integration, and because of the questionable durability of network morphologies when set against other, more conventional, communal, societal and governance architectures (Axford, 2004; Chandler, 2009; Albert, 2007; Knorr-Cetina, 2007; Castells, 2008). There is also the related question of what constitutes the ontology of global networks and whether they constitute anything more than mere connections extended over greater and greater distances (Holton, 2008; Thompson, 2003; Axford, 2009).

Castells' work on globalization and, in particular, his analysis of the network society are of great significance in understanding the dialectic of networks and borders in the political and cultural economies of global space. Of course, there are criticisms. The breadth of theoretical ambition in his work is not always matched by the quality or depth of empirical analysis needed to substantiate it. In part this results from the sheer scope of the enterprise and also turns on his treatment of informational capitalism, which, at one and the same time, is too dismissive of other modes and also technologically determinist, because it assumes that there is a social logic carried by information technologies and networks. Much of his treatment of networked capitalism and of state power traffics a curiously dated or mechanical conception of power and inequalities in power. This conception owes much to rationalist and modernist theories that may have little purchase on the vagaries of 'postmodern' network connection and networked identities, for all his sense of the space of flows as being elementally chaotic.

Yet Castells' great contribution to the debates on globalization allows us to think of the globe as a highly, indeed systematically, connected space. Moreover, his perspective stresses the unfinished business of both global and European integration. It rejects any sense of ontological closure and regional boundedness largely because of the topologies of network connection. Even if the notion of Europe as a network state is counter-intuitive, it permits Castells to identify the rescaling of territory (and of state power) being effected through connectivity. The upshot is actually a very qualified transformationalism, because even though the EU is organized around the dynamics of mobility and interconnection, as an institutional order it is also engaged in the business of managing and regulating movement and flow, and the same may be said of national states.

Conclusion

By identifying interrelated themes – the question of territory and state space, the issue of scalarity and the dialectic between networks and borders – we have been able to address some of the changing, multiple, layered forms in which space and place are imbricated in social reproduction and change. Socio-spatial theory has often suffered from a willingness to treat these categories separately, whereas the spatial turn is most useful when their mutually constitutive ontologies are acknowledged (Jessop et al., 2008, 392). Writing in 2001, Peter Dicken and colleagues, tried to demonstrate that global commodity chains and inter-firm networks are, at the same time, scaled and territorialized, while Sassen's references to global networks of local activists carries the same conviction (Bulkeley, 2005). On the other hand, Castells, for all his analytical vision, has been accused of 'network-centrism' because of his 'one-sided focus on horizontal, rhizomatic, topological and transversal interconnections of networks, frictionless spaces of flows and accelerating mobilities' (Jessop et al., 2008, 391).

Finally, intimations of a 'networked globality' (Axford, 2005) draw heavily on the notion that culture, as the realm of meaning and context for identity formation, can be seen as a property of networks of interaction – trans-territorial and global – as well as being an attribute of place. Such a take is at odds with the reified concept of culture found in positivist and functionalist sociology and with the treatment of 'authentic' sources of culture as shared meaning previously found, and to some extent still visible, in what Friedman calls 'globalized anthropology' (2000, 641). For students of global structuration, the issue of the production of shared meaning that is not tied to place, particular histories and so on is critical to understanding how globalization proceeds and how globalities subsist. Through processes of globalization we can infer a growing weakening of the implied necessity of connection between culture and territory. Demonstrating this is not always an easy task, because a lot of normative baggage about the claimed isomorphism of culture and territory gets in the way (Melucci, 1996; McAdam et al., 2001).

CHAPTER 5

Theories of Globalization and Culture

Introduction

At one and the same time culture can be seen as a major force in social, economic and political transformations (Held and Moore, 2008, 1; Buzan, 2010) and, more prosaically, an interpretative framework that attaches to 'our daily practices, our relations with others, our desires and our hopes' (Steger et al., 2009, 31). In this chapter we will address four related themes that have been significant in the cultural turn in globalization scholarship. These are (1) debates over the existence of global culture(s); (2) the imbrication of, or antinomy between, global and national/local cultures, including 'methodological glocalism'; (3) cultural convergence, differentiation and hybridization; and (4) the matter of communication and culture, or the symbolic production of culture through media and consumption. In different ways each theme exemplifies aspects of core problematics in globalization research and in theorizing globalization: the tensions between connections (including flows, liquids, mobilities) and the barriers to them, the dialectics of mobility and stasis and the nexus between agency and structure.

But let's start on a cautionary note, for we should be in no doubt that how culture is treated in theories of global change in large measure reflects how it has been used elsewhere. Sometimes this makes for sorry reading. When employed in explanations of social stability and change generally, more often than not cultural variables have assumed dependent status. In much of this scholarship, which is either broadly or explicitly functionalist, the assumption is that culture functions as a general value system for society. As a kind of social cement, culture is presumed to hold societies together by providing shared meanings, while serving to delineate insiders from outsiders by exemplifying the 'reality of a particular past' (Wallerstein, 1991, 190). Applied to the global context of social relationships and consciousness, as well as to normative prescriptions for various global futures, such tenets are problematic to say the least, primarily because assumptions about the isomorphism of territory, people and culture are now insecure.

Much scholarship on globalization and culture still obeys functionalist reasoning and moves to the implicit logic of methodological territorialism. When discussing the consequences of economic globalization and market liberalism in particular, there is also a regrettable tendency to treat culture – usually particular cultures – as the victim of globalization. As Jean-François Bayart puts it, this time rather elegantly, '[t]he usual view of globalization is that it involves dispossession, alienation, anomie' (2007, 83), which effects are often subsumed under the rubric of 'Westernization', reducing globalization to a form of 'occidentosis' (Al-e Ahmad, 1962).

That said, it does not do to minimize the range of analytical positions available about culture and globalization. Under the rubric of the cultural consequences of globalization, the theme most rehearsed in the literature (Tomlinson, 2007), there is a wealth of argument around claims to discern cultural homogenization (Barber, 1995; Ritzer, 2004; 2012), cultural polarization (Huntington, 1996, and critics) and cultural hybridization/creolization (Pieterse, 2003; 2009; Cohen, 2007; Inglehart and Norris, 2009; Turner and Khonder, 2010; Breidenbach and Zukrigl, 2000). And as a challenge to the oversimplified notion of global culture being no more than the diffused Western cultural account, the prospects for alternative or many (cultural) globalizations is entertained in a growing body of research (Arnason, 2008; Berger and Huntington, 2002; Turner and Khonder, 2010). Such fecundity of approach is both energizing and confusing, but still a long way short of demonstrating that all experience is, in some way, culturally constituted. But at the least, studying culture should enrich our understanding of globalization in ways not usually countenanced in, or even recognized by, all neo-liberal and most neo-Marxist theories of globalization.

One more point before we proceed: even in the recent past, scholarship had a penchant for treating cultural phenomena either as avatars of 'thin' (though often oppressive) global homogeneity or the expression of 'thick' local identities under pressure and/or disposed to resistance. This stark dichotomy does help to distinguish the role of cultural factors in promoting or resisting globalization processes from the impact of globalization on received notions of culture (Tomlinson, 1999). At the same time it predisposes to the intuitively appealing, but probably skewed, depiction of globalization as playing out a simple domination–resistance model of interaction. Here, globalization is viewed either as a slide into nihilism or nothingness (Ritzer, 2007) or a corrosive dialectic in which hegemonic global consumer culture spawns primitivism and/or fanaticism, as well as less visceral forms of resistance (Barber, 1995; Appadurai, 2006). In much of this kind of discourse a considered, and certainly a multidimensional, treatment of globalization is vitiated by reducing 'generalized mutual interaction to a zero-sum game of identities: if you are a democrat you are less of an African; if you eat McDonald's burgers you are less French', and so on (Bayart, 2007, 25). So it is one thing to claim that, as a component of social explanation, cultural factors should be accorded due weight and quite another to portray and then to explain the imbrication of cultural, economic and political variables in the structuration of contested globality.

Global Culture(s)

Two of the more charged sub-themes apparent in the study of global culture(s) are those of globalization as cultural homogenization and as a form of cultural imperialism. Both are shorthand for the notion of globalization as Westernization and/or capitalist commodification. Such processes are held, on the one hand, to meld particularities under the ideological banner of universalism and, on the other, to spawn a politics of resistance in defence of local, national and even civilizational cultural identities. The polemical nature of interventions around these sub-themes sometimes hinders dispassionate reflection, so, first of all, it is necessary to ask what is meant by 'global culture'. Here we need to retrace our steps for a moment.

What is often reified as culture should be understood as the contextual expression of interpretative practices by agents (Axford, 1995). At the same time, what might then appear as no more than a constructivist or phenomenological conceit has to be weighed against the sense that reality construction actually takes place in the context of cultural scripts or cultural structures (Benhabib, 2002). Agents experience cultural rules as objective or constitutive because the rules have been successfully institutionalized to become part of the inter-subjective understanding of the conditions for action (Giddens, 1990). Rules or structures have both an ontological aspect, 'assigning reality to actors and action, and a significatory aspect, endowing actor and action with meaning and legitimacy' (Meyer et al., 1987, 21). So culture is an interpretative framework or context, a source of identity and, although this is a tad simple, a means 'of telling people who they are' (Lash and Urry, 1994, 129).

But is there or can there be such a thing as world culture (Wallerstein, 2006; Featherstone, 1990)? The question reeks of scepticism about the possibility of culture as a property of non-territorial spaces, though in Immanuel Wallerstein's thesis, for example, that is not the main point. There, culture is treated as the realm of ideological support for hegemonic power, or, in special cases and particular conjunctures, a rather forlorn means of opposing it. Wallerstein points to the world-integrative power of the 'geo-culture' of neo-liberalism, and this is not so far from other neo-Marxist accounts which see globality as uniformity of culture and both as the necessary fallout from the spread of capitalist commodification. In such discourse, Westernization/Americanization as a form of cultural imperialism proceeds through energetic exchange and consumption. Global culture then reduces to a battery of convergent tastes, most obviously in branded mass entertainment, clothing and fast foods – a largely material gloss – although we might include communicative and aesthetic practices such as downloading movies from the Web, or tweeting styles and etiquette, under the same rubric.

If culture is the 'production and the experience of meaning through symbolization', the assumption must be that the way in which people consume these goods and participate in other forms of symbolic exchange and consumption profoundly influences the ways in which they construct their 'cultural worlds and make sense of [their] lives' (Tomlinson, 2006, 9). There has to be some truth in such claims but, as John Tomlinson also notes, prima facie, they seem to 'ignore the hermeneutic appropriation which is an essential part of the circulation of symbolic forms' (see also Schafer, 2007).

In their critical examination of the idea of global culture, John Boli and Frank Lechner (2005; Lechner, 2009; Boli and Thomas, 1999) offer a sophisticated and robust analysis of the origins and consequences of world culture. Their intervention attempts to marry the insights of world polity theory as elaborated by the Stanford Group to Pittsburgh School ideas about the cultural constitution of the global system (Boli and Thomas, 1999; Boli and Lechner, 2005). While critical of some popular accounts of globalization built around broadly cultural themes – a clash of civilizations, the joys and depredations of McWorld and the promise of 'Lexus' cultures represented by 'Davos Man' or the 'TNCC' (Barber, 1995; Friedman, 1999; Sklair, 2002) – they acknowledge that such work nonetheless 'affirmed and shaped growing consciousness of the way the world was growing together, or might implode, culturally' (Boli and Lechner, 2005, 30).

The key component in Boli and Lechner's analysis is the possibility that the globe may have a culture of its own that constitutes a 'reality' worthy of study. World culture contains 'meaningful frames for organizing social life', including the globally diffused and widely legitimated model of the nation-state (Lechner, 2001). It also comprises a set of global norms, for example those promoting human rights and sustainable development. Global culture has distinct vehicles too, with numerous international organizations and INGOs among them. At the same time it remains highly contested, although much cultural conflict is structured by global consciousness and constraints. Clearly this thesis owes a good deal to world polity models of how global cultural scripts are instantiated and sustained, and in this genre there is a strongly performative element, whereby cultures have to be reproduced through enactment. So, at first, it seems a moot point as to whether the global, as used by Boli and Lechner, is an autonomous cultural field, a 'self-evident global scale' as Sassen has it (2007, 7), or no more than the articulation of local cultural conditions and practices (Friedman, 2007; Berger and Huntington, 2003).

However, Boli and Lechner's critique of some other prominent contributions to the study of cultural globalization (notably Tomlinson, 1999; Berger and Huntington, 2003) gives clearer pointers to their 'strong' interpretation of global culture. Tomlinson is criticized because, allegedly, he misreads the concept and thus misconstrues what has transpired. While his scepticism about the potential to achieve a global culture is deemed understandable from a social-scientific standpoint, his take on what might comprise global culture relies on a limiting case definition that is both unrealistic and analytically unhelpful. In Tomlinson's account, global culture refers to 'the emergence of one single culture embracing everyone on earth and replacing the diversity of cultural systems that have flourished up to now' (1999, 71). Boli and Lechner deny that this is the only way to represent global culture because, paradoxically, it supports either the hyper-globalist conceit that the world is, or can be, (culturally) homogenous (Friedman, 2004) or the sceptical position that because such convergence is inconceivable, there is no point talking about it.

While rejecting the depiction of global culture as presumptively monolithic, Boli and Lechner are also at pains to query the seemingly more permissive model offered in Berger and Huntington's case-study based analysis of *Many Globalizations* (2002). This volume rehearses the ways in which various aspects of world culture – Japanese and American business models, popular music and English as a lingua franca – are 'localized' through different patterns of accommodation and resistance. The overall argument of the edited volume is that there is no single pattern of cultural globalization and that diversity remains the default position for what others present as a totalizing process. The purpose of the research was to study national variations in the reception of cultural globalization. While such an approach is legitimate it ignores what Boli and Lechner deem of most significance when trying to understand cultural globalization, namely the common factors that subvent all the individual cases. The 'local multiplicity of global cultures' is not what makes 'global cultures global' (Boli and Lechner, 2005, 34). Instead, these authors focus on what turns universal ideas into a form of global civilization (Breidenbach and Zukrigl, 2000).

The message from Boli and Lechner's work into the meaning of cultural identity in a globalized world is unabashed, but nuanced. Cultural globalization is a double process; beyond doubt it differentiates through processes of localization or indigenization, so that '[p]eople interpret globally circulating symbols very differently according to their own needs and customs' (Boli and Lechner, 2005, 35). At the same time these differences are played out in what is, and in what is seen as, a common framework. The world now has a common set of standards or a symbolic 'reference system' (Breidenbach and Zukrigl, 2000). Much of what takes place locally is thus only intelligible when set in a global context. So global culture is not all embracing, since many lifestyles are not incorporated and many differences not spanned. In global culture, differences are fluid and relative. Global culture is not an 'alien' force suppressing difference, because when global symbols are 'freely appropriated' (a telling qualification?) they can be part of anyone's 'authentic culture'. Overall, global culture 'organizes diversity' and provides 'ideas, symbols, concepts and models that seep into daily life and thus add a layer to people's experience' (Boli and Lechner, 2005, 36).

These observations echo one of the most intensely debated themes in the study of globalization, namely the 'analytical and empirical degrees of freedom that may be discerned in how local cultures engage with the global' (Giulianotti and Robertson, 2009, 31). In this debate the usual binary distinctions, or antinomies, of universal and particular and of local and global are often invoked. Richard Giulianotti and Roland Robertson (2009) refine the nexus in a complex, multidimensional account of globalization and football (the round-ball version). Their argument is that 'any particular experience, identity or social process is only comprehensible with reference to universal phenomena' (2009, 32). The 'globalwide nexus' of the particular and the universal then produces two complex interrelationships.

First is the 'universalization of particularism', wherein particularity has been valorized since the late nineteenth century, with the result that its appearance in almost any area of life is greeted with approbation. In these authors' specific field of interest, this interrelationship is manifest in the 'cultural arenas' constituted by international football tournaments that enact national-societal particularisms within the framework of a set of global rules. Second is the 'particularization of universalism', which refers to the ways in which global standards, rules and practices actually serve to identify and underwrite particularisms. For example, global communications technologies and the rules governing their use enable the instantaneous presentation of bespoke personas and identities, as sport fans, corporate bond traders, devotees of social media and so on (Tomlinson, 2007; Axford and Huggins, 2010).

The global culture so observed is not bereft of roots or floating in panoramic space, even if some adverse commentary assumes that it encourages agents to 'forget history' (Ardener, 1989, 17; Axford, 2001). Rather than seeing global culture as a kind of 'free-wheeling cosmopolitanism' (Smith, 1990, 22) and possessed of essentialist qualities, particularly where ethical considerations are concerned, Giulanotti and Robertson underscore the 'banal' or 'rooted' nature of the global cosmopolitan (Beck, 2005; Tarrow, 2002).

World polity models emphasize that structures and processes involved in global system making – the commonality of the human condition, the principles of rationality, and a highly scientized conception of nature – tend to isomorphism, although this should not be taken to imply simple cultural convergence or homogenization. Nonetheless, diversity is played down in such models, whereas in some anti-globalization literature standardization has been interpreted negatively as part of a systematic process of Westernization reliant on the insidious appeal of consumerism or appeals to an ersatz cosmopolitanism. So cosmopolitan 'contamination' may well be the modus operandi of a globalized world, at least where that refers to the effects of interconnectivity, or the kind of 'banal' cosmopolitanism found in routine encounters with others across borders. But defenders and opponents of national cultural particularism still engage around the ideal of a strict binary division (Appiah, 2006). The terrain of their disagreement is sometimes epistemological; more often than not it is ideological.

The Imbrication of, or Antinomy between, Global and Local Cultures

In a world that is de-territorialized, transnational and diasporic (Appadurai, 1990; 1993), nationalism remains an elemental political force, and national identity a symbolic boundary to be defended, even though the unity of the nation may be 'imagined' or constructed (Anderson, 1983; Arnason, 1989). National culture, however contrived, musters as a source of meaning and identity for citizens, anchoring the otherwise rational and individuated modern subject by way of foundational myths, through the invention of tradition and via appeals to the timeless and natural character of the nation (Axford, 1995; Hall, 1992). There is also the seeming paradox of a world-wide culture of the nation-state (Ramirez, 1987) – itself properly taken as a facet of global culture – and the extent to which apparent global isomorphism legitimates national and local autonomy and difference.

All this is important because, with the exception of realism, scholarship on the global spread of the nation-state as part of the cultural and geo-political dynamics of the global system still treats the identity of states largely as the outcome of their own history and culture. At the same time, while ties to the past and to myths about the past underline the authenticity of national and local cultures, the effects of extra-national, even global, cultural mores and symbols are presumed to be either relativizing or, with less of a benign feel, culturally debilitating. Nation-building was the seminal political-cultural process of Western modernity and it was, and in some respects remains, a tortured journey almost everywhere. Nationalist and nationalizing projects – the integrative revolution spoken about by students of comparative politics – have been repeatedly challenged in their attempts to control and amorphize the identities and experience, as well as the sense of history, of indigenous peoples, localities and regions. Some modern nation-states were built around what Anthony Smith calls 'dominant ethnic cores', but through adoption of the principles of universalism and pluralism, they have been able to fashion at least a jobbing multiculturalism, if not considerably more than that when respect for difference is codified in law and convention (1990).

The point here or, more accurately, the point of comparison and relevance is that like world-making processes, those of nation- and state building are eminently cultural. But there is no easy parallel in the experience of national states and societies for what is happening globally. The integrative revolution that produced political modernity in the global North was (and elsewhere in the world to some extent remains) an oppressive and sometimes bloody process. To date the current phase of global cultural integration has not proceeded in anything like this way, although some critics point to the destruction of local cultures and identities, with material inequalities – also held to intensify under globalization – compounded by cultural impoverishment.

Local and global: Methodological glocalism

So it is understandable that discussion of local/national and global cultures often takes for granted an elemental or ontological tension between the two. The assumption of a binary division has many variants and, at its most vehement, sees globalization as incompatible with local, regional and national difference. This 'methodological globalism', as Bob Holton reminds us, was common in first wave theorizing, but subsequent scholarship invests in more exotic and nuanced images and metaphors to capture the different articulations of local and global (Holton, 2005). All reject the Orwellian tendency to see local *or* global as good or bad by definition; as mutually destructive, or else mutually exclusive.

In disciplinary terms the treatment of these binaries is instructive, in part because they throw light on the ways in which disciplines have dealt with the challenges of methodological globalization. For example, early anthropological thinking on the impact of modernization on indigenes and indigenous cultures assumed that tribal peoples and their cultures were doomed to annihilation. Later scholarship tended to reify local identities as isolated cultural communities beset by national and global constraints. More recently, as Peter Phipps notes, the blanket idea of constraints has given, or is giving, way to an understanding that indigenous peoples exist 'in a global framework, both self-consciously drawing on globalized strategies of rights and identity, as well as being objectively situated through international legal frameworks' (2009, 28; Kearney, 1995).

Within a sociological frame of reference, Roland Robertson claims that globalization brings locales closer together materially and ideationally through various spatio-temporal transformations (1992; Giddens, 1992). In this process localities 'cease to be things in themselves', but the very *idea* of locality gets reproduced and valorized globally (Robertson, 1994, 38). The local is where pressures for global convergence are articulated with the vernacular, both actually and metaphorically. The outcome is new cultural hybrids or syncretic forms, and these are *glocal* (Raz, 1999).

But presenting glocalization this way could suggest a rather mechanical relationship between the global and the local, such that, 'the global penetrates the local, the local reacts, and the glocal emerges' (Roman, 2006, 3). In fact, Robertson's account is nothing like as simplistic as this critique suggests. In recent empirical studies, he and Richard Giulianotti have paid greater attention to the imbrication of homogeneity and heterogeneity in the construction of a glocalized world (Giulianotti and Robertson, 2006; 2007; 2009). Theorists of glocalization rebut the assumption that globalization processes always endanger the local. Rather, 'glocalization both highlights how local cultures may critically adapt or resist "global" phenomena, and reveals the way in which the very creation of localities is a standard component of globalization. There is now a universal normalization of "locality", in the sense

that "local" cultures are assumed to arise constantly and particularize themselves vis-a-vis other specific cultures' (Giulianotti and Robertson, 2006, 134).

In their study of football and globalization, Giulianotti and Robertson
employ a helpful analytical scheme that describes four categories of cultural
glocalization. First is *relativization*, where social actors try to preserve their
cultural institutions, practices and meanings within a new environment,
underpinnning differentiation. There is also *accommodation*, where actors take
up the practices, institutions and meanings associated with other societies,
a pragmatic accommodation made to maintain key elements of the prior
local culture. *Hybridization* occurs where social actors synthesize local and
other cultural phenomena to produce distinctive, hybrid cultural practices,
institutions and meanings; finally, there is *transformation*, where social actors
come to favour the practices, institutions or meanings associated with other
cultures. In this case, 'transformation may procure fresh cultural forms or,
more extremely, the abandonment of the local culture in favour of alternative
and/or hegemonic cultural forms' (Giulianotti and Robertson, 2006, 135).

Robertson and Giulianotti also talk about the 'glocalization projects' or
strategies of local cultures, and this is some way from seeing the local as a
reified entity and the global as an abstract and totalizing process. Rather, the
emphasis is on outcomes that may be an uneasy mix when national and local
identities and cultures are (1) eroded through cultural homogenization of the
sort described by George Ritzer (2004; 2007); (2) reinforced in a politics of
cultural resistance to globalization; or (3) replaced by hybrid cultures, which
are the result of the interpenetration of local and global (Hall, 1992). Obviously,
such outcomes are not predicated on the immutable properties of either
localities or globalization processes.

Cultural Convergence, Differentiation and Hybridization

When discussing the idea of global culture, the themes of convergence, differentiation and hybridization dominate both research and polemics. In practice, analytical and normative riffs cut across these broad themes and in
particular contexts may reveal any or all of them at work, as well as invite
different judgements about their relative propriety and effects.

Convergence

In world polity accounts, global isomorphism occurs through the more-or-less
enthusiastic and conscious engagement of actors with wider cultural rules.
The acceptance of these rules globally may then legitimate some forms of
diversity as a global cultural script or standard (Boli and Thomas, 1999). Much
of this reasoning assumes a cognitive engagement between actors and cultural rules or structures, such that rules are instantiated and reproduced
through conscious practice. Yet it is clear that global isomorphism, even

homogeneity, can be realized behind the backs of agents, through unconscious everyday practices and experiences. Here we can return to George Ritzer's *McDonaldization* thesis, with its powerful demotic feel (2010; 2012). Ritzer's argument, derived in no small part from Max Weber's theory of societal rationalization, has it that McDonaldization is the process whereby the principles that guided the fast food restaurant chain to global supremacy are dominating not only American society, but also the rest of the world.

It is easy to caricature this thesis, so let's be clear about Ritzer's argument. The idea of convergent consumption patterns as features of *grobalization* is important for his understanding of global processes, and McDonaldization is a multidimensional process moving to a number of principles. These are *efficiency*, the systematic attention to ensuring cost-effective means–ends relationships; *calculability*, the precise quantification of time spent on, for example, preparing and serving food, and the time taken to consume it; *predictability*, which means that the product is uniform and fit for consumption anywhere in the world; and *control*, with an emphasis not only on standardization of product, but on the behaviour of employees in the workplace.

Finally, there is the *irrationality of rationality*. This portmanteau category refers to the consequences of applying the first four principles and encapsulates Ritzer's critique of the grobal process of McDonaldization. In his words, the 'irrational' outcome of rationalization processes, despite the obvious intent of the businesses that practise them, is to standardize practice regardless of local conditions and tastes and to degrade the experience of workers and customers (2010). Other studies have carried Ritzer's insights into the McDonaldization of higher education (Hayes and Wynyard, 2002) and social work (Dustin, 2007), while Ritzer has, of late, alluded to the McDonaldization of sex through the global use of drugs used to combat male erectile dysfunction (2010).

So conceived, McDonalidization is a debilitating grobal process injurious to diversity. Ritzer also delivers an aesthetic critique because, Viagra notwithstanding, the process is generally seen as damaging to good taste and civility. Of course, in other hands the features of McDonaldization he describes might be taken as indicators of a growing and generally progressive global isomorphism. Even Ritzer is at pains to point out that although it implies convergence, McDonaldization does not mean that the world is becoming completely homogeneous, and certainly not at a uniform rate. At one remove the principles are often indigenized, at another they may be resisted, while, in a kind of reverse cultural imperialism, non-US corporations built on American models of retailing now market to US consumers in their own shopping malls and virtual shopping spaces. While such shifts may still constitute what Ritzer calls the 'globalization of nothing', in that the social and cultural forms produced are 'devoid of distinctive content', the enemies of difference (2010, 267), they still stand as a more contentious and variable model of global process than is countenanced in simple hyper-globalist accounts.

Traversing similar terrain, Benjamin Barber (1995; 2007) denounces the same empty banality of consumer capitalism that exercises Ritzer. For Barber, material plenty disguises spiritual poverty, and the ideology of consumer choice comprises a subtle form of tyranny. In fact, Barber's work on this theme starts with a stark warning about the prospects for global polarization, rather than homogenization, that reside in the tensions between consumer capitalism and religious fundamentalism, with each possessing totalizing potential (1995). *Jihad vs. McWorld* is a bleak vision for our age, envisaging either tribalism or globalism. In the forces of tribalism Barber discerns the 'jihad' principle, where 'culture is pitted against culture, people against people'. The pressures of homogenizing globalization, that 'onrush of economic and ecological forces that demand integration and uniformity, that mesmerize the world with fast music, fast computers and fast food', deliver only McWorld. On his account, neither of these forces respects democracy, nor have they any moral currency with which to initiate or sustain it.

Seemingly, McWorld does hold out the promise of prosperity and stability, but at the cost of autonomy, community and identity. Jihad valorizes these qualities but cannot redeem marginalized peoples from irrationality, poverty and other inequalities. Barber's pathological image of a globalized world roots the crisis of late modern societies in questions of motivation and identity. America and the West in general have squandered reserves of social capital on an easy life of consumption. By contrast, jihad may deliver vibrant, even visceral identities, easy social and political mobilization and a strong sense of tradition and community, while incurring debilitating costs – parochialism and an enduring suspicion or hatred of strangers.

Barber reprises at least some of these tensions over a decade later and in a world made rather more unsafe and unpredictable by global warming, the war on terror and the beginnings financial meltdown. He looks even more closely at American society and culture as the forcing ground for the ideology of consumerism that 'infantilizes' culture. In *Consumed*, (2007) he presents a somewhat crude political economy in which global inequality has left the planet with two kinds of potential customers: the poor of the undeveloped world, who have great and unsatisfied needs but lack the means to fulfil them, and the first world rich, who possess disposable income but have few real needs. Today's consumerist economy sustains profitability by creating needs, convincing us that the brands of electronic culture – iPhones, Wiis and so on – are necessary. It has done so by promoting an ethos of infantilization, a modus of 'induced childishness' manifest in adult tastes and spending habits.

While this may look like a designer hair-shirt philosophy, Barber has an important message derived from his earlier work on the conditions that promote democracy. The advent of 'radical consumerist society' has pitted capitalism and democracy against each other, with deleterious consequences for both. In the USA and increasingly elsewhere, 'me' cultures relegate civic mindedness and social responsibility to the ideational scrapheap, while the idea of the public sphere and public investment in social progress is denigrated or accorded also-ran status to private virtues (vices) and interests. These interests now invest everything from the conduct of warfare, through the use of private companies selling security, to the commercial management of state provision in education, health and penal justice.

Capitalism, says Barber 'seems quite literally to be consuming itself, leaving democracy in peril and the fate of citizens uncertain' (2007, 168). He blames the slide into decadence on rising productivity in the West. In the past, 'productivist capitalism prospered by meeting the real needs of real people'. By contrast today, 'consumerist capitalism' nurtures 'a culture of impetuous consumption necessary to selling puerile goods in a developed world that has few genuine needs' (2007, 173). These are fell words for any belief that global capitalism exerts a benign modernizing influence. They are also a caution for those who see global cultures as no threat to difference.

Difference or polarization?

For Barber, globalization is limitless consumption in the economies of the global North and anti-systemic/alter-systemic resistance elsewhere. This is not an unusual view of cultural dynamics today, but even in Barber's own terms it can be challenged. A substantial body of comparative research on 'postmaterialist' attitudes and values suggests that the 'emphasis on economic achievement as the top priority is giving way to an increasing emphasis on the quality of life' (Inglehart, 1977; Inglehart and Norris, 2009). The desire to accrue consumables has commuted to a search for less tangible satisfactions and meaningful experiences, for proper work–life balance and for self-actualization (Trentmann, 2004).

In addition, Barber's one-size-fits-all model of global consumer culture rather underplays diversity except in its more pathological variants. By contrast, differences in consumer motivations and behaviour are widespread and mostly benign, evidence of a cultural tapestry that subsists quite easily in what might otherwise be portrayed as an increasingly and irrevocably uniform world. This benign image of cultural diversity morphs with little difficulty into depiction of a more impure, but still largely pacific world, which is hybridized or creolized. But there are also more abrasive and polarized accounts of cultural differentialism.

In the wake of the collapse of the Soviet world-empire, the world seemed ripe for globalization made in the image of Western liberal democracy and attendant neo-liberal economics. Samuel Huntington, a conservative student of democracy and comparative modernization, published a critique of the assumed cultural hegemony of Western modernity, including its narrowing of history to a treatment of the emergence and consolidation of nation-state forms and national identities (1996; 2004). Indeed, *The Clash of Civilizations* is a decidedly non-state-centric argument, although its intellectual and emotional origins lie in a deeply particularistic – American – view of the world, and its message is aimed at preserving and strengthening that heritage (Huntington, 2004).

Huntington argued that the conflicts of the post-Cold-War era derive not from statist ambitions or political ideologies but from civilizational differences rooted in religious traditions and ethnic and racial divides. Civilizational identities – Western, Sinic or Confucian, Japanese, Islamic, Hindu, Slavic-Orthodox, Latin American and perhaps African – will be the sources of conflict in the twenty-first-century, superseding the Western model of international politics and the stand-off between hegemonic blocs characteristic of the decades after World War II. His thesis turns on whether civilizational 'fault lines' have resurfaced and are revealed in the rediscovery of more fundamental identities in recent decades.

It is Huntington's views on the threats posed by the global resurgence of Islam that have attracted most attention and which, post-9/11, have persuaded some analysts and policy makers to depict the conflicts in Afghanistan and Iraq as local and particular manifestations of the clash of civilizations. None of this is surprising because, according to Huntington, (1) conflicts will always occur along the fault lines between civilizations, and these are now more visible and less effectively managed than in the recent past; and (2) the pursuit of Western universalism (democracy promotion, consumer culture, nuclear arms control and so on) is vitiated by the declining ability and resolve of the West to make its writ effective. But even after 9/11 and the ravages of Afghanistan and Iraq, much of the evidence marshalled by Huntington struggles to carry the analytical burden placed on it.

First, the awesome façade of civilizations may be no more than conceptual shadow play, or a potent form of geo-nostalgia. As Fouad Ajami opines, as a legacy of (Western) modernity, 'furrows run across whole civilizations' (1993, 5). Where one civilization ends and another begins cannot be stipulated with any certainty, and the call to protect civilizational identities relies more on polemic and ideology than on hard historical and sociological evidence. Second, despite Huntington's strictures, multiculturalism can be held up as a success story in many societies, while the unforced movement of people across borders (across civilizations), or the maintenance of translocal ties in the shape of diasporas and other networks of affect, are evidence of a world in process, where 'fault lines' are bridged. Third, even if civilizations exist they are not monolithic, and in the case of Islam this is manifestly true.

Cultural hybridization as a global icon

Understood by some commentators to express the cultural logic of globalization, the concept of cultural hybridization identifies the mixing of cultures affected by globalization and the creation of new, sometimes unique, hybrid cultures that cannot be designated either local or global (Kraidy, 2005; Ritzer, 2010; *Globalizations*, 2007). Hybridization is the default position of globalization optimists and those who want to use the concept as a way of understanding the complex and contradictory facets of cultural globalization (Hutnyk, 2006). It is quite easy to depict cultural globalization *as* hybridization by seeing it as the cultural structure of globality and a rich process of intermingling. Jan Pieterse says that globalization is 'structural hybridization or the emergence of new, mixed forms of social cooperation and cultural hybridization, or the development of translocal mélange cultures' (2003, 46; 2009; see also Bhabha, 1990). Set against some predictions of a global future based on more-or-less pathological forms of identity politics, a tide of cultural relativism or fractured postmodernity, this is a wholesome brew.

Pieterse describes hybridization as the mixing of cultures and the emergence of translocal cultural forms that include diasporas, virtual connectivity and food menus that mix cuisines (2003; 2005; 2008; 2009). Cultural hybridity appears in the 'global melange' of fusions produced throughout history, and its most potent feature is to challenge and reinvent boundaries. We can think of hybridity as '*layered* in history, including pre-colonial, colonial and postcolonial layers, each with distinct sets of hybridity, as a function of the boundaries that were prominent at the time and their pathos of difference' (Pieterse, 2007, 2). Hybridization as a process is as old as history, but nowadays, 'the pace of mixing accelerates and its scope widens in the wake of major structural changes, such as new technologies that enable new forms of intercultural contact' (2007, 3). Contemporary accelerated globalization is just a new phase, and what is critical is that the phenomenon accelerates the shift from anti-colonial to post-colonial social orders and politics.

Quite rightly, Pieterse says that there are many forms of hybridization, but that they all challenge boundaries, whether local or civilizational, phenomenal or imagined. Hybridization also runs against the grain of hegemonic projects, including the more diffuse global convergence implied by the McDonaldization thesis. Cultural syncretism rather than cultural synchronization becomes modal and in this regard, there are many exemplars. Pieterse mentions East–West fusion cultures, the Latin American idea of the 'mestizo', of in-between identities and cultures found in creole communities, and the 'melange' cultures of global cities. The sheer creativity of cultural hybrid formation is presented as a transformative social dynamic, although we should not assume that prior to hybridization, immaculate cultural enclaves existed everywhere, at least not as evidenced in the historical record (Buzan, 2010).

In more recent work (2007; 2009) Pieterse is very aware of the intense debates that the concept of cultural hybridity has aroused. One of the most cogent criticisms is that by articulating a powerful non-essentialist credo, he and others (Benhabib, 2002) exaggerate the fluidity, permeability and renegotiability of culture, and actually introduce their own form of anti-essentialist essentialism (Kompridis, 2005, 319). Another criticism dismisses claims to discern hybrid cultures as, at best, trivial and denies that there is any real analytical mileage in the thesis that all cultures are, to some degree, mixed. As Paul Gilroy opines, 'I try not to use the word hybrid . . . cultural production is not like mixing cocktails' (1994, 54–5). Pieterse would argue that the case for hybridity still needs to be made in face of the erstwhile dominance of essentialist positions that not only dismissed cultural hybrids as analytical categories, but despised them as 'impure' or despicable features of social worlds.

More telling than either of these considerations is the obvious criticism that the production of culture requires more than a constructivist act of interpretation to render all identities malleable and boundaries permeable. But Seyla Benhabib counters even this point by arguing that the narrative construction of cultures can occur where there is some room for renegotiating identities and when a repertoire of cultural opportunity structures is available. She acknowledges that such repertoires cannot be assumed and neither can the capacity of agents to 'voluntarily self-ascribe' or opt for a cultural identity (2005, 386). Because most work on cultural hybridity stops some way short of the postmodernist conceit that identity formation is simply a matter of cultural manufacture, or a convenient, lifestyle-conscious decision to reinvent a cultural persona, this may be a weighty qualifier.

For many critics the major failing of research on cultural hybridity has been its neglect of power and inequality (Hutnyk, 2006). As Pieterse admits, '[i]n notions such as global mélange what is missing is acknowledgment of the actual unevenness, asymmetry and inequality in global relations. What are not clarified are the *terms* under which cultural interplay and crossover take place' (2007, 4). Unequal power relations may be reproduced in any cultural melange, or assume new, but still unequal forms. There should be no a priori assumptions about emancipatory effects. At the same time, processes of cultural hybridization do point to a more polycentric world than can be entertained in the usual binaries of East–West or North–South. This recognition is not simply a statement about the revamped phenomenon of 'Oriental globalization' as a reversal of cultural flows and influence, but an acknowledgement that cultural globalization flows in circles: East–West, West–East, East–West and so on, over millennia. Hybridities now appear as circular and layered, 'braided and interlaced, layer upon layer, to the point that it is difficult to decide which is which' (2007, 8).

Communication and Culture, or the Symbolic Production of Culture through Media Consumption

In making hybrid identities and in the making of culture more generally, processes of communication are crucial (Kraidy, 2005). The study of culture and communication, which includes analysis of cultural production and consumption as well as cultural convergence and difference, is important for building a more nuanced account of globalizing processes and for comprehending the role of different kinds of agency, including the agency of different audiences, in their enactment (Axford and Huggins, 2010; Orgad, 2012). Issues we have rehearsed above – those of cultural imperialism, indigenization and glocalization, as well as the nature of symbolic power and cultural change – all involve processes of communication.

When discussing communication and globalization, two discourses occupy centre-stage. The first employs hyper-globalist or transformationalist language about the boundary-destroying and relativizing qualities of 'new' and fluid forms of communication (see Holton, 2005; Axford, 2001; Axford and Huggins, 2010). At the other extreme lie sceptical positions in which even dramatic changes in communication technologies and formats are no more than adjuncts to usual politics and established patterns of social intercourse (Hirst et al., 2009). While the language of transformation is powerful and even plausible, caution is still necessary because, as Kai Hafez notes, a good deal of media content underwrites rather than transcends the national mode of address regardless of the technology (2007). So it is important not to overstate the role of 'new', and especially digital, media in allegedly reworking sociality, transnationalizing communication and facilitating the creation of a global civil society or global public spheres.

At the same time, massive changes in communication technologies are clearly instrumental in reshaping the cultural economy of the new millennium. John Tomlinson emphasizes the part played by such 'impatient and immoderate' media technologies in constituting global 'cultures of immediacy' (2007, 131). In this regard the Web is only one facet of the systematic *telemediatization* of culture now observed, variably, across the world. It is, however, an increasingly important facet when assessing the impact of connectivity on the personalization of communication and consumption and when weighing the impact of trans-border connections on social practices. Telemediatization is the process through which electronic communication and different kinds of media systems play an increasing part in the framing and constitution of everyday experience (Hjavard, 2008; Castells, 2000a).

Tomlinson's larger project concerns the ways in which the modern culture of speed is being superseded, notably in the global West, by a culture of immediacy. Consumerism has become modal through the 'enticements' of marketing and branding and by the interaction of producers, advertisers, marketers, citizens, consumers and fans through ever faster and interactive media. Impatient and immoderate media facilitate consumer immediacy by offering instant and increasingly bespoke delivery. Indeed, without giving way to technological determinism, it might be said that such technologies frame how we engage with them and each other by promoting and embodying the value of speed, immediacy and bespoke consumption as cultural aesthetics (Castells, 2000a).

The aesthetics of new media are those qualities that promote immediacy and interactivity, greater scope for reflexivity and the dominance of images over text. Fast and interactive media increase the element of hyper-reflexivity between actors in a way that confounds, or at least profoundly alters, the conventional distinction between the producers of output and those who consume it. Indeed, the great selling point of digital media is the claim to erase signs of mediation, providing immediacy and a sense of control by disguising the machine–user interface in a fusion of art and technology. Unlike conventional mass media, internet technologies, especially in Web 2 and 3 formats, also facilitate dialogical communication by permitting a range of one-to-one, one-to-many and many-to-many exchanges. Paul Virilio's corrosive take on social-technical change has it that machines, including the hardware and cultural software of media technologies, increasingly constitute our environments (1991), and even in less disturbing interpretations we are enjoined to engage with modalities which cross the seeming boundaries of technical and social, human and non-human, to comprise a world 'always in process' (Leyshon and Thrift, 1997, 126; Lash and Lury, 2007).

This is an important way of summarizing the cultural repertoires of possibility available through digital communication. It is also a warning that accelerated lifestyles and the valorization of immediacy may be injurious to deliberative practices and reflective engagements, whether in interpersonal relationships or democratic procedures. So deceleration is now bruited as a new global, social good, a stance visible in resistance to fast capitalism and fast foods (Tomlinson, 2009; see also Connolly, 2002). Of course, any politics of resistance may be a politics of nostalgia and sometimes regressive. William Connolly warns against yearning for what he calls the 'long, slow time' (2002, 162). While 'slow' may be the watchword of banal and harmless nostalgia, it is also a sub-text for fundamentalism, scapegoating and 'accusatory' cultures drawn to the myth of a centred, stable world, suspicious of change.

Barry Wellman's research on digital media and the rise of networked individualism also details the 'social affordances' available through internet connection, and these underscore the sense of cultural boundaries being shifted, though without the angst that attends many a *cri* about the cultural and psychological damage done by new communications technologies and formats. In this respect the key affordances are *always being connected*, or having the capacity so to be; the *personalization of communication*, such that 'the ensuing interactions are more tailored to individual preferences and needs, furthering a more individualized way of interacting and a way of mobilizing as fluid networks of partial commitment'; and *globalized connectivity*, where this 'facilitates transnational connectivity, be that migrants staying in touch with their homeland or transnational networks mobilizing around issues' and matters of common interest (Wellman et al., 2003, 3). Other research on the existence of global civil society or on forms of transnational activism (Keane, 2003; Keck and Sikkink, 1998; Gaventa and Edwards, 2006; Crack,

2008) endorses the idea that quite robust and enduring networks of actors and audiences are capable of being mobilized and sustained through media connection (see Axford, 2004; 2005).

For all this, media globalization may still be a myth, albeit a necessary one, says Kai Hafez. It is necessary because it forms part of the reorientation of scholarship away from the nation-state and national cultures to the prospects for cross-border communication and trans-cultural social formation. It is a myth because the quality of data available makes it hard to substantiate claims about the dynamics and consequences of media globalization. Simple, though compelling notions such as cultural imperialism or Westernization through media are flawed, but so are claims to discern systematic patterns of indigenization or glocal forms of media content.

Hafez' work is a cautionary statement about the possibilities of global cultural convergence through media, but it rather smacks of the kind of elite nostalgia found in many commentaries on the adverse consequences of tele-mediatization. For him the internet has brought 'a new subtlety to the global array of information', but this generates only 'virtual cosmopolitanism' and is a long way short of the 'true' variety (Hafez, 2007, 170). Usefully sceptical as this is, it is also designer anxiety about the authenticity of identities and cultures formed through mediatization, and especially digitization (Tarrow, 2002).

Debates such as these inflect the discussion of media effects more generally, so that ambivalence may be the only intellectually and emotionally sustainable response when faced with claims from cyber-enthusiasts and the special pleading of 'old' media advocates and devotees of nationally regulated public service broadcasting. In large part the critique of the role of media in transforming culture and politics stems from Theodor Adorno's account of the *Culture Industry*, a treatise in sync with post-World War II concerns about the spread of mass, industrial or 'Americanized' culture and the prescription for (national) cultural policy to protect European cultural traditions from these perceived threats (1991; Hall, 1971).

Economic trends in the developed world led to the liberalization of economic policy by the 1970s, and in the 1980s to the increasing fragmentation of consumer demand and markets. These, along with flexible production techniques (Miege, 1989; Lash and Urry, 1994), facilitated a shift away from the idea of self-contained national economies and cultures towards the model of a global cultural economy based on exchanges delivered through interlocking networks (Castells, 2000a; Harvey, 1989; Soja, 1989). This change constituted not just a cultural turn in the constitution of the world economy, but also a significant spatial turn. Today, culture and economics are closely intertwined. Increasingly, markets appear based on the demand for symbolic goods, with the internet and the deregulation of traditional media providing the means for bespoke consumption. Scott Lash and John Urry (1994) stressed the increasing role of symbolic consumption and 'aesthetic reflexivity' as central to the processes of identity construction (Giddens, 1990), while the culture industries have become the expression of what these authors describe as flexible 'economies of signs and space', of disorganized capitalism.

Fredric Jameson argues that under flexible, globalized, capitalism, communication acquires a 'whole cultural dimension' because communication as culture carries two, seemingly contradictory, charges (2001, 56). First, it promises standardization in many areas of symbolic consumption, of 'forced integration . . . into a world-system from which "delinking" . . . is henceforth impossible and even unthinkable and inconceivable' (2001, 57; 1991). Second is the potential for a more 'joyous' cultural pluralism seen in the blossoming of alternative lifestyles, the visibility of previously marginalized and unheard minorities, and a 'falling away of structures that condemned whole segments of the population to silence and to subalternity' (2001, 57). In the first, communication technologies and formats stand as economic signifiers that reinforce the baleful image of the Americanization and standardization of culture. In the second, they appear as carriers of quotidian cultural heterogeneity, sometimes grounded in the ideologies of resistance to globalization, sometimes in the surge of utopian and libidinal energies released through 'individual hyper-consumption' (2001, 57).

Conclusion

The arguments canvassed in this chapter point up the need to treat with culture as a constitutive dimension of most globalizations, and provide important concepts and tools for a culturally inflected understanding of globalization. While this is some way short of truly multidimensional theory, there is a growing body of work that takes that injunction seriously. Giulianotti and Robertson's preference for 'middle-range' issues and explanations exemplifies that prescription, while world polity researchers, with their focus on the cultural content of world-making processes, deliver important empirical insights into world-making practices and global cultural rules and standards. Research around the important themes of cultural convergence, difference and hybridity, whether applied to consumption patterns or to local and civilizational identities, often provides a detailed historical and empirical focus on the actual interplay between different agents and structures, although powerful ideological and normative currents still inform such work. Most important, all this work provides an important countervailing thrust to the simplistic notion of globalization as a form of material connectivity.

CHAPTER 6

Theories of Globalization and History

Introduction

Much scholarship on globalization is rooted in events since the early 1980s, and thus feels distinctly 'chrono-fetishist'. An uncomfortable notion, chrono-fetishism is a form of theoretical presentism, a condition in which events are deemed explainable only through recourse to 'present causal variables' (Hobson et al., 2010, 16). Here, globalization appears as entirely novel, dislocated from the past and purportedly dislocating in its effects. Such portraits are not unusual in globalization scholarship. But increasingly it is considered necessary for research to provide a historical perspective on change of global proportions, delivered through the use of rigorous historical method, and sometimes informed by sociological theory and techniques.

By and large this prescription springs from the, admittedly banal, sense that 'history matters', even if it is not always apparent what that means. If the injunction is to be at all meaningful, it has to offer more than a chronological narrative, a 'vague preamble to the current moment', and identify some important, even crucial mechanisms and processes of social change (Adams et al., 2003, 2; Abrams, 1982; Mazlish, 1998). And if contemporary globalization had no precedent, we would still need a way of distinguishing its novelty and explaining observed discontinuities (McNeill and McNeill, 2003). In this chapter the premise that history matters to the study of globalization will be explored as follows. First is the question of what we mean by global history. This will be followed by a critique of civilizational analysis as a historically informed paradigm, with particular reference to the debates on multiple modernities and emergent globalities. Last we will examine the contribution of historical sociology to the future of the discipline of IR and of state-centric inquiry into globalization.

History and historical method are central to the scholarship of long-term, large-scale social and political change. Such scholarship includes macro-historical research on those processes that might explain change for all societies and civilizations (Snyder, 1999; Mann, 1986), and clearly there are variants of such generic intent. For example, Karl Polanyi, whose historical problematic has been appropriated by at least one student of contemporary globalization, offers a heuristic device by which to comprehend historical 'great transformations' such as the shift to a free market society at the start of the nineteenth century. In his account, history proceeds by way of a series of 'double movements' so that, in the case of marketization, the dominance of free market principles has been countered by movements and ideologies aiming to protect society from market expansion and market failure (Polanyi, 1944; Munck, 2006; Harvey, 2003; 2005b).

By contrast, the kind of comparative micro history found in the work of the *Annales* school and of historians such as Carlo Ginzberg places the emphasis on small social and cultural units and how people conduct their lives within them. Here the research seeks 'answers to large questions in small places' (Ginzberg, 1980, 26; 1983; Braudel, 1979; Elias, 1969; 1982). For example, Fernand Braudel's pioneering work, sometimes labelled the 'new' historicism, lies more in the tradition of historical scholarship which privileged specific social contexts – time, place and local conditions – against the notion of fundamental, generalizable laws of social change. Modernization theory, theories of imperialism and the insights of the Dependency School (Frank, 1998) all look to the historical record to substantiate their claims.

Within and between these theoretical strands are important differences, some of which turn on the key issue of whose history is being portrayed or held up as seminal in the emergence of global modernity (or modernities). The most potent illustration of this tension is the charge of 'Eurocentrism' levelled at pretty much the whole gamut of Western thinkers from Marx and Weber, through Douglass North and Milton Friedman, to Immanuel Wallerstein and even Gunder Frank, at least in his early work (Denemark, 2009; Hobson, 2006). Eurocentrism, it bears repeating, is the tendency to reinterpret the world from a European perspective. As Robert Denemark says, 'once Europe had risen to dominance, then its scholars conveniently forgot the rest of world history and began theorizing about how "others" were deficient (whether in property rights or in stripping the means of production from their immediate producers)' (2009, 235).

While this may be a somewhat polemical summary of a complex scholarship, it is also a salutary reminder that 'history' should not be seen as singular and uncontested, and this includes how it is recorded. In more polemical vein, Samir Amin refers to Eurocentrism as one of the major 'ideological distortions' of our time, one that has had great economic, political and cultural consequences for the demeanour of the modern world (1989). His argument is that Eurocentrism distorted both Greek rationality and Christian doctrine to justify a newly created capitalist social and moral order, the West's economic, political, cultural and military conquest of the world. and its systematic exploitation of all non-European humankind.

The use of historical method is not confined to one school of thought. In many sceptical accounts of globalization, historical detail has been used as a stick with which to beat true believers of either a hyper-globalist or a transformationalist persuasion (Hirst et al., 2009). Tensions between disciplines and the existence of different theoretical frameworks invest the vogue for historical sociologies of globalization and of international relations, notably with regard to the debates about modernity and the role of the territorial nation-state in its making (Adams et al., 2005; Rosenberg, 2006; Abrams, 1982; Giddens, 1984). The question of how societies became (become) modern is not only a concern for historians but at the very core of sociological theory, even if the very idea of 'becoming modern' is contested (Weber, 1958; 1968; Marx, 1967 [1867]).

In fact, the engagement of sociological theory with history displays some quite striking shifts. As sociology developed as an academic discipline from the early twentieth century, especially in the USA, its commitment to historically informed theory gave way to a-historical models and theories of social change and modernization. By way of structural-functionalism and rather schematic and abstract approaches to modernization, detailed historical and contextual analysis commuted to a focus on identifying and classifying trans-historical features of social change aligned, for the most part, to the emergence of modern societies in Europe (Parsons, 1966). But a further shift occurred from the late 1970s and signalled a return to historical inquiry, initially with a Marxist and then a Weberian problematic (Skocpol, 1979; Trimberger, 1978; Evans et al., 1985). Still informed by readings of the classic texts on historical change, a new and more inclusive research agenda has since become apparent. It embraces 'a heightened attention to institutions, theorization of agents and signification, gendered analysis and rejection of Eurocentrism' (Adams et al., 2005, 3; Hobson, 2006). Much of this scholarship is still located in the debates on how to deliver a historical sociology of modernity and the transformations associated with it. So the challenge for historical sociology in relation to globalization is whether to imagine a past not indebted to and a future beyond or apart from capitalist modernity, or to treat the allegedly transformative effects of global processes and ideologies as a further playing out of modernizing and universalizing liberalism (Adams, et al., 2005, 66; Morris, 2010; Fukuyama, 2011).

What Is Global History?

Perhaps surprisingly, the study of global history need not presume 'an affirmative history of singular transformation' (Schafer, 2007, 517). Rather it constitutes the 'main historiographical answer to global change' and canvasses both historical affinity and divergence as these appear over centuries, even millennia. And if we construe history as natural history, historical change of global proportions is as old as the planet. For long periods human history was intensely local before it resembled anything that can be taken as global, at least where the latter is understood as a spatial phenomenon rather than, or simply as, a form of consciousness. In 1998 Bruce Mazlish argued that it is also crucial to make a distinction between *world history* and *global history* (see also Mazlish and Buultjens, 1993). Though not accepted by all scholars in the field (see Crossley, 2008), this distinction runs through much historiography on the global. World history effectively deals with pre-global times and has a longer pedigree than global history, with its roots in the work of Oswald Spengler (1918) and Arnold Toynbee (1934–61). In many respects it is the child of 500 years of post-Columbian Western history, although in more recent guise and through the work of contemporary historians it acknowledges that Eurocentrism is no longer a viable perspective through which to comprehend modernity.

In fact, Spengler's magnum opus, *The Decline of the West* (1918), predicted the demise of Western culture as part of the millennial life-cycle of all civiliza-tions. Toynbee's version of world history has less of a cyclical quality than is found in Spengler, but he too discerns 'rhythms' in the playing out of civili-zational destinies that tend to entropy. But, in his account, the West – Western culture – is not doomed to fail, which leaves the fate of his 'postmodern' Latin Christian civilization still moot. On any accounting this is big history, and while it is true that civilizations have been world history's primary unit of analysis, as we shall see, the focus can be problematic given the difficulties in specifying and demarcating civilizations as cultural wholes.

By and large, global history denotes a quite recent and different field of historiography, or potentially so. It is characterized by alternative concep-tions of space beyond territorial nationalism, Eurocentrism and universalism. To that extent, it mirrors wider shifts in the scholarship on globalization, including third world history, post-colonial studies, feminist history and recent treatments of empire. Whereas world history often embraced theories of societal and civilizational convergence and linear trajectories of social change, global history (sometimes called translocal history) challenges these assumptions, though not always to the point of complete rupture (Ireyi and Mazlish, 2005).

Of course, once one departs from theories of convergence and linearity the difficulty lies in being able to 'tell a story without a centre', as Pamela Crossley puts it (2008, 5), and it is hard to do this unless one accepts the quotidian reality of different global narratives. Crossley points to four such analytical/narrative categories: *divergence* (things diversifying over time and space from a single origin); *convergence* (the narrative of different and widely separated things assuming similarities over time); *contagion* (the narrative of things crossing boundaries and changing their dynamics and identities as they do so); and finally, *systems* (the narrative of interacting structures changing each other at the same time).

There is also the matter of temporality. When we first alluded to this in chapter 3, it was to refer to the de-historicization of the complex processes that produce modernities as these are found in much globalization theory. In this regard, the treatment of the state and theories of the state system often convey a very static conception of historical time (Teschke, 2003; Rosenberg,

2005; 2006). Thus political realism, as Duncan Bell argues, 'forecloses the possibility of substantial global transformation; consequently it annihilates the future through denying any possibility of transcending the obdurate trajectory of the past' (2003, 807). Most explanations of social change that invoke path dependency might also plead guilty in this court.

In *Globalization in World History* (2002) and *Global History* (2006), Tony Hopkins, evangelist for the cause of studying globalization historically, aims to deliver a 'truly global history of globalization' (2002, 3). The former volume is important because contributors try to assess the past from a global, rather than a national standpoint. Hopkins is at pains to underline the claim that historians are uniquely placed to comment on the novelty or otherwise of globalization and to reveal how attention to global history also poses new questions for the study of history. Two key points emerge and, in *Globalization in World History*, they are then threaded through the various contributions to the book. The first is that globalization is a more multidimensional and historically variable process than much scholarship allows. While this is no real news for advocates of macro-historical sociology and strains of WSA, it is a useful counterpoint to any form of 'presentist' or essentialist globalization theory.

The second point, by now a mantra, is that globalization is not simply a Western phenomenon. In remapping the intellectual geography of the subject in both books, Hopkins and others examine ancient and modern, as well as Occidental and Eastern, facets and currents of globalization. This broad prospectus includes the idea of a global Muslim community, other appearances of diaspora and diasporic politics, and social movements. The theme of empire also weaves through the narrative, though mostly in a guise that would be unrecognizable to writers such as Hardt and Negri (but see Colas, 2005). Empires have been crucial vehicles and conduits for spreading people, ideas and institutions across the world, and this has rarely been a simple West–East or North–South process. Over time, the agents and facilitators of globalizations have included religious leaders and ideologies, merchant adventurers and other capitalist gamblers, flamboyant monarchs, networks of itinerant scholars, diaspora and the forced movement of people, often as slaves.

In *Globalization in World History*, Hopkins and his contributors argue that globalization took four different historical forms, three of which conform to the standard periodization of (Western) modernity. This allows these authors to formulate a typology of historical globalizations, with each different in its form, extensiveness and intensity. The historical categories are *archaic, proto, modern* and *post-colonial*, none of them discrete, because the new is always indebted to and parasitic on the old. Archaic globalization covers the period before industrialization and the rise of the nation-state. In many ways it is the most problematic of the categories, simply because of the span of time it encompasses, the possible range of exemplary cases available for study and, in some instances, the incompleteness of the historical record.

A number of themes are apparent and these can be seen as precursors of proto-globalization. The first is the variety of ways in which expansionary urges emerged in quite different cultures. Christopher Bayly sees proto-globalizing pressures in the ways in which the emergence of the Atlantic plantation system subsumed and overtook all economic systems through expanding markets and consumption. Amira Bennison (2002) demonstrates how a non-Western world-system, that of Islam, which contained 'universalizing elements' in the shape of the Arabic language and the ideal of a universal Muslim community (the *umma*), acted as a vehicle for Muslim globalization. Second is the importance of universal belief-systems, mainly religious, which combined with changing patterns of production and consumption to create world-spanning networks of culture, communication and trade. These areas of increasingly intense connectivity appeared mainly between key regions – the coastal zones of Africa, India, China and Europe. Moreover, *Globalization in World History* syncs with other work on the emergence of non-Western world-systems prior to 1500 (Abu-Lughod, 1989; Chaudhuri, 1990).

Proto-globalization occurred between 1600 and 1800, when major geopolitical changes took place. Principally these relate to the emergence of territorial states and the state system, but also to massive changes in both manufacturing technology and trade (Morris, 2010; Kennedy, 1989). Not only is this the period when the modern nation-state was established, but it is the forcing ground for Western expansion. Tony Ballantyne refers to the 1760s as a decade of globalization (2002), and this is not just a statement about material connections. Cultural aspects of globalization/hegemony are also important, evidenced in the spread of Western ideals of civilization and in the diffusion of new practical and technical knowledge. Of course, the regressive consequences of these avatars of Western expansionism include slavery, conquest, cultural impoverishment and, on some accounts, underdevelopment.

Modern globalization (1800–1950) is presented as the confluence of statist, and sometimes imperial, developments and ambitions, nationalism and the spread of industrial capitalism. New technologies permitted greater mobility and economic growth, but universalist and cosmopolitan ideals gave way to intense forms of national rivalry and imperial ambition, notably between the European 'great powers'. Vestiges of cosmopolitan ideals survived into the twentieth century in both intellectual currents and world-community prescriptions such as the League of Nations. Indeed, they muster today in the vogue for global governance and global civil society. Interestingly, America's globalization as depicted by David Reynolds (2002) is historically distinct, achieved through a combination of its position as an initiator and beneficiary of the 'massification' of production, consumption and communication and its geo-political clout applied through economic dynamism and military hardware.

Throughout the two volumes, the theme of 'decentring' Europe and/or the West is ever present. Its message is three-fold. First, indigenous cultures usually react, rather than just succumb, to the manifestations of Western dominance. Second, the concept of 'Western' civilization hides a much less monolithic reality. Finally, each period of globalization is not only layered on top of previous modes, but inflected by them as well (Pemberton, 2001). The post-colonial period, from about 1950 onwards, sees the playing out, and possibly the transformation, of modernity as a process of 'organisation and ungoverned energy' (Pemberton, 2001, 112). As to the future, despite predictions of a new Chinese century, it may not be a case of history simply repeating itself through further hegemonic cycles of expansion and decay (Bell, 2003). These are important qualifiers to linear, Western models of historical development. As Duncan Bell says, global history 'can help to render contingent that which is so often naturalized as inevitable, as inescapable' (2003, 813).

Civilizational Analysis as a New Paradigm

The historical sociology of globalization has to be set in the context of significant changes in sociological theory and in the study of comparative history since the 1970s. These changes cohere under the rubric of civilizational analysis. Themes rehearsed under that rubric throw light on the 'constitutive patterns and long-term dynamics of civilizations' and on how these influence historical transformations, including the transformation that is seminal in much globalization scholarship: the movement into and possibly out of modernity (Arnason, 2008, 2).

While this focus is necessary, it is also problematic, both because it is empirically hard to identify, demarcate and then classify civilizations, and because the concept is deeply rooted in European thought and lends itself too easily to strategic and ideological projects to universalize the Western civilizational account as a justification for hegemony (Wallerstein, 2006). There is one further lesson for globalization theory. In Martin Wight's seminal analysis on the *Systems of States* (1977), he reflects on the relationships between patterns of culture – civilizations – and international society, seen as the society of states. Wight underlines the importance of historical-cultural factors in constituting society and hints that the instability of international society is traceable to the absence of a shared culture.

In their volume on civilizational analysis, Said Arjomand and Edward Tiryakin note that it is usually employed to facilitate the imbrication of theoretical and historical approaches to the comparative study of civilizations (2004; Arnason, 2007). Although its provenance is quite recent, as we intimated, there is also a classical sociological tradition of civilizational analysis as well as a historical scholarship found, most obviously, in the work of Spengler and Toynbee. Classical sociological theory in the style of Marcel Mauss and Emile Durkheim (1998 [1913]) was also drawn to the idea of plural historical civilizations primarily rooted in religious differences and configured in a tranche of regional, socio-cultural complexes – Eurasian, Western European, Byzantine, Islamic, Indian and East Asian. Both Durkheim and Mauss were at pains to distinguish civilizations from societies on the basis that the former were large-scale and long-term socio-cultural formations comprising many societies.

But the emphasis on plurality found in such early works on civilizations was neglected in much mid-twentieth-century sociology, where themes such as modernization and development worked with an, at least implicit, assumption that *civilization* referred to a singular universal-historical (and in some work, evolutionary) process subject to law-like patterns and forces. In fact, the assumption of an emergent singularity can be traced to Enlightenment thinking, and this too underlines the European roots of still potent ideas about the provenance of modernity (Devezas et al., 2007).

By contrast, Max Weber's comparative studies speak of diverse and plural 'cultural worlds', rather than civilizations, although the two may be taken – largely – as equivalent. Weber was interested in the different historical trajectories of civilizations, but his main concern was to describe and explain the historical and cultural factors that had enabled the Western breakthrough to capitalism. His historical sociology examines the ways in which Western cultural worlds paralleled, but also diverged from, those of non-Western civilizations that had not experienced such a transformation. In this regard, processes of rationalization, which include capitalist practices, bureaucratization and the scientization and secularization of social worlds, are deemed critical. Crucially, Weber never claimed that non-Western cultures were devoid of rationality. His legacy remains potent, a precursor to the rediscovery of civilizational analysis since the early 1990s (Weber, 1958; 1968).

But as Johann Arnason points out (2007, 7), Weber's project, while not 'imprisoned within an ideological universe of discourse', also carries a strong Eurocentric strain. To reiterate, this tendency appears too in accounts of social differentiation as the key feature of post-Enlightenment modernity as depicted in all forms of structural-functionalism. By contrast, the civilizational turn in sociological theory and historical sociology is an attempt to grasp the complexities of plural cultural worlds or multiple civilizations and their historical trajectories, by privileging cultural factors over the more bloodless categories and claims of structural-functional theory (Arnason, 2003; Eisenstadt, 2000; 2004; Arnason et al., 2005; Holton, 2005).

Axial transformations and multiple modernities

Starting in the mid-1980s, Shmuel Eisenstadt's work builds on the traditions of historical cultural analysis and the history of ideas found, initially, in the writings of Karl Jaspers after World War II (Eisenstadt, 1986; 1996; 1998; 2000; 2006; 2009; Jaspers, 1949; Carr, 1961). The 'new' civilizational turn that his work presaged emphasizes the divergent historical paths of major civilizations and the theoretical paucity of unilinear models of social evolution, including those of modernization. The civilizational turn exemplified in Eisenstadt's corpus attempts to refurbish a quite venerable concept found in the history of ideas and religions, so as to deploy it in a sociological analysis of modernity (Arnason, 2007). The historical focus is on hugely significant 'cultural mutations' (Arnason, 2007, 4) that took place in separate civilizational centres at crucial periods in their development. These mutations, which involved major shifts in religious beliefs and philosophy, constituted a cultural and spiritual revolution that is claimed to be of world-historical significance.

Central to Eisenstadt's thesis is a concept he takes directly from Jaspers, the idea of 'Axial civilizations' (Jaspers, 1949). Axial Age civilizations were those that formed during the half-millennium or so between 500 BC and the end of the first century of the Christian era (Eisenstadt, 2000). The process of formation, which Eisenstadt calls 'crystallization' (2000, 4), took shape in ancient Israel (Judaism and Christianity), in ancient Greece, by way of Zoroastrianism in Iran, in early imperial China, as well as through Hinduism, Buddhism and – outside the Axial Age proper – Islam.

The burden of the cultural and spiritual changes that occurred during the Axial period varied from place to place and culture to culture, but in generic terms comprised the following. First was the growth of personal and social reflexivity and a spirit of self-questioning. In the political realm this process was manifest in the changing nature of and justification for rule, whereby the tradition of the king-god, the embodiment of both cosmic and earthly orders, was replaced by more secular and accountable versions. Second, and strongly related to this more demanding mentality, was the emergence of new social actors – philosophers, literati – often laying claim to knowledge not derived from notions of sacral infallibility and tradition. What these signify is the emergence of 'autonomous elites' as bearers of new civilizational visions and as champions of heterodoxy, protest and change in both the social and political realms (Eisenstadt, 2000, 6). Taken together, these features of Axial Age civilizations carried huge transformative potential, not least in their embrace of the prospects for and desirability of wholesale – indeed transcendental – change.

At this point, Eisenstadt takes a further analytical step, one that allows him, and then others, to demonstrate how Axial Age civilizations opened up new forms of interaction between cultural and social patterns, and this insight remains crucial for all types of civilizational analysis. His understanding of Axial Age civilizations allows that there were significant cross-cultural affinities, but notes continuing diversity in those historical paths and formations that were largely context-dependent. He then goes on to explain modernity as a new and distinctive form of civilization. In this he is only partially successful, but his insights still allow us to examine the possibility of multiple modernities under the rubric of civilizational analysis.

At the same time as Axial civilizations became institutionalized, a new form of intersocietal and intercivilizational world history also began to emerge. All Axial civilizations exhibited a tendency to expansion driven by the almost missionary zeal found in their revolutionary world-views, notably in religion. Such expansion could be geographically isomorphic with that of religion, but not always, and certainly not of necessity. The key point is that expansionism gave rise to a much greater consciousness of civilizational frameworks and identities by encompassing many different societies and diverse ethnic and political groups. Eisenstadt talks of these new civilizational frameworks 'impinging' on pre-existing political and primordial formations and identities. Crucially, this was a highly reflexive process.

The expansion of Axial civilizations entailed the possibility of new civilizational ontologies because they had the capacity for internal transformation. Eisenstadt. says that Christianity, Buddhism and, to a lesser degree, neo-Confucianism all developed out of the potential for heterodoxy contained in their respective 'original' Axial civilizations (2000, 9). So the post-Axial world is not the product of a single world history. Rather, encounters between non-Axial/pre-Axial formations and Axial civilizations produce a multiplicity of 'different, divergent, yet continuously mutually impinging world civilizations, each attempting to reconstruct the world in its own mode, according to its basic premises, and either to absorb the others or self-consciously to segregate itself from them' (2000, 9). For students of globalization and global history the most dramatic transformation was the emergence of modernity, first crystallized in Western Europe and then 'expanded to most other parts of the world, giving rise to the development of multiple, continually changing modernities' (2000, 11).

Eisenstadt's view of modernity and of modernization is made in contradistinction to the version at least implicit in 'classical' studies of modernization, which not only stressed the convergence of industrial societies, but sometimes envisaged teleological progress towards that goal across political, economic and cultural realms and diverse societies (Preyer, 2007). As Gerhard Preyer notes, the idea of multiple modernities is a kind of antidote to the 'self- prescription of Western society as a normative orientation and general prototype for all societies' (2007, 10; Amin, 1989). In the same vein, it is also an indirect response to much theorization on globalization and global systems since the 1980s (Eisenstadt, 2009). The universalism bruited as an axial component of contemporary globalization is, on some accounts, also a form of particularism, given its provenance in ideas about and prescriptions for Westernized or American modernity (Robertson, 1992; Lash and Urry, 1994; Ikenberry, 2011). Although they may differ in degrees of approbation, in such accounts modernity is a product of the modern world-system that emerges from the West to spawn a singular global modernity, with global convergence delivered through evolutionary change.

The notion of multiple modernities offers a different paradigm. Its core idea is that features of modernity can emerge, develop and find expression in different ways in different parts of the world. In and of itself this claim does not reject the historical and current impacts of 'modernizing' processes as these manifest around the globe: the industrial revolution, the urban revolution, the scientific revolution and so on. But what some construe as the ideological components of the modernization thesis – uniformity, standardization and, of course, Western superiority – are given short shrift. Put simply, the idea of being modern does not require that everywhere looks like, or thinks like, Britain, France or Sweden in matters of religious belief, culture, morality and even science and philosophy. At the same time, it is obvious that valorizing diversity in this way might look like yet another form of non-essentialist essentialism, or a rather naive kind of normative prescription. There is also the danger of denigrating the valuable empirical findings of world polity research on global standardization and rationalization, on the a priori grounds that they mask a profoundly ideological view of the making of world society (Schmidt, 2006).

For all that, some modernization theorists and proponents of multiple modernities share the assumption that modernization is a 'continuous and open-ended process' (Kumar, 1999, 72) and accept that once the modern project had become established in the West it spread globally. Where they disagree is in the assumption that societies experiencing modernization tend to converge over time. Rather, those who champion multiple modernities emphasize the continuing salience of cultural and institutional differences that obtain despite modernization. Let us be clear here; the apparent logic of the multiple modernities thesis is that, as a consequence of its catholicity, the 'open-ended' project of modernity must admit the possibility that there are as many modernities as there are societies which have modernized. This apparent logic has, say, British or French or Norwegian modernities as bona fide evidence of the quotidian historicism at work in what might otherwise look like a universal and unremittingly convergent process. Echoes of this debate also appear in pragmatic versions of the multiple modernities argument. Here the emergence of China as the global hegemon in waiting, or of Russia and China as hard evidence of historical particularisms both resisting and accommodating global liberal doctrine, are taken as illustrative of different and viable routes to modernity and, of course, of the return of history (Ikenberry, 2010).

But is this what proponents of the multiple modernities paradigm really want to argue? Their core position is that modernities exist outside the Western paradigm. The provenance of these modernities cannot be understood in terms of categories and analytical tools employed to make sense of Western modernity, and there should be no assumptions made about these modernities' inevitable convergence with the institutional and cultural forms of the West. For the most part this still subsists as a variant of civilizational analysis, though with a more obvious historicist gloss, in that modernities in the plural still cluster or crystallize around the main human civilizations (Huntington, 1996). These civilizational identities leave significant imprints on the institutions and practices of particular societies and thus qualify simple diffusionist or evolutionary models of social change, by pointing to a more polycentric view of global history.

Modernity now appears as less than universal, or as subject to some kind of logic of evolution, and subsists more as a feature of variable structural change in different social systems (Preyer, 2009). The theoretical consequence of this for any refurbishment of theories of modernization is that the process no longer needs to be seen as singular or plural, universal or particular. Rather, it emerges out of the variable processes of expansion common to all social systems. Of course, difficulties of cultural translation, along with other barriers, may set limits to such expansion and thus dilute the impact of exogenous and/or universalizing forces or cultural scripts on particular places. All of which syncs with a good deal of anthropological and sociological analysis on globalization, allowing indigenization, vernacularization and hybridization to be seen as suitably modest versions of the multiple modernities thesis, along with the whole critique of cultural meta-narratives (Preyer, 2009; Pieterse, 2009).

For critics, the emphasis on difference, notably in culture and religion, is understandable and possibly appropriate for a nuanced treatment of globalization. At the same time, noting difference is one thing, establishing its significance for explanatory purposes is quite another; unless, of course, the object of the exercise is the valorization of *any* differences which appear to redeem local history and culture. If it is not, then it remains of key analytical concern as to whether the differences observed between, say, India and the West are so obvious, or unique, as to warrant talking about the former in terms of its civilizational distinctiveness. By contrast, how much weight should be given to the factors that allow the analyst to treat India or Japan as part of a 'common family of industrial societies' (Schmidt, 2006, 81)?

Do contemporary India or Japan have much more in common with their respective pasts than they have with contemporary Britain, Germany or Canada? If cultural differences translate into a markedly different pattern of accommodation with twenty-first-century globality, then the multiple modernities thesis has a strong case. If not, then the normative project that lies at the heart of the thesis can still succeed, but its analytical purchase may be questioned. Jan Pieterse recognizes this tension when he talks about '[r]eal existing modernities' as mixed social formations, in that they straddle past and present, and import and translate styles and customs from other cultures. Modernities are layered; some components are shared among all modern societies and make up transnational modernity, 'while other components differ according to historical and cultural circumstances' (2009, 19).

But is this still only obfuscation with an ideological motive? Drawing on work from the 'varieties of capitalism' literature out of new political economy (Hall and Soskice, 2001; Yamamura and Streeck, 2003), Volker Schmidt (2006) notes differences in modernizing patterns and all institutional (as opposed to just cultural) forms. However, such differences are presented as variations on a theme that displays more significant 'family' similarities. These span economic institutions, social policy regimes, even political, or at least constitutional, systems. Analysed in relation to modes of capitalism – liberal Anglo-American, non-liberal Japanese and European, as well as possibly new forms of the 'Oriental' – the relative weights of affinities and differences produce variations on a singular modernity, not multiple modernities defined solely through specific historical-cultural factors (Ikenberry, 2010).

Notwithstanding its rather integrationist slant, this take on the ontological singularity of modernity as globality, or globality as a form of modernity, does at least point to some conceptual and empirical problems with the multiple modernities thesis. Principally these turn on the need for comprehensive historical and comparative analysis across cultural, economic and political spheres of life. Across-the-board comparisons, as Schmidt writes, then allow for any outcomes: intra-civilizational divergence or convergence, the possibility that societies look more like or have more in common with those in other civilizations than with their own, the sense that ascribed differences between modernities do not actually exist, and so on. Really to speak of multiple modernities, research has to find clusters of modern societies (civilizations) with 'coherent patterns of institutional co-variation' (Schmidt, 2006, 88), and because such a research design has yet to be delivered, the case remains at best moot. So contemporary issues that fall out of civilizational analysis and the multiple modernities debate, or are informed by it, abound and constitute a prospectus of global scholarship's current preoccupations. They include the weakening of US hegemony and the rise of rival or successor powers, the emergence of a more fluid multi-polarity, and the crisis/transformative potential in the existing order of (Western) modernity. Modernity, as Pieterse notes, remains very much a theme for our times (2009, 19).

Historical Sociology, International Relations and Globalization

Historical realities are complex, and if we put aside the simplifying normative intent of the multiple modernities school, its considerable virtue is to qualify views of world history that over-privilege the systematic at the expense of contingency, unevenness and contradiction (Denemark, 2009). The universality implied in the concept of modernity and that of globalization is qualified by differences in the rates and patterns of diffusion and differentiation and in the appearance of what Michael Mann calls the sources of social power, whether ideological, political, economic or military (1986; 1988; 1996; 1997;

2006). Agreeing that this may be so does not render the concept of modernity an 'empty designate' or a purely descriptive category (Anderson, 2000). But the problem for world historians and for historical sociologists remains that of identifying and explaining the linkages between different periods of historical stasis and transformation and the sources and impacts of change within and across particular places.

The critique of Eurocentrism finds expression too in what John Hobson and his co-authors label the 'second wave' of historical sociology applied to the discipline of IR – HSIR (Hobson et al., 2010). The second wave of theorizing musters not only in opposition to the Eurocentric cast of much social theory, but as a critique of – until recently – theoretically moribund IR scholarship. Our task now is to unpack the strains of HSIR and identify the implications for globalization theory.

Some preliminary caution is necessary. HSIR of whatever provenance aims to rescue IR scholarship from both realism and neo-realism's a-historicist and deeply unsociological treatment of social change (Waltz, 1979). Understanding, even countenancing, the idea of globalization, let alone globality, is at best an adjunct to this goal. Nonetheless, once the realm of 'the international' is problematized in IR theory, such that the modern international system can no longer be 'treated as an ontological given', the scope for theoretical transformation vastly increases (Hobson et al., 2010, 19). Having said this, many of the proponents of HSIR still experience difficulty in imagining a world beyond the world of states, even if their understanding of what states are, and why they behave as they do, has been modified. It is clear that anything resembling traditional IR theory cannot provide a purchase on the globalized world of late/post-modernity, and HSIR is clearly an attempt to go beyond traditional IR theory. But does it do service as a global historical sociology (Shaw, 2000)? Indeed, to the extent that at least some of its practitioners retain a commitment to the ontological centrality of the state form, can it do so?

HSIR is now a recognized feature of IR scholarship. But this may amount to no more than a ritual acknowledgement of the need for the specificity of historical inquiry, and a bow to the eminently sociological idea that understanding social behaviour means attending to how social relationships are structured, as well as to the perceptions and motivations of various agents so engaged. Outside realist and neo-realist IR theory, none of this seems earthshattering in its implications for scholarship, but applied to that realm a number of quite significant shifts in attempts to theorize the international – though rarely the global – have taken place. These attempts, again summarized as 'waves', reveal much that is good in the maturation of IR theory, but also point up the enormous task of reconciling aims that include identifying deep-lying structural 'patterns that explain important historical processes', rejecting realism's a-historical and a-historicist assumption of anarchy as a trans-historical logic, and recognizing the importance of contingency as part of the constitutive process of international relations (Hobson et al., 2010).

The first wave of HSIR emerged in the late 1980s and drew on Weberian and neo-Weberian thinking found in earlier work on comparative macro history. This work tried to shift the sociological enterprise away from 'societalist' interpretations of social order and change that privilege the idea of the state as kind of social relation, or else as an instrumentality in thrall to dominant and usually materialist interests. 'Bringing the state back in' in the manner prescribed by Theda Skocpol (1979) and by Peter Evans and others (1985) involved specifying the actual conditions under which and the resources with which states might act autonomously. Many such attempts are either explicit or closet forms of Weberianism and emphasize the subjectivity and anthropomorphized 'self-interested' behaviour of states as organizational actors (Skocpol, 1979; Trimberger, 1978; Giddens, 1984; Mann, 1986).

For critics of realism this was quite a heady brew. All forms of IR theory treat with the world beyond the territorial state, but realism is as unconcerned theoretically with the significance of endogenous forces on state action as many societalist accounts out of mainstream political sociology have been with the contexts in which the nation-state is embedded. Realists have emptied the concept 'state' of anything that might suggest that the behaviour of states is a product of human intervention, of motivation and of inter-subjectivity. Rather, the 'reality' conjured is that of the anarchic state of nature, with state behaviour rooted in the unalterable logic of an international system reproduced through the survival strategies of egoistic actors (Wendt, 1994; 1987; 2004). In this milieu, works such as Theda Skocpol's *States and Social Revolutions* (1979) seemed to offer a novel perspective on the interaction between the national and the international. In Skocpol's organizational-realist account of dramatic social and political change, the analytical charge for students of IR is her depiction of seminal events in recent world histories, where the idea that pressures from the international state system influence the shape of national societies is acknowledged, but tempered by a good dose of sociological realism pointing to the still considerable room for manoeuvre enjoyed by national actors.

Skocpol (1979), Trimberger (1978), Mann (1986), Tilly (1990) and others were sociologists and/or historians rather than students of IR. Their views were shared by IR scholars trying to link developments in the international realm to domestic conditions (Rosenau, 1990). State autonomy was linked not just to international pressures but – to mitigate what might otherwise look like realism or even hyper-globalism – to endogenous and frequently unique sources of power; not least to what Michael Mann calls the 'transcendent' power of ideology. Of course, not all of these insights can be seen as directly or uniquely Weberian; witness the writings of the *Annales* school, the seminal ideational account of social and political change provided by Barrington

Moore (1966), and a tranche of neo-Weberian, neo-Marxist, neo-Gramscian and critical theory interventions around the same theme (Anderson, 1974; Teschke, 2003; Cox, 1987; Gill, 2008; Linklater, 1998).

The Weberian motif was dominant. Yet despite its merits, Weberianism also presents a considerable problem of conceptualization for revisionist IR scholars. Neo-Weberian historical sociologies of IR still embrace an ersatz realism to depict the international realm, a realm where the behaviour of states is predicated on the timeless constraint provided by the geo-political logic of anarchy. Of course, such criticism of neo-Weberian historical sociology underplays the more nuanced insights of Michael Mann and Theda Skocpol, where the intersocietal dimension of relations is critical and subject to forces much more contingent and context specific than the inexorable logic of anarchy. The identity of states as actors is seen as a negotiated condition moving to domestic vagaries, and a matter of reflexive engagement with larger, sometimes exogenous, cultural and structural scripts. It is also a product of particular histories. States may not be entirely self-made, as in some constructivist conceit, but neither are they timeless, ontological givens.

Nonetheless, discontent with Weberianism produced a second wave of HSIR theory, this time ridden by mainly IR theorists. The main thrust of this scholarship is to debunk chrono-fetishism and its fellow-traveller *tempocentrism* (Hobson et al., 2010). Tempocentrism is the tendency to underplay or ignore past discontinuities in the historical record. Instead, current circumstances are extrapolated to the past. As Hobson et al. say, this 'is an inverted form of path dependency which renders previous epochs and international systems as homologous to the present' (2010, 17). Examples are not hard to find. Hobson et al. mention the fallacy that antiquarian imperialism is akin to that found in modern Europe after 1492 and the claim that European feudalism equates to the functioning of the modern system of states. In tempocentric accounts, time, space, particularity and contingency all meld or are rendered nugatory.

The antidote to both these fallacies, especially the latter, is to employ a more obviously historicist approach, such that the possibility of a sustained historical narrative is entertained while the impact of contingency, unintended consequences and context are admitted. So far, so good; but the prescription now runs up against the usual problem of permissive solutions to explanations of historical change; namely, how to fit diversity and contingency within a more encompassing theory of history and how, or whether, to make them subject to universal laws. The idea of a sustained historical narrative isn't all that hard to conceive, but it does impose exacting criteria on any attempt to overcome tempocentrism, and these students of HSIR may struggle to meet.

For all that, a robust scholarship has developed drawing on different intellectual traditions. These range over neo-Marxist interpretations of the ways in which different types of class relations produce distinct forms of international order (Rosenberg, 1994; Teschke, 2003; Lacher, 2006); neo-Weberian interventions on how particular state–society relations impact on 'external' modalities, for example in trade patterns and regimes (Hobson, 2007b; Lawson, 2005); and constructivist approaches to the state and to sovereignty (Wendt, 1994a; 2006). In much of this work, but especially that indebted to Marxism, the immanent tension in recognizing diversity in historical forms and outcomes, while insisting that this diversity is part of an ontological whole, is tangible and possibly theoretically debilitating. At the same time, given their varied provenance there is no doubt that many of these developments have contributed or are contributing to more of a 'trans-disciplinary agenda for IR' (Hobson et al., 2010, 20). They also do service in pursuit of the holy grail of establishing a true historical sociology of IR, principally by challenging and, to some degree, overcoming the 'categorical separation of domestic and international spheres of enquiry' (Hobson et al., 2010, 21) and by strengthening an already extant sociology in which intersocietal relations are deemed an integral part of the remit of sociological theory (Giddens, 1985).

In the third wave of theorizing, the shift away from anti-sociological and a-historicist international theory is given further impetus by closer attention to the nature and constitution of 'the international'. Principally, this third wave theorizes the international in terms of two features basic to historical development (Rosenberg, 2006). First, it sees development embracing a multiplicity of different societies, whose variable 'internal' dynamics make for a process of uneven development. At the same time, because such societies coexist in space and time they influence each other, thus exhibiting features of combined development. In Justin Rosenberg's plea for a rigorous international historical sociology (IHS) (2006) and in his more polemical work on globalization theory (2000; 2005; 2007), these processes are rehearsed as part of a Trotskyist theory of historical change.

Writing in 2006, Rosenberg is at pains to underline the complexity of 'multiple instances' of societal and statist development in the international system, while stressing the need to see such diversity – indeed to see diversity per se – as part of an ontological whole (unevenness). The consequence is that

> one would have to abandon at the deepest theoretical level any notion of the *constitution* of society as analytically prior to its *interaction* with other societies. For '[i]n reality, the national peculiarities' which seem to pre-exist and govern international relations are themselves in each case not pre-interactive essences, but rather 'an original combination of the basic features of the world process' (Trotsky 1962:23) of human development – that is, of its uneven and combined character.

Rosenberg's use of Trotsky is a considered attempt to revive IR theory but, from the point of view of both HSIR and globalization theory, it simply lessens without wholly relaxing the tension in the relationship between what is historically specific or contextually variable and what is theoretically encompassing. This tension is apparent also in Rosenberg's attempt to depict the current phase of globalization as a conjunctural anomaly, not subject to any sustained historical narrative and growing out of the unlikely concatenation of a set of events and processes that interrupt the flow of history in the late twentieth century. Here he has recourse to the anodyne observation that 'when we refract the elements of the conjunctural method through the "level" of geopolitics, we find that the abstract, linear quality of the organic tendencies is interrupted – perhaps we should say "overdetermined" – by the specifically international mechanism of their operation in the context of a plurality of societies' (2005, 41). True, he notes diversity in state and societal forms, which is at the heart of HSIR, but does not carry this insight to its proper conclusion, which is that once diversity in 'stateness' (in independence, authority and capacity) is introduced into the analysis, it is not possible – indeed, there is no need – to retain the alleged antithesis between states and globalization. And when all is said and done, the very idea of diversity, of stateness, is part and parcel of the historicity craved by third wave theorists.

Other, albeit related, variants of third wave IHS rehearse the familiar critique of Eurocentrism and expound a model of historical development that is more obviously attuned to global currents and dialogues, rather than simply extolling the virtues and unmediated impact of Western institutions and cultural scripts (Hobson, 2007a; 2007b). Instead, the emphasis is on the ways in which West and non-West exhibit reciprocities or, as Hobson et al. put it, engage in the 'dialogues of civilizations' (2010, 24). These dialogues may involve straightforward exchange, assimilation of alien practice and, of course, forms of hybridization. They also reveal agency at work in the resistance to imperial ambitions and practices. Above all, the significance of intersocietal transmission is stressed, along with the sense that domestic and international are not separate spheres of existence, but mutually constituted.

At this point any simple binary, especially one based on scalar separation, looks redundant, or incapable of capturing the interaction of different kinds of agency with varieties of wider social practice (structures). In common with recent work in the sociology of globalization, students of HSIR look increasingly to middle-range or meso levels of investigation to substantiate their arguments. Sometimes this takes the form of historical network analysis of the kind practised by Charles Tilly (2005) that explores patterns of social network formation and dissolution across time and space (borders). In a reversion to a more conventional form of historical analysis combined with quantitative methods, historical institutionalists and some world polity researchers have reconstructed the event history of different world cultural scripts in fields such as climate change, world society formation and policy on human reproduction, mapping the interests, networks and organizations implicated in constructing and promulgating them (Thelen, 2004; Ramirez, 2001; Mann, 1988). This focus on 'eventful IHS' allows, or should allow, students of IR to explore how historical events 'enable social formations to emerge, reproduce, reform, transform and break down' (Hobson et al., 2010, 25). Critically, it seems to dispense with the need to use 'entities', such as civilizations and binaries like state–society or structure–agency, as the limiting starting points for analysis.

Such is the gloss, at any rate. In practice, many of the tensions we refer to above continue to dog these laudable attempts to break free of disciplinary conventions. A case in point is Justin Rosenberg's attempt to employ a historical sociology of the emergence of the international system of states as a way of demonstrating the theoretical indigence and a-historicism of globalization theory (Axford, 2007a). He does so by pointing to the reliance of globalization theory on the 'deeply unsociological' and a-historical concept of the 'Westphalian system'. He then looks to relocate a theoretical understanding of state sovereignty in the historical emergence of modern societies (and states). This is bruited as an authentic historical sociology rooted in a Marxist theory of historical (uneven and combined) development (Teschke, 2003; Spruyt, 1994; Hall, 1999; Mann, 1986).

But the state has long been a theoretical sticking point for Marxism, leading some scholars to argue that exploration of the state points up Marxism's limitations as a theory of politics and the political, because the state is often the source of anomalies which have to be squared with the main theoretical thrust of the argument (Easton, 1969; Hindess and Hirst, 1975; Gouldner, 1978). Comparative macro history, especially in its early forms, seemed to endorse this critique, but shied away from attempting or endorsing theoretical transcendence. Understandable in the 1970s and early 1980s when academic Marxism was riding its own wave, this reluctance is less explainable now. Rosenberg also comes very close to, but abjures, apostasy. He reveals as much when he refers to the huge theoretical difficulty of combining general theory and empirical explanation, for as he says, there is never an unbroken line from theory to historical explanation. Which device lets Marx off the hook but not, in Rosenberg's estimation, globalization theory.

Conclusion

In this chapter we have examined some of the main currents in historical treatments of globalization and the application of historical method to globalization, international relations and the debates over multiple modernities. The appropriation of historical approaches to globalization provides, at the least, a much-needed dose of detailed empiricism to rather abstract and ungrounded reflections on the origins and career of global processes. At the same time, serious problems remain. The multiple modernities thesis, while plausible and necessary in terms of its reassertion of non-European routes to modernity, also flirts with relativism and a rather too cautious historicism.

In 1990, James Rosenau called for recognition of the growing significance of 'post-international politics', a shift that orientates IR to the global (Shaw, 2000; 2003; Hobden and Hobson, 2002). For all its promise in this respect, it is not clear that HSIR, or rather its main practitioners out of IR, has embraced or is capable of embracing that shift. Partly this is the necessary consequence of a continuing absorption with the ontological centrality of the territorial state and, as a corollary, the reluctance of proponents actually to take on board the consequences of their own prescriptions for what to investigate and how to do it. In the next chapter we will examine work on the state and on governance that offers a more nuanced global historical sociology. Here the repositioning and even transformation of the state is given greater credence in discussions of global governance.

CHAPTER 7

Theories of Globalization and Governance

Introduction

In this chapter we will begin by looking more directly at the territorial state and the changing character of *stateness*. Then we will turn to the liberal international order of states and raise questions about the efficacy of new institutions of global governance and the prospects for world society. No discussion of these features of the contemporary world order can ignore claims that we are in a process of transcending the boundaries of political community and the identity spaces of the state and national societies. These claims inform prescriptions for cosmopolitanism, which is a powerful normative treatise that may have implications for the conduct of governance and democracy.

The State and Stateness

To reiterate: in political science, debates about globalization tend to focus on the future of the state. At one remove this focus can be treated as a purely empirical matter and turns on whether the state is in decline, being 'repositioned' or undergoing transformation; with each as potent, but still very imprecise and often polemical, attributions. The empirical referents have always been contested. If the state is embattled, how and over what period of time do we gauge that condition and thus the steepness of decline? How should we assess the consequences for the architectures and conduct of government, for the emergence and shape of non-state governance, and for the location and character of political community? If the state is being transformed, what are the indicators and the consequences? Empirically contested, these concerns are also normatively potent. Even desiccated concepts such as regionalization and multi-level governance (MLG) are not just descriptions of organizational form and change but, in some work, prescriptions for new orders of governance.

When discussing the work of Saskia Sassen we noted that the effect of her 'new geographies of power' is to bring into question what constitutes a political community or a social and cultural order, where the boundaries of such constructs lie and who are to be ascribed roles as legitimate actors in them. Sassen suggests that there has been a 'denationalization' of governance functions through the instantiation of global institutions and practices. Quite often this pattern of globalization takes place through the agency of states acting both individually and collectively, as well as through the offices of a host of non-state actors. Her conclusion is that states are not simply bit players side-lined by the forces of history and current exigencies.

Examples of continued potency include states' roles in implementing the rules and standards laid down in international law, and the significance of state compliance for the legitimacy and effectiveness of regime-governed behaviour in various policy and issue areas. Global constraints, as well as forms of advanced multilateralism, are increasingly visible in these undertakings, but they are often reliant on the agency of individual states to make them work. Undoubtedly Sassen's is a transformationalist position where the state is concerned, but it does not traffic a simple version of states in decline (Cerny, 2010).

The lesson here is the one bruited, but not always heeded, by students of IHS with respect to the ontological status of the state: there are no simple analytic dualities that can provide a purchase on the complex imbrication of national and global. Moreover, states cannot – should not – be treated as a uniform category for purposes of analysis. Rather, any regard for historicism counsels respect for the idea of 'stateness', of diversity, and in turn this requires us to treat the relationships between states and globalization as subject to empirical investigation and not presumed on the basis of a priori reasoning or ideological commitment.

If we entertain the idea of stateness, we have to accept the inference that under globalization some states prosper while others do not (Weiss, 2006). Variation appears in each and all of the qualities that contribute to the *stateness* of states. Bertrand Badie and Pierre Birnbaum list these as independence, authority and capacity (1983; Ruggie, 1993), while Sassen talks of the historical relationships between territory, authority and rights that have traditionally allowed us to identify bordered states and societies and signify them as effective actors in the international system. At the same time, she also talks of 'foundational changes' that are taking place in these relationships because of globalization. Michael Mann's concept of state power seen as 'infrastructural power' is also relevant, and points up variability in the capacity of states to penetrate, extract and coordinate resources within a territorially defined space (1986; 1993; 1997). Changes in the demeanour and performance of individual states as practitioners of and participants in governance functions can be mapped along Badie and Bertrand's dimensions, and that is true of hegemonic or 'preponderant' states as well as for those barely clinging to the status (Clark, 2011).

Commentary on the nature of and the variations in state power and state capacity are not new. For Max Weber, the sphere of action of any state was territorially bounded, and nation, state and territory in turn define the limits of society. Even Michel Foucault can be read historically, as it were, as a theorist of Fordist modernity, with the disciplinary society of which he writes confined to a historical period – of discrete welfare states and national economies – now said to be in retreat (Foucault, 2004; 2006; Fraser, 1981; 1997; 2003; 2008; 2010). Nancy Fraser's treatment of Foucault has it that the rise of post-industrial society and especially of neo-liberal globalization, with its organizational emphasis on deregulation and financial, labour market and institutional flexibility, decentres the kind of power crucial to Foucault's thesis, not least in relation to the significance of the national frame of reference.

Thus globalized governmentality is not nation-state centred and comprises a 'dispersed collection of entities including states, supranational organizations, transnational firms, NGOs [non-governmental organizations], professional associations and individuals' (Fraser, 2003, 168). The very idea of 'governance without government' is that of a multi-layered regulatory ensemble, not always and certainly not easily correlated with the nation-state. Indeed, whether one is talking about security arrangements, aspects of criminal law and policing or the rules governing trade, there is seldom any single 'locus of coordination' (Rosenau and Czempiel, 1992; Fraser, 2003, 167). Instead, the typical post-Fordist governance regime tends to govern at a distance (Hardt and Negri, 2000) through 'flexible, fluctuating networks that transcend structured institutional sites' (Fraser, 2003, 168; Neumann and Sending, 2010).

Whether derived from classical sociological theory, French Marxism or historical institutionalism, pretty much all such reflections are a world away from realism proper, which treats the matter of state power and thus the identity and motivations of state actors as entirely unproblematic. Yet, if power exists in social relationships that are less and less located within the national frame of reference, but are, as Castells says, 'global and local at the same time' (2009, 18), not only the boundaries but the very idea of what constitutes society change (Fraser, 2008). The palpable need is thus to transcend both endogenous frameworks, wherein state power and state actions are ordered by societal forces to meet particular goal states or functional needs, and models that favour crudely exogenous imperatives, whereby state power has been irretrievably compromised by the forces of globalization (Held and McGrew, 1992). The question for globalization theory has always been how to transcend methodological nationalism without completely jettisoning the state as a crucial part of the ontology of a globalized world (Hay, 2007).

In the first two volumes of his treatise on the social sources of power (1986; 1993; *Millennium*, 2006), Michael Mann argues that we should treat states as nodes (albeit key nodes) in political, institutional, military and economic interaction networks – local, national, international and transnational – that are sometimes contained by, but also cross, territorialized societies. He distinguishes these categories too from 'genuinely global networks', which are themselves variable in intensity and scope and which cover most, if not all, of the world. His answer to the question posed at the outset of this chapter – 'is the state in decline?' – is couched instead in terms of the relative shifts taking place between more-or-less local, national and international interaction networks and those operating transnationally and globally.

Mann's response is suitably cautious as well because he does not discern an unqualified shift to universalisms or the emergence of global isomorphism through networking, even if there is a crystallization of power along network connections. The actual force of transnational and global interaction networks is moderated by issue area and, of course, by the type of state and by its capacities (Weiss, 2006). Of course the intriguing question is whether the growing ubiquity of such interaction networks challenges or even undermines the very idea of society as a stable form of social organization. On this Mann is also cautious, going so far as to suggest that where matters of identity are concerned, global networks may actually reinforce local networks and local particularisms. This too syncs with the findings of those who point to the conjoint relativizing and essentializing effects of global processes. And for students of globality a further important question concerns the extent to which network ontologies and what Castells calls the 'relatively stable configurations built on the intersection of these networks' can redefine and relocate the very notion of 'society' (Castells, 2009, 19; Axford, 2012).

Mann's own assessment of the relationship between state power (its infrastructural power) and globalization turns on the extent to which growing interdependence compromises the state's organizational autonomy and restricts its capacity to penetrate, extract and coordinate resources within its territory. Mann has yet to publish the long-awaited third volume of his trilogy on the changing basis of social power, but in his 1997 article on globalization he argues that on the evidence available it is clear that globalization's impact is variable because states display varying degrees of stateness. Moreover, globalization is not a singular phenomenon, or one that is simply imposed on state actors.

None of which is particularly radical as a depiction of either states or globalization, although Mann blazed a much-needed trail by his willingness to countenance a positive relationship between globalization and the growth of infrastructural power, rather than point to the latter's necessary attenuation (Weiss, 2005; 2006). This insight relies on two related propositions. The first is that transnational networks (for example in financial markets) have grown apace with national ones, not one at the expense of the other. The second proposition is that global and national networks of interaction are intertwined, or mutually reliant, and not parasitic or competing for the same interaction space.

Mann's understanding of states as significant players in global networks resonates with more obviously sceptical treatments of the alleged 'retreat of the state' found in second wave globalization theory and seen too in discussions of the variable resilience of welfare nationalism when faced with market forces (Strange, 1996; Hirst et al., 2009; Glatzer and Rueschmeyer, 2005; Lechner, 2009). For the moment we should underline the importance of keeping an open mind about the direction of influence in relationships between the global and sub-global and about the variation in experiences of retrenchment or opportunity that they entail.

For the present in Mann's work, insights on the interrelationships between states and global networks remain allusive, which both enhances their plausibility and raises questions about the robustness of some of the historical research underlying all the claims. At the same time, network approaches to understanding the problems of governance, organizational change and even global order are widely bruited (Axford, 2009). Linked to the theme of democratizing world politics through the trope of 'global civil society', network interaction bears directly on the changing nature of governance in the millennial period of globalization. Against the still relatively stable configuration of the state and the (liberal) international order of states, network models of global governance and sociality look decidedly volatile. Obviously, they express a powerfully transformationalist strain in global theory (Axford, 2009). Before we address such matters there is related analytical terrain to cross. The alleged decline or transformation of the state has to be seen in the context of a wider issue. That issue is the durability of the liberal international order of states and of cooperative but still state-centred institutions of international governance, along with the emergence of institutional/political structures and processes summarized as *global governance* (Lechner, 2010).

The Liberal International Order

In Mann's discussion of the relationships between global interaction networks and nation-states, he rehearses four areas of supposed threat to the latter as effective institutions of governance (1997). These are global capitalism, environmental danger, identity politics and post-nuclear geo-politics. His conclusion, trailed above, is that such constraints impact differentially on states in various parts of the world and possessing variable capacities (Lechner, 2009). Globalization is both state weakening and state strengthening. Well and good; but what Linda Weiss labels the 'enabling logic of globalization' (2005, 533) has not been a significant theme in too much scholarship on the subject.

At the same time, the sense of threat or enforced transformation has not disappeared. Indeed, when faced with the rigours of the early 2000s one might be forgiven for thinking that as far as states are concerned, matters have become decidedly more difficult to manage. The liberal new world order bruited at the time of the collapse of the Soviet world-empire, complete with the universalisms of liberal democracy and neo-liberal-inspired economic prosperity, now looks somewhat threadbare. Since the launch of the War on

Terror, some core liberal democracies have behaved less like guardians of freedom and more like surveillance states (Thompson, 2007). Moreover, the wealth gap both within and between states has grown, and is still widening.

Humanitarian and cosmopolitan intervention, hymned so boldly in the later 1990s, took on a different, and possibly more sinister, hue in the Afghan incursion from 2001 and the second Gulf War. And it is not yet clear whether the democratic uprisings across North Africa and the Middle East that began in 2011 will necessitate and – more to the point – re-legitimate such interventions by the international community, and if so, where, on what scale and for what duration. Meanwhile the position of the USA as either the anchor of or incubus on the liberal world order seems vitiated, with the unipolarity that emerged after the end of the Cold War giving way to something more resembling a state of flux or a shift to a new era of great power conflict – perhaps a new realism – with illiberal states as the main movers and shakers (Mearsheimer, 2006).

All this is some way from the relatively benign if dispiritingly uniform 'end of history' envisaged by Francis Fukuyama in the early 1990s and, on some accounts, is seen as threatening to liberalism as the paradigm expression of a post-ideological world. The liberal order of states and liberal ideals extended to economic and social progress have been the most stable features of world politics since the end of World War II. Of late the language of stagnation or crisis attaches more easily to this order. Yet, as the editors of the journal *Millennium* note, rather than immanent fragility, it is resilience and adaptability that still strike many commentators (2010). Writing in the same issue of *Millennium*, John Ikenberry argues that, while experiencing crisis, the core of liberalism as a global script not only remains intact, but is capable of further instantiation across the world. Noting challenges to the liberal script, he predicts more rather than less liberalism as a result. By this he means an 'open, rule-based relations system organized around expanding forms of institutionalized cooperation' (2010, 173).

This prediction rests on four claims. First, the contemporary liberal order is dependent not on US hegemony, but on cooperation between liberal democracies over the conditions of open trade and collective security. Second, the very openness and rule-driven nature of the liberal regime make it easy to join and render it less reliant on the good offices of any one actor to make it work. Third, new powers, even proto-hegemonic ones, want to be part of this arrangement, rather than seeking to destroy it. Finally, for all the doom-laden talk about nuclear proliferation and the unpredictability of rogue states, nuclear weapons and the dominance of democracies as possessors of these have made the period since World War II unparalleled as a period of 'great power peace'. American preponderance is diminishing, but this is discommoding rather than terminal for the liberal order. The weight of these arguments remains open to scrutiny in the wrack of the current crisis.

In many ways the new world order bruited by Fukuyama and by George Bush Senior in the early 1990s relied on a partial abrogation of state power in favour of a more pronounced and systematic multilateralism, despite the continued special role played by the preponderant power as the guarantor. Multilateralism entails the 'coordination of the behaviour of states on the basis of generalized principles of conduct' (Ruggie, 1992, 562). Rules governing behaviour may be codified in different domains of interstate relations, through international regimes and international organizations, but can appear too as forms of 'diffuse reciprocity' (Ruggie, 1992, 584) that are not in any way codified. Principles of conduct include norms employed by trading regimes to establish reciprocities in traded goods and services, or in security regimes that uphold non-aggression pacts.

All multilateral regimes, whether the North Atlantic Treaty Organization (NATO), the World Bank or the IMF, imply a great deal of complex interdependence, and this extends to the form of advanced multilateralism observed in the EU. While the EU institutional complex is also described in quite different ways – as supra-national, perhaps as a network state, or vilified as a super-state – it remains a very sophisticated form of non-state governance, and the most developed attempt to achieve a transnational community of affect using methods for integrating societal entities lacking a common culture but displaying ever more functional interconnections. But neofunctionalist logic applied to the displacement of governance functions from national to international, supra-national and global institutions and practices has many pitfalls, not least the diminution of agency that such logic implies, since it does not require that agents endorse and then enact the rules that both regulate and constitute their lives (Haas, 1961; 1958; Rosamond, 2000).

In all this the state remains a key consideration. Writing in 1993, just after the formal completion of the single internal market process in Europe, John Ruggie talks about the potential in a model of governance whereby 'the sovereign importance of place gives way to the sovereign importance of movement' (173). But with appropriate caution he also refers to the continued centrality of member states in the EU's decision-making arenas. Twenty years on, and after protracted debates about the necessity for a constitution for the EU, similar questions of institutional balance and competence still hold sway. The Eurozone crisis lends a particular, and possibly deadly, frisson to this debate.

The idea of governance without government, widely trafficked since Rosenau and Czempiel first coined the expression in 1992, captures the essence of these debates. Applied to the ways in which the management of public affairs may be conducted without the involvement of state government, this designation covers both within-state governance and the transnational character of various governance functions under globalization. Couched thus, its greatest analytical charge is that the national scale is being decentred, or 'unbundled' in John Ruggie's homely expression (1992; Sorensen, 2006). Social ordering ceases to be entirely nationally bounded and coordinated, and many regulatory functions of governance – though less so the distributive and redistributive ones – have been reassigned to agencies with different spatial remits, whether local or sub-national, regional or global. Indeed, some of the functions of governance in an increasingly interconnected world are imaginable and deliverable only in this disaggregated and rescaled form (Cutler, 1999).

To say that the nation-state is reduced to being just one level of governance among others may be to flirt with hyper-globalism. Nonetheless, as Nancy Fraser says, this globalizing mode of regulation 'brings a considerable dispersion of governmentality' (2003, 167) that is multi-level and increasingly networked; both rule-governed and dispersed at the same time. The very idea of MLG carries with it a whiff of statelessness. But while radical in some respects, its linear metaphor of scales stretching from micro to macro levels remains basically territorialist in conception. Moreover, transnational MLG delivered through (policy) networks does not dismiss territoriality as such, so much as build structures of governance that operate in a network-like fashion to create cross-border joint action or cooperation, producing what Bob Jessop (2004, 34-5) calls 'inter-localisation', even 'inter-regionalisation' (Strihan, 2005; Lissandrello, 2003).

Global Governance

The idea of global governance partakes of all these variants of reworked governmentality. Used descriptively it refers to the attempts to build institutions that order some common aspects of world affairs without state control, or, more accurately, without direct and routine control. It is also a normative concept, both in terms of the implied prescription to transcend, if not to abrogate, sovereign power and because it invests in a world order built around the idea of universals. For sceptics and many black-letter lawyers this prescription is without any real foundation since, for them, rules, especially when codified as law, can be effectively implemented only through the agency of a sovereign power. Without such agency the rules have little authority because they lack the coercive means required to enforce them. Nonetheless, the notion of international law, or rules governing international behaviour, has a quite long and respectable provenance, suggesting that what we now call global governance is not simply the outcome of various contemporary globalizing tendencies.

Indeed, the modern idea of international society can be traced at least as far back as the Dutch legal scholar Grotius' *On the Law of War and Peace* (1625). Grotius was writing at the time of the first wave of what we would now call globalization, or modern world-system development, and the core of his seminal text is that sovereign powers are still subject to rules which are grounded in natural law and thus applicable to all humanity (Bull, 1990; Brown, 2007). Then, as now, the sticking point remains the enforceability of that dictum, notably when applied to the (still contested) principle that intervention in the affairs of a state, up to and beyond the point of war, is admissible where that state has violated the norms of good governance, visited unwarranted suffering upon its citizens and threatened its neighbours.

Grotius' doctrine is not a template with which to trace the scope and vicissitudes of contemporary international law and society, but it does offer a framework for a pattern of rule or a system of governance which institutionalizes shared norms to produce visible and sometimes realizable international solidarity, while acknowledging that states have the right to govern themselves – thus producing an immanent tension. States are seen as caught up in rule-sanctioned action, or disposed to inaction, on the basis of their shared commitment to international society norms, by the legitimacy conferred through their membership of international institutions (such as the UN today) and, sometimes, by their fear of reprisals should they become delinquent.

And there's the rub, since the status and force of international society as a moral order, at least as applied to the limiting condition of humanitarian intervention in the affairs of a sovereign power, is vitiated by the absence of a fully institutionalized and legitimate body of law and the institutions and will to enforce it. Yet more ambitious, 'thicker' conceptions of global governance are still bruited based on the principles of normative cosmopolitanism, complete with a Kantian vision of world society (Kant, 2008; Held, 2010; Archibugi, 2008a). David Held's widely cited corpus fits reasonably well with liberal conceptions of international society and law (2003; 2004; 2005; 2010). But it is of an altogether more cautious variety than can be found in some strains of idealist thinking, being a blend of normative prescription and legal argument linked to specific (and often quite modest) institutional reforms.

Other proponents of cosmopolitanism advocate the whole philosophical package of universal trans-cultural authority that is the hallmark of Kantian ethics. Martha Nussbaum (1996), with due acknowledgment to the Stoics but little regard for matters outside the ethical domain, insists that rights, obligations and commitments do not stop at the borders of a nation. She counsels a primary allegiance to the world-wide community of humanity, where educative processes and the exemplary behaviour of multilateral institutions gradually narrow the gap between particular and broader loyalties and between the local and humanity as a whole.

As Chris Brown notes (2007, 177–8), the immanent tension between the universal particularity of sovereignty and universalism exemplified in the doctrine and politics of human rights reveals what might at first appear as quite incompatible models of world society and global governance. But let's be clear: the tension between one set of rights and another has been an enduring feature of discourse on international society for two to three centuries.

On balance, both legal and philosophical opinion has supported the prescription that the rights of states to behave as they see fit does not extend to gross violations of human dignity, and this – at least since the latter part of the twentieth century – includes loss of material wellbeing as well as degradation through judicially sanctioned torture or the massacre of civilian populations.

The furore surrounding the legality of the second Gulf War reflects these tensions and is part of a longer-term and elemental theme being played out over the shape and demeanour of international society and global governance. Dramatic instances of multilateral intervention and post-conflict resolution throw this tension into relief, though it moves to more routine but consequential shifts in the locus of governmentality, delivered through the decisions of international courts, the work of regimes that regulate commerce and other exchanges, various manifestations of 'private governance' and the fleeting solidarities established by global issues. Perhaps the limiting case in such developments is the claim that a tipping point has now been reached and that international society has commuted, variously, to a form of global community, a world state, some form of global state complex or, from a neo-Marxist perspective, a transnational state, which proves not to be a state at all.

Alexander Wendt argues that a *world state* with a global monopoly on the legitimate use of force is 'inevitable,' given the nature of the struggle for recognition that always underlies the realist logic of anarchy (2003). A world state is inevitable because technological changes in the conduct of warfare make it too difficult and too costly to prosecute war and to organize the state to execute it. Because of this the self-sufficiency of states is threatened to a degree where the only 'logical' outcome is a world state (2003, 493; Deudney, 1999). The relative incapacity of states will trigger a rational shift towards world state formation characterized by 'a universal security community' in which members look to resolve conflicts peacefully rather than through force; a 'universal collective security' system that ensures the protection of each member should 'crimes' occur; and a 'universal supranational authority' able to make binding, authoritative decisions about the collective use of force (Wendt, 2003, 505).

A much less systemic variant of this thesis is available in Martin Shaw's theory of the global state (2000; 2001). The global state complex is not *a* state in any conventional guise, albeit institutionalized in various ways. It is more an admixture or bundling of Western state power to manage geo-political turbulence; a functional solution to new and acute problems of order and of how warfare and political violence are managed. The argument shares with realism the ontological centrality of martial states and the interstate system, but it does not tally with much writing on states, governance and globalization out of Marxist IPE, or with softer variants mediated through Gramsci and critical theory. At root, Shaw's is a form of neo-Weberian historical sociology; a strand of scholarship devoted to bringing the state back in to comparative historical sociology, but to a point where its role is not seen as 'over-determined' by material forces, nor its ontology fudged through treating it as a mere social relation or arena in which class conflict is played out.

Bill Robinson challenges all state-centric positions on globalization (2004; 2006; 2008; Harris, 2005; 2009; Sklair, 2002; 2007). In addition, he favours a radical, though not complete shift away from depicting the world as ordered economically and politically by domestic capitalisms. Twenty-first-century capitalism is truly global capitalism and requires governance structures and supportive geo-political strategies to match. The burden of Robinson's argument is to take globalization seriously as a set of forces restructuring capitalist domination and how it is reproduced 'beyond the logic of the inter-state system' (2007, 5). His thesis is based on two potent, but still imprecise, concepts – the transnational capitalist class (TNCC) and the transnational state (TNS) – and is some way from classical Marxist accounts of class relations and production functions and their translation into political form.

The concept of the TNCC has its provenance in work on the sociology of elites and ruling classes, and is cognate with empirical research on spatial mobility among professionals and others as a factor in fashioning cosmopolitan or global lifestyles and identities. Used by Robinson, it is inflected with radical analytic intent because he employs it as the primary mechanism or agency through which the TNS subsists. The TNCC is a class of professional managers occupying key positions in global institutions (public and private). It is the agent, or at least the interlocutor, for promoting those conditions most propitious for the 'new global capitalist production system' (2006, 48). In this guise it constitutes a 'transnational ruling bloc', which in effect, and sometimes deliberately, sets aside the idea of national interests.

Robinson's account of the TNS is a proper invitation to think about governance beyond the state and about the de-territorialization of rule. His TNS has no centralized forms but subsists in both transnational institutions and the transformation, perhaps the de-nationalization, of contemporary nation-states in familiar ways. Transnational bodies such at the WTO and World Bank work together with national states to rescale and (de)regulate labour relations, financial institutions and circuits of production into a system of global accumulation. Critically, it is the TNS that manages and implements the rules and conditions needed to sustain global capital, not the USA or any other state actor.

In some respects this argument is instrumental, even reductionist. The role of the TNS is functional for global capitalism in the same way that a tranche of vulgar Marxist arguments reduced the role of individual states in capitalist societies. True, Robinson qualifies the idea of a uniform and implacable functionality to insist that the TNCC is not a monolith, but consists of fractions of key personnel located in different national contexts. These fractions are crucial to the power of transnational capital because they are able to mobilize support for the transnational project in individual states – especially core states – where there might be local opposition. While transnational capital still relies on the agency of individual states to make it work, its relationship with states is contingent on the strategic clout, bargaining power and motivational skills of transnational class fractions.

None of the three positions canvassed is willing to abrogate the role of the state entirely. So transnational governance in the guise of a world state, a global state or a TNS looks rather like an amalgam of global institutions, nation-states and a smattering of other actors. In Robinson's account, it is a functional response to prevailing crisis conditions. Interestingly, all the arguments rehearsed above cleave to highly selective, even ascetic, models of governance beyond the state, still rooted in the multilateral institutions reliant on cooperation between states and a tranche of more-or-less incorporated interests. Third sector organizations and social movements either rehearse the usual politics of insiders and outsiders in their dealings with such institutions or try to enact 'genuinely political activity at the global level *apart* from the system of states', as John Ruggie opines (2004, 5; Wapner, 1995).

Global Civil Society and the Democratization of Global Governance

In a growing body of literature on global governance and world society formation, subaltern forces are increasingly referenced, their interventions bruited as new forms of global governance or oppositional politics from below. Indeed, the likelihood of progressive globalization is said to reside in the ability to challenge, subvert, bypass or reform the institutions of usual politics and the interests tied to them (Jaeger, 2007). The romantic gloss that often attaches to discussions of this sort of politics is a feature of globalization debates, but it is not always helpful in formulating sound theory about the emerging ontologies of the global system (Ruggie, 2004; Keohane and Nye, 2000).

Raymond Vernon's seminal *Sovereignty at Bay* (1971) was among the first to advert the importance of TNCs as non-state players, while in the 1980s international regime theory began to explore the role of other non-state transnational actors – epistemic communities, business or industry peak associations and the like – in various governance regimes, for example in environmental pollution control and financial regulation (Krasner, 1983; Kratchowil and Ruggie, 1986). In political science it was not until the 1990s that the study of transnational civil society organizations was married to still novel conceptions of global governance. Then, Keck and Sikkink's pioneering work on transnational advocacy networks and human rights politics extended the study of interest group mediation – the classic politics of influence – to the transnational arena (1998; Cerny, 2010).

Seeing transnational civil society organizations as interest groups still leaves states at the centre of analytical attention. Indeed, Sidney Tarrow's extensive body of work on transnational activism reminds us that Western states in particular are 'deeply implicated in the funding and promotion of transnational actors' (2002, 18). Moreover, state policies trigger activism because they remain the 'prime targets and fulcra of political exchange' and thus of oppositional politics (2002, 3; Melucci, 1996; McAdam et al., 2001). This is a usefully sceptical view of the actual prospects for what Tarrow defines as real transnational action that scales beyond the state and is not predicated on its centrality. His caution underlines the need for careful typology and more careful inference.

Typologists distinguish between global or transnational social movements, INGOs, transnational advocacy networks, epistemic communities and publics constituted only through virtual networks. Some movements and groups consciously address the world scale and may revel in the sense that they are articulating new visions of world order – perhaps alter-globalizations. Others are resolute in their defence of purely local interests and see the global instrumentally, as an arena in which to raise visibility and mobilize support for local causes. By proceeding with some empirical caution, good social science can assess differences in the aspirations, objectives, resource pools, membership, tactics, political demeanour and spatial reach of such associations and thus their contribution to politics beyond the nation-state (Boli and Thomas, 1999).

The importance of good typology also underpins any shift away from describing and explaining a world ordered solely or largely by state behaviour, to one that demonstrates 'world civic politics' not predicated simply on the existence or capacities of states (Wapner, 1995). John Ruggie locates such change as a part of the restructuring of the global public domain in which states are embedded in a broader and deeper transnational arena. This transnational arena of activism and governance is constituted through the meshing of global civil society with more formal institutions of world governance. In other words, global civil society complements, rather than displaces, the institutions of world society (Lechner, 2009, 149). Yet there is a radical sting in the tail of this proposition because activists and volunteers might now be seen as prototypical world citizens who informally enact the cultural rules of a world polity.

If they exist, world citizens may well be critical citizens. Indeed, in much of the literature on globalization it is the agonistic qualities of global civil society that stand as its most notable feature. For students of globalization and globality both the concept and the practices of global civil society are charged, because on the one hand they seem to embody the very essence of globality as a normative ideal practised through real politics, while on the other hand the nationalization of social scientific concepts and principles still makes it difficult to entertain the idea of *global* society and thus to locate this politics theoretically.

In various accounts, global civil society is used as a descriptive category denoting various forms of activism and organization across borders. Inevitably there is some definitional imprecision about its composition and scope. More contentious is its status as a normative prescription with a bearing on the presumed qualities of democratic politics and the conduct of governance both within and beyond territorial states. Finally, it musters as an analytical category, a component of multidimensional theories of globality. But as an analytical construct, global civil society often suffers from the tendency for commentators to blur the boundaries between empirical evidence and normative claims a little too easily for comfort (Chandler, 2007; 2009, Axford, 2012).

Usually, civil society is seen as the 'sphere of institutions, organizations and individuals located between the family, the state and the market, in which people associate voluntarily to advance common interests' (Anheier et al., 2005, 27). There remains some dispute about whether for-profit organizations are eligible members, but objections to their inclusion appear to turn on ideological conviction rather than scientific classification (Keane, 2003). A usefully permissive definition is one that captures the historical sense of the idea of civil society, namely that it comprises all social activities and organization beyond the family but not controlled by the state.

On first appraisal the idea of *global* civil society appears just to extend that permissiveness across borders and onto the world stage. John Keane writes about a 'dynamic non-governmental system of interconnected socio-economic institutions that straddle the whole earth, and that have complex effects that are felt in its four corners' (2003, 8), which is suitably inclusive, if rather vague (see too Boli and Thomas, 1999; Lechner, 2009).

Of note is the extent to which global civil society organizations are deemed to diverge from the more conventional organizational and decisional models of hierarchy and market (Thompson, 2003; Holton, 2008). Keane identifies a complex pattern of global connectivity comprising face-to-face encounters, networks, pyramid-shaped organizations and hub-and-spoke structures as well as chains. Perhaps more than any of the other features of global governance, global civil society is a description of a fluid world, a world in process. But despite its progressive and transformative connotations it does not stand apart from, and should not be seen as necessarily in opposition to, the architectures of usual government and governance.

The claim that the emergence of global civil society may constitute a shift in the locus of power, away from states and inter-governmental organizations (IGOs), is an empirical claim as well as a normative prescription. But the latter is not reliant on actual referents to give it legs. As such, global civil society can be all things to all people. On the one hand it is held to ameliorate the excess of markets, of neo-liberal globalization from above, while on the other hand it compensates for the systemic anarchy of states and the weak performance of the institutions of global governance, especially where justice is concerned (Edwards, 2011; Clark, 2003). On the side of the angels because of its un-co-opted and anti-systemic feel, it also rounds out eminently respectable and 'thin' liberal assumptions about the character of the global polity and the role of citizens in it.

At the same time it offers hope for those who aspire to thicker cross-border ties of solidarity, and who see in global civil society the possibility for democratic renewal and the creation of strong global publics (Castells, 2008; Dobson, 2006). Hardt and Negri's incurably romantic gloss on the 'multitude' and that subset of NGOs and INGOs that 'represents the least among us' (2000, 13; 2004) is really just a cool version of 'traditional' civil society. Both the exotic and the quotidian – the latter in the shape of NGOs and INGOs that act in a consultative role inside the UN, the IMF or the Association of Southeast Asian Nations (ASEAN) – are features of global civil society and, on some accounts, are contributing to a shift in the nature of governance and the balance of power in world society (Lechner, 2009; Scholte, 2005a; 2008).

Inevitably there are cautionary voices as well as outright dissent. In WSA, 'anti-systemic' forces kicking against the pricks of a systemic global geo-culture of neo-liberalism are seen as heroic, but poor drivers of revolutionary change, except in times of acute crisis when they can assume world-historical significance (Wallerstein, 1991). Even in accounts not mired in theoretical pessimism, globalization from below in the shape of transnational social movements is still seen as a weak, though welcome, countervailing force to globalization from above. Richard Falk's *Predatory Globalization* (1999) depicts global civil society as a means of offsetting the tendency for national governments to be co-opted by top-down market forces. Transnational social forces represent an innovative and variegated type of politics, one that increases the number and range of interests contesting the way global public goods are managed.

Yet Falk remains cautious, even pessimistic, about the impact of such changes. He sees the growing incidence of transnational activism as weakening citizenship in many states. This is an interesting argument predicated on the decline of social capital and national institutions and forums as a direct result of the intensification of bonds of interest and solidarity across borders (1999; 2005). Because the 'logic of market opportunity' no longer coincides with the 'logic of territorial loyalty', elites are more likely to create links and allegiances across borders than within them. There are shades of the TNCC model here, although Falk is not exercised by that debate. Citizens determined to resist or augment the forces of globalization then follow suit, organizing locally and transnationally. As a direct consequence, the nation-state and national democracy become pigs in the middle of this respatializing of interest and affect. Falk still sees this as an alternative form of globalization, part of a political adjustment to the de-territorialization or hollowing-out of the state.

Regardless of normative preference, if one accepts the force of Falk's arguments, the interesting question then becomes whether the alleged transfer of social and political capital from local and national to global can be seen as supporting an emergent cosmopolitan political culture. But here too Falk treads carefully (2005), seeing transnational activism as, at best, a countervailing force battling with the extra-territorial power of business and finance. Like Tarrow, he points up the logistical and resource problems that attend the mobilization of subaltern politics beyond the territorial state. And the danger of turning relatively resourceless victims into heroes is well illustrated in Nancy Fraser's take on 'subaltern counter cultures' (1987, 124) as 'parallel discursive arenas where members of subordinated social groups invent and circulate counter-discourses . . . interests and needs' (1993, 123). She argues that a growing number of competing interests and publics will only improve the quality of democratic life, but all this may achieve is to increase the number of players, turn up the volume of discourse and glamorize the status of victims. Of course, the romantic in all of us might cavil at such inferential caution.

Finally, let's turn to the status of global civil society as an analytical category. From our discussion so far, it can be seen that reservations attach to the use of global civil society as a categorical description of some kinds of voluntary association, although not as a normative goal. We would do well to consider Sidney Tarrow's jeremiad on whether 'transnational civil society' is a concept tied to clear empirical referents or just part of a 'strong' version of 'global speak' that 'congeals' and confuses the complex relations between non-state actors, international institutions and norms, transnational activist networks and transnational social movements (2002, 1). In similar vein David Chandler takes both liberal cosmopolitans and their post-structuralist critics to task for having quite developed political projects, but very little in the way of evidence or convincing theory with which to validate their claims (2007; 2009; Axford, 2004).

Chandler defends a parsimonious definition of global society through specific and demanding attention to the factors that underpin political community. He argues that liberal cosmopolitan and post-structuralist positions on world society and political community constitute a 'degradation of the modern liberal conception of the rights-bearing subject: [because] once the connection between citizenship and political community is broken then political community lacks any clear conceptual grounding' (2009, 17). Cosmopolitans cleave to a universalist discourse using a social constructivist framework that privileges the 'power of ideas' and the importance of global information networks. By contrast, in post-structuralist arguments, cosmopolitanism is seen as just another version of repressive biopower, masquerading under the banner of a progressive politics that will emancipate the universal subject. Emancipatory potential does exist, but it must be harnessed to a real politics 'from below', in order to escape co-optation and subordination by various types of statist and some non-state regulatory mechanisms. For Chandler, both sets of argument are derived less from empirical investigations than from their own normative aspirations. None of this adds up to nostalgic communitarianism or the brute realism it might first appear, although Chandler clearly is wedded to the isomorphism of state, society and political community.

No doubt his argument carries weight as a critique of liberal cosmopolitanism and post-structuralism applied to the idea of political community. The flight from the situated rights-bearing subject of liberal modernity is characteristic of both cosmopolitan and poststructuralist frameworks. But in Chandler's schema, political community cannot be constituted without the rights and duties of citizenship, and these are reliant upon the specific political and legal framework of liberal rights found in territorial states and societies. Because flight or transference is essential 'to enable the move to post-territorial constructions of political community' (2009, 24); in its absence, and *ipso facto*, radical accounts must be flawed.

Convincing as all this first appears, for our forensic purposes it judges the prospects for global or world society by criteria designed to underpin the national variety, and thus falls prey to its own normative agenda. The logic, of course, is impeccable. If citizenship and the basis for the rights of the universal subject can be secured only in specific bounded institutional and normative contexts, and if both these are the necessary underpinnings for political community, then there can be no such thing as post-territorial world society or any of its look-alikes.

Globalization, Democracy and Normative Cosmopolitanism

The idea of global civil society challenges received wisdom about the nature and boundaries of political community and of sociality. Network approaches to the construction of cross-border affect point to the affordances available through routine connectivity. Empirical research also reveals 'thicker' affinities in some kinds of networks and exchanges. An argument key to the normative burden in such claims is that, in a globalized world, people are more willing to enter into 'relationships of justice' or 'causal responsibility' with those who are 'at a distance'. Such ties of obligation invest mere cognitive awareness and connectivity with thicker and longer-term affinities (Dobson, 2006, 173). Global citizens claim rights as members of a common humanity but they also have responsibilities. This is the meat of the cosmopolitan ethic and expresses the strategic and normative goals of liberal or 'new' cosmopolitanism (Keane, 2008; Archubugi and Held, 2011; Axtmann, 2003).

In a recent exegesis full of normative intent, Daniele Archibugi, a scion of 'new' cosmopolitan thinking, claims baldly that '[d]emocracy can and must become the method of global governance' (2008a, xv). This credo owes everything to the sense that globalization puts great strains on the ideal and practices of democratic self-rule. So new cosmopolitanism is as much an answer to perceptions of a profound and increasing democratic deficit caused by globalization as it is a contemporary manifestation of the goal of establishing universality of justice found, most notably, in Kant's work (2008). While cosmopolitan theory today is informed by the threats and opportunities for reform afforded through global compression (Anderson-Gold, 2001; Held, 2004), it remains indebted to Kant's original idea that a federation of nations espousing universal principles of right is at the heart of the search for global justice. Underlying much contemporary theory from Jürgen Habermas (2003; 2006; Fine, 2007; Tambakaki, 2009), Daniele Archibugi and David Held (Held, 2003; 2004; 2010; Archibugi et al., 2011; Archibugi and Held, 2011; Rumford, 2008) is the Kantian notion that reason is the universal standard by which to judge moral conduct, and thus should inform attempts to rescue and reform the practices and institutions of governance charged with realizing that universality.

Under globalization, almost every feature of sovereign power, including behavioural autonomy, is subject to international and global constraints. Multilateral institutions such as the UN, the IMF the World Bank and the WTO have taken on more and more authority, and the EU, through 'positive' integration such as monetary union, has curtailed the decisional autonomy of member states. Similar statements about the growth of private interest governance or the ability of global markets to influence domestic economic policy all echo this theme. Once again this is not a message of unremitting state decline, but in the work of both Archibugi and Held, the burden of the argument is that all such developments are producing a growing democratic deficit. This outcome is partly the result of the power of non-state actors having outstripped the capacity for democratic control by national institutions, and partly the related consequence of having effective governance taking place beyond the state, leaving only a residue of democratic legitimacy within it.

Held argues that in the face of globalizing pressures two core elements of the liberal democratic theory of sovereignty have become difficult to sustain (Held et al., 1999). The first, a political community of fate, can no longer be located within the boundaries of the nation-state and national society. Second, the locus of effective political power has shifted from national governments to a host of international regimes, regional organizations and TNCs. The general trend is towards a pattern of global governance in which there is overlapping authority and divided, or perhaps multiple, loyalties; a conclusion that is not very contentious, save for died-in-the-wool realists and globalization sceptics. These changes have not been matched by sufficient attention to how they can be controlled through democratic procedures and institutions.

In more recent work, both Held and Archibugi have addressed the risks to democratic governance in relation to key policy and issue areas (Archibugi,

2008a; Held, 2010). Writing about the global governance of finance in the wake of the financial crisis of 2008, Held notes that interconnectedness of any kind has the inevitable consequence of dispersing risk on a large scale (2010, 188). The problem is that national institutions and regulatory provision either did not anticipate the crisis, or else were powerless to prevent contagion; while multilateral institutions, such as the International Organization of Securities Commissions and the Bank for International Settlements, were also weak and unprepared. Global finance has been relatively lightly monitored and regulated when compared to other policy areas, such as the environment, but Held's overall judgement is that the institutions of global governance remain too fragmented, or else too dominated by core states, to be effective instruments of accountability. For the most part they also lack visibility and democratic legitimacy among (world) citizens subject to their remit.

Neither Held nor Archibugi is prepared to countenance a world government as a solution to the democratic deficit, however benign and accountable. Rather, they look to the instantiation of a governance system based on the principle of democratic autonomy within a framework of democratic public law entrenched across borders. For Held this would produce a 'radicalized' democracy, but one that still relies on existing institutional structures to deliver good governance. In fact, and certainly in Archibugi's writing (2008b), the main thrust of the reform programme is the democratization of existing global institutions and the strengthening of a global judiciary. In practice this would require equal status for all states (not just core actors) and wider representation (co-optation?) of NGOs and INGOs in international organizations and forums.

The UN is still seen by Archibugi as 'the pivot of the entire world judicial and political system' (2008a, 156), and he advocates the need for a truly 'World Parliamentary Assembly' similar in composition to the European Parliament. In his work there is relatively little emphasis on globalization from below, on global civil society as an uncompromised source of countervailing politics and the catalyst for a transnational public sphere, *pace* Castells. Rather, Archibugi has a quite conservative stance on the procedural incorporation of civil society organizations and groups into multilateral institutions, and his account underestimates how incorporation might simply reproduce a politics of insiders versus outsiders. Neither does he engage with the concern that exercises Richard Falk, namely the concurrent need to refurbish democratic practices within states, or else ensure that transnational activism and selective representation of activist groups on multilateral bodies does not further vitiate participation and democracy at the national and local levels.

David Held is more attuned to the importance of 'informal' cosmopolitanism of the kind canvassed by Ulrich Beck, for at least rounding out what otherwise looks like a reworked form of democratic elitism (Held et al.,

1998). Held has also gone beyond philosophical as well as legal and political cosmopolitanism to explore the realm of culture (Held and Moore, 2008). His cultural shift includes instances of routine cross-border interconnectedness and, echoing the idea that global consciousness is a vital precursor to building a sense of shared humanity and shared fate, the idea that awareness will promote collective solutions to common problems. Such consciousness and the cultural affinities allegedly promoted can be seen too in Jürgen Habermas' long-term support for a formal EU constitution that can demarcate a discrete political space and thus foster a common value orientation (2001; Kant, 2008).

Conventional as Archibugi and Held's prescriptions appear, along with other cosmopolitan good intentions, they have suffered from paying insufficient attention to the means by which the goals are to be realized. In past writing it has seldom been made clear just how global institutions are to be democratized and those designated as global citizens actually mobilized. Leaving aside normative objections to the cosmopolitan thesis, these are considerable qualifications of the empirical plausibility of the argument. The global commonwealth of citizens, seen by Archibugi as central to the democratizing of world politics, may be significant only as a hortatory device. But in a recent paper he and Held address these lacunae in their prospectus (2011) by asking directly, 'who are the agents that might promote cosmopolitan democracy?' and what the conditions are that might mobilize or deter them (2011, 3; Koenig-Archibugi, 2010).

Their exegesis attempts to link the contexts of and paths to cosmopolitan democracy. The aim, previously spelled out by Archigbugi, is to make cosmopolitan democracy less of a 'planetary fantasy' and more a realizable project with obvious strategies. The pathways and, in some cases, the actors are states as agents of cosmopolitan democracy; international organizations undergoing reform; global judicial authorities reinforcing complex global norms; lawful forms of conflict resolution; international administrative courts that arbitrate in disputes in commercial and competition law; and formal citizen representation in global politics through the arena of the World Parliamentary Assembly.

With the exception of the last item this is a list of features already extant, and singly none of them may be able to shoulder the burden of expectation they carry. The litany of agents mustered which 'might' (Archibugi and Held's usage) play a part in reforming these institutions and practices includes mainly subaltern forces or constituencies because, these authors argue, the hunger for political change is more likely to come from those on the margins of societies and political inclusion. They advert the dispossessed of the Earth, migrants, so-called 'cosmopolitan' groups such as mobile professionals, global civil society organizations, globalist political parties such as Liberal International, trade unions and multinational corporations. Lest we dismiss all this as no more than a wish-list, it should be said that Archibugi and Held are at pains to identify the barriers to effective, or any, mobilization. They do not suggest that just being able to identify contexts, pathways and potential actors actually produces cosmopolitan awareness, momentum or reform. In short, these are no more than the ingredients of potential consciousness and thus still a politics *manqué*.

Conclusion

In this chapter we have examined some important themes and key interventions in the scholarship of globalization and governance. The matter of the state and its future are woven through this scholarship, along with elements of a putative power shift in the conduct of governance and the scope and quality of democratic participation. The burden of all but hyper-globalist scholarship is that states are both winners and losers in terms of how they accommodate globalization. Notions of society and its locus can no longer be confined to national territories, although when such discussion ventures into matters of allegiance and identity, the evidence is contested. Disputed too are claims about continuities or discontinuities in the shape and demeanour of the international order of states, multilateral institutions and hegemonic powers. Very few such claims are based on the consensual interpretation of agreed evidence, especially where they entertain alternative models of that order and of the possibilities for world society. Some of the claims made, notably about cosmopolitan futures, are highly contestable because of their irreducible normative content. While the meaning of the concept of 'global civil society' is also fraught with definitional imprecision and its significance disputed, there can be no doubt that its appearance in the scholarship of globalization discommodes conventional understandings of political space, action and identities.

CHAPTER 8

Theories of Globalization and Capitalism

Introduction

In this chapter we will look at the relationships between globalization and capitalism. We will begin with an examination of recent theorizing about the changing character of the global economy. While the debate about the existence or novelty of a truly global economy has produced a good many intellectual dead ends, it raises substantive issues for globalization scholarship. Among these are questions about the origins and drivers of a system of long-term, large-scale global change seen mainly as a process of economic expansion and integration. As well as revisiting WSA, we will canvass more conventional Marxist political economy and accounts of 'new' imperialism applied to the global age. Because debate about the capitalist world economy is not confined to internecine disputes within academic Marxism, we will also address strongly integrationist arguments.

The last will involve revisiting neo-liberalism as a policy agenda rather than an ideology, and then reflecting on its many 'discontents', as evidenced in selected activist positions and in third wave theory out of IPE. In the latter, economic globalization is seen as an ideological project, a constructed reality. Subjectivist approaches to economic globalization should not be treated lightly since they can help us to understand the mentality of state elites abroad in a sea of global flows. Throughout we will distinguish treatments of globalization as a facet of capitalist expansion from those accounts that see the latter as a world-historical force, but decline to take the idea of globalization seriously.

Let's preface these considerations by expanding on the role of the state in global capitalism. States are enduring actors in processes of global convergence and differentiation. Relativized by forces blind to territorial borders, they still express, or aspire to, an essential quality, reflecting deeper imaginings about identity and community. In some sceptical accounts of economic globalization the state has been re-branded as a bastion of difference, even exceptionalism, the protector of welfare nationalism and a prophylactic against the brute rationality of neo-liberalism. But some opponents of neo-liberal capitalism are critical of such readings and the state-centrism they express. Bill Robinson sees even the TNS as a function of the needs of global capital. His account is only one of many to interrogate the relationships between states, capital and globalization (2006; 2008).

Among recent contributions to Marxist theories of imperialism – rooted in Leon Trotsky's concept of uneven and combined development, and mirrored in the third wave of IHS – the burden of the argument is that uneven spatial patterns of global capital accumulation tend to sustain a plural system of states rather than promote, let alone require, a single global state (Trotsky, 1962; 1964). If accurate, this suggests the persistence, rather than the demise, of quite different forms of geo-political competition, not only between different states, but between different capitalisms as well. In turn, processes of global capital accumulation are not seen as monolithic, but display territorial and geographic clusters of investment, markets and labour in specific areas of the world economy (Arrighi, 2007).

Robinson is also scathing about recent Marxist analyses of imperialism, and of the idea that the dynamics of global capitalism can be explained by reference to the competitive strategies of national capitalisms augmented through the agency of individual core states. By contrast, Alex Callinicos has argued, 'the centrifugal pulls generated by the inherently geographically uneven distribution of resources under capitalism play an irreducible role in keeping the state system plural'. Preponderant powers also play a role in this system because they can 'provide public goods for all states'. But in coming to terms with deeper, structural patterns of global capitalism and its attendant politics, the system is better understood as 'inherently conflictual, presupposing and generating antagonisms of interest between workers and capitalists and among capitals, and unleashing economic crises and self-reinforcing processes of uneven development' with 'extreme geographical concentrations of economic power' (Callinicos, 2007, 545, 547; Neumann and Sending, 2010).

Such arguments are contested both within the Marxist canon and from outside it. But in much of the literature from Marxist IPE and neo-liberal theory, globalization is equated with the spread of capitalism as an economic system of accumulation, exploitation and economic governance, and this includes its appearance in a new form of imperialism. In turn, capitalist globalization is seen as spawning more-or-less dynamic alternative globalizations and a raft of countervailing activism. These are powerful motifs because they take capitalist globalization (especially neo-liberal capitalist globalization) to be the dominant global system at the start of the twenty-first century. The politics of globalization then appears as an elemental struggle between dominators and resistors, with victims caught in the press. Indeed, in most accounts from Marxist and non-Marxist sources, the political economy of globalization is seen as moving to the vagaries and rhythms of capitalist expansion and by systematic and contingent responses to it.

The Idea of a (Capitalist) Global Economy

In his standard text on *Global Political Economy*, Robert Gilpin defines political economy as the interaction of the market and powerful actors, including states (2001, 45; Strange, 1996). Disarmingly simple because it appears so obvious, this formulation still captures the dynamics of world economic integration as it occurred in the decades following World War II. Viewed from a longer-term perspective, however, the dualism may be too neat. Gilpin describes himself and the message of his book as 'realist' or state-centric, in that he discerns a continuing role for state actors in influencing economic outcomes. At the same time, he acknowledges the important roles played by a growing range of non-state actors in both facilitating and regulating the processes of capital accumulation.

Here, as always, the devil lies in the detail of interpretation, notably between those taking their cues from classical economics and others schooled in varieties of IPE. In globalization literature these differences often appear as a clash between apologists for neo-liberal economics and its opponents. What is often remarked on as an elemental tension in the relationships between states and markets then imparts an ideological gloss to any understanding of the working of the global political economy.

In previous chapters we referred to historical treatments of globalization and particularly to the origins of world-systems. In this scholarship the provenance of capitalist and certainly of market-led globalization is either traced back to early modern times in Western Europe, or related to various precursors found in pre-modern societies and civilizations. There is, of course, a third position that roots the current phase of globalization, perhaps globalization *tout court*, in circumstances and trends extant only from the mid-to-late twentieth century. For the moment we need to concentrate on the first two strands of thinking. We will begin with WSA. Our focus will be its treatment of capitalism as a historical world-system and how far, or whether, this can be seen as a theory of globalization (Wallerstein, 1974; 1979; 1989; 2000).

Like others of the world-systems persuasion, Immanuel Wallerstein is very uneasy about labelling WSA a theory of globalization, let alone a fully fledged theory of history. But the question *when did globalization begin?* is important to discussions on the origins of capitalism and for theories of modernity as either linear or disjunctive. For example, some of the features described by Wallerstein and others as unique to Western modernity – the ceaseless accumulation of capital through exchange relations and the centre–periphery structure of exploitation – are considered by students of civilizations to be features of all historical systems (Frank and Gills, 1993; Robinson, 2009). WSA engages in a history and critique of capitalism as a system that spread across the entire world over the past 500 years to realize a single modern world-system. In this it is hardly novel or, at least where orthodox Marxism is concerned, particularly revisionist.

There is clearly a Marxist intellectual genealogy to Wallerstein's corpus that stretches back through Lenin, Rudolf Hilferding and Rosa Luxemburg to Marx himself. However, Wallerstein's definition of capitalism springs from a quite distinctive interpretation of the dynamics of world-system integration, and this has implications for his dismissal of globalization as a discrete or novel phase of capitalism. As defined by Wallerstein, capitalism is a system of commodity production in which there are different forms of class relations: wage labour in the core of the world economy and more repressive forms of surplus extraction in the periphery. Global capitalism is realized through commodity chains established between peripheral and core producers and consumers, while commodity production is defined as production for price-setting markets. All this imparts a strongly Weberian feel to how capitalism is defined by Wallerstein, in that production for exchange and profit in competitive markets are taken as capitalist. Because of this definitional permissiveness it is not necessary to limit capitalist relations simply to those structured through wage labour.

With writers of the Dependency School, Wallerstein is at pains to depict capitalism as a global system from the sixteenth century onwards, not one confined to the core economies of the European landmass. But his is not a progressive model of world-capitalist development in the style of post-war modernization theory, or one indebted to Marx's writings on the energizing impact of capitalism on India. The lack of conventional, even expected, development in the periphery is explained by how economies and societies there were integrated into the world economy and not as a result of their separation from it or their innate 'backwardness'. The modern world-system of capitalism is an economic unity fashioned through unequal exchange between strong core states and economies and weaker ones in the semi-periphery and periphery. Indeed, the world-system of capitalism is reproduced through the core–periphery hierarchy and by the agency of states and markets. These features constitute its 'deep essence'.

Unlike the earlier and dichotomous model of core and periphery used by the Dependency School (Frank, 1969a; 1969b) Wallerstein's world-system of capitalism exhibits a three-fold division of labour between states and economies located in the core, semi-periphery and periphery of the world economy. The relationship between these zones is characterized by unequal exchange and successively more repressive and labour-intensive systems of production for world trade. In this model the semi-periphery ameliorates the destabilizing effects of what would otherwise be a world economy polarized through unequal exchange between high-wage, capital-intensive manufactures in the core states and low-waged extraction of raw materials in the periphery. Economies in the semi-periphery trade with both core and periphery, and the inclusion of this in-between zone imparts a curiously voluntaristic element to what, certainly in dependency theory, looks like an immutable positioning of states as either winners or losers. Semi-peripheral states are either on the way into the core or the periphery or on their way out of them, and, on the face of it, such indeterminacy means that the system is dynamic and therefore mutable.

For all that, there is also a strongly functionalist cast to Wallerstein's argument. The 'axial' division of labour between core and periphery is a necessary component of world-system reproduction and is expressed too in a geographical division of labour between different world regions. Surpluses move from periphery and semi-periphery to core regions and the upshot is that the core is enriched at the expense of the outer zones and regions, which remain systematically underdeveloped. This is a schematic that has to be taken seriously because it identifies the structural dynamics of the capitalist system and thus provides an explanation for global inequalities, as well as debunking mid-century modernization theories (Robinson, 2009; 2011). It is also cast in pretty much the same mould as classical theories of imperialism, in that interstate rivalry, notably among core states, fuels the struggle for world markets, and territorial aggrandizement is a means of accessing and controlling labour and raw materials.

Wallerstein's analysis relies on a basically economistic and developed, but rather crudely spatialized interpretation of world-system integration. Its merit lies in treating world-level structures and constraints as integral to any understanding of social change. At root, it is a coherent testimony against methodological nationalism, although states remain as essential components of world-system dynamics. Perhaps its most telling contribution is to examine the ways in which capitalist integration structures on a world scale. While its devotion to systemic analysis sits uneasily with all manner of deconstructivist and action-centred positions on pretty much the same global themes, this is still a monumental piece of social-scientific inquiry. And yet, leaving aside Wallerstein's own reservations, is it a theory of globalization, let alone a sound theory, when judged in the light of recent and current trends and circumstances?

For all its emphasis on world-level constraints, when pared down, WSA relies on a territorial model of zonal competition based on a hierarchy of states. To be sure, this is hardly a full-blown realist account, in that states are not simply ontological givens, but the equation of state strength with location in the functional division of labour imparts a markedly realist feel to the analysis. For many current observers of global capitalism, indeed of globalization, this essential structural feature of the world-system, along with others key to Wallerstein's model, is out of kilter with (at least) recent trends.

These trends reveal a world economy that has become much more globalized than internationalized in areas like production and finance. Particular locations now appear as nodes in networks of interaction and exchange, and these changes make the axial features of the world-system as depicted by Wallerstein quite redundant. Geographical definitions of core and periphery have less analytical purchase in a world characterized by transnational connectivity (Castells, 2000a; Cox, 1989; Robinson, 2008). In other words, concepts such as 'core' and 'periphery' cease to have obvious geographical points of reference, even if the terms still symbolize important functional characteristics of capitalist exploitation (Cox, 1989). Robinson (2004) and Sklair (1991) also say that WSA is simply too state-centric to capture the structural features and dynamics of twenty-first-century capitalism, when the idea of competition between strictly national capitalisms is on the wane.

Other key tenets of WSA also seem at odds with models of an interconnected, relatively stateless and post-hegemonic world. The idea of hegemony, central to Wallerstein's unfolding of historical categories through cyclical rhythms, is predicated on a state-centric model of world-system structure. But instead of reproducing the hegemonic cycle through competition between core states, in an age of globalized production there may be other visible forms of transnational hegemony such as the TNCC, which operates through states, multilateral institutions and epistemic networks. With the decline of the USA, we may be entering not another hegemonic cycle but an era of world and regionalized markets firmly established within, but also outside, the Western core of the capitalist world-system (Arrighi, 2007).

Shifts in global political economy?

Criticism of WSA as a historical and theoretical treatment of capitalist expansion could be taken to prefigure sceptical accounts of globalization – though not entirely, since at least some of Wallerstein's critics are sympathetic to the globalization hypothesis, albeit not to hyper-globalist versions. The burden of hyper-globalist accounts is that globalization is a recent phenomenon, the fruit of particular trends emergent in the latter part of the twentieth century and the first decade of the new millennium. Its appearance is novel and its intensity unprecedented, even though it may not be quite the rupture with earlier capitalist modernity sometimes claimed. The referents for these claims are said to lie in the radically changed constellation of the world economy since the late 1950s.

Following World War II a global transformation in the demeanour and balance of the world economy took place. When attempting to periodize global integration, these decades and the interlude of intensive economic integration from the 1970s onwards are often described as the third wave of globalization, and there is no doubt that over that period the world economy exhibited powerfully integrative tendencies around key institutional clusters. These tendencies include the shift from 'organized capitalism', in which production, consumption, money and labour circulate nationally, to 'disorganized capitalism', where circuits became increasingly global in scope (Lash and Urry, 1994, 322–3).

So what are the key trends in the alleged reshaping of the capitalist world economy since 1945, and do they have consequences for globalization and for its scholarship? Disorganized capitalism is a spatial shift in the key circuits of capitalist accumulation. This spatial shift has been accompanied by changes in the nature and meaning of work, in the creation of a much expanded service economy increasingly based on the 'knowledge' and 'culture' industries, and in patterns of consumption especially, though by no means exclusively, in the global North. Usually these changes are understood as the transition from a Fordist to a post-Fordist political economy, and as well as having economic significance they have triggered enormous shifts in the organization and conduct of social and cultural life. Finally, as we noted earlier, the trends have forced us to modify rather simplistic models of centre and periphery as a description of the economic, political and cultural geography of the world.

This litany of trends endorses or affords a number of possible interpretations of the condition and direction of the world economy of capitalism. These comprise full-blown apologies for neo-liberal globalization (Friedman, 2007), reformist positions around the dominance and desirability of free markets (Stiglitz, 2002), outright attacks on market fundamentalism and hegemonic power (Harvey, 2005b) and critiques of the 'awful logic' of these when visited on developing countries (Stiglitz, 2002, 185). In addition to ideological arguments are those that question both the historical novelty of events and processes and the extent of economic de-territorialization (Hirst et al., 2009). At the core of differing interpretations is the question of just how convergent or divergent the capitalist world economy is. Let's examine this question by way of some key interventions before taking up the meat of the seminal integrationist argument provided by neo-classical economics. While each intervention musters very loosely under the 'sceptical' label, they have quite different intellectual origins and, perhaps less obviously, serve different normative and/or ideological agendas.

Sceptical Accounts of Capitalist Global Political Economy

In a classic statement on what they insist remains an international economy, Paul Hirst and his co-authors (1996; 2000; 2009) question not only the inevitability and durability of globalizing neo-liberalism, but also the descriptive accuracy of the concepts of global or globalized economy. The third edition of their book acknowledges recent dramatic changes in the international economy – 'new' players in the guise of Russia, China and India, each, in different ways, resistant to the logic of unfettered markets; the distorting influence of sovereign wealth funds on the pattern of international investment; the impact of the banking crisis on financial architectures – but takes these changes to endorse the authors' previous sense of continued state and interstate influence in shaping the international economy. While open to criticism, their thesis stands as the most developed and empirically grounded sceptical argument against the inevitability of strong globalization (2009, 5–11). For them, the international economy is capitalist, but not monolithic or hegemonic. Diversity (certainly) and exceptionalism (possibly) remain key features.

Their argument is simply stated. Economic globalization is not an independent, exogenous variable of sufficient power simply to meld, let alone dissolve, independent national economies. Moreover, trends – particularly in volumes of trade and investment – bruited as unique, or else greatly intensified in the latter part of the twentieth century, were either matched or exceeded in previous periods of international economic integration, notably between the 1860s and World War I. Apologists for neo-liberal hyper-globalism see an unremitting integration of the world economy in recent decades and applaud it, but Hirst et al. curb any ideological enthusiasm and factual certitude.

Hirst et al. note, first, that truly transnational companies are the exception, not the rule. Most companies that are successful internationally enjoy the benefits of national legal identity and rely too on other national attributes and domestic conditions to underpin their performance and reputation. Second, capital mobility is not global, and certainly has not produced huge shifts in investment and employment opportunities from advanced to developing economies. Foreign direct investment remains concentrated in the advanced industrial economies, and the successful development of newly industrialized countries (NICs) through investment and trade has produced few success stories. Third, the global economy is far from being global in reality. Most trade, investment and finance flows between the triad economies of North America, Europe and Japan, though these authors acknowledge that this is changing as China and India make their presence felt. Finally, the concentration of economic flows in three privileged regions enables these powerhouses to exert effective regulatory pressure on financial markets and on other globalizing 'economic tendencies' (1999, xiii). In other words these states, whether individually or in concert, are still potent in face of global flows.

Long after the dog days of hyper-globalist thinking such wisdom looks much less eye-catching. Today, very few theorists of globalization subscribe to the demise of the state thesis, not even when the state is viewed just as an economic actor. However, even in their third edition, Hirst et al. still betray a quite startling naivety about the nature of globalization and its meaning for different actors. Nowhere is there real sensitivity to the importance of subjectivity when assessing the impact of globalization on the identity and behaviour of actors. For example, it is true that the location of headquarters, the siting of research and development (R&D) facilities and the number of 'foreign' employees who occupy senior management positions may be useful indicators of the global-ness of a company, but quantitative measures can often miss the point. Many commercial organizations, especially those with aspirations to do business on a world scale, consider themselves as operating in a global market. Crucially, this market may not be homogeneous in the sense that firms are catering for an undifferentiated consumer, or that tastes and standards are uniform.

But the taxonomic status of a company as global, rather than national or international, may turn on the management style and corporate culture of the organization and how it identifies itself in relation to changing competitive environments. Similar considerations relating to the subjectivity of actors in their dealings with wider cultural scripts inform both world polity accounts of global convergence and constructivist arguments on the role of ideational factors in conditioning responses to globalization. Constructivist positions, some with a Marxist provenance, traffic at the limits of sceptical thinking on globalization. At the same time they still work within the frame of a limiting model of neo-classical economic globalization, while claiming to transcend the brute materialism of works like *Globalization in Question*.

Hirst et al. offer a robustly sceptical view of the globalization hypothesis, but our second intervention is sceptical in a rather different way. More than that, it is a striking variant on WSA and on the prospects for the world-system as a capitalist system. Giovanni Arrighi's argument in *Adam Smith in Beijing* (2007) is that the obvious failure of the US neo-conservative programme to ensure American dominance for the next century, along with the successful economic growth of China, suggest that Smith's notion of 'world market' is a more accurate picture of current and future trends (Denemark, 2009; Abu-Lughod, 2007; *Journal of World-Systems Research*, 2010). The world market is based not on hegemony or on the dominance of the West, but on greater equality among global regions.

Arrighi pays attention to China as the prime mover in what he calls an 'East Asian-centred world-market society' (2007a, 32), because this development is changing the nature of the global capitalist world economy (Abbeloos and Vanhaute, 2011). Unlike the received model of a 'Great Divergence' between European industrializers and 'The Rest', we are now witnessing a 'Great Convergence', one bringing world regions much closer to the Commonwealth of Civilizations prefigured by Adam Smith. In previous work, and notably in *The Long Twentieth Century* (1994), a treatise indebted to the pioneering research of Fernand Braudel (1979), Arrighi identified China's 'subordination to Western commands'. But in *Adam Smith* he portrays China's survival as a hybridized economy, revealing two patterns of development. One is capitalist (with historical China as a subordinate and peripheral player during the period of the Great Divergence) and one market-oriented, but not capitalist, and having a much longer pedigree. Arrighi contends that two distinct world economies – capitalist and non-capitalist – were extant on the east and west of the Eurasian landmass well into the nineteenth century. When these two world economies came into contact the Great Divergence ensued, and in this his interpretation is not so very far from

Frankian dependency theory and the core position of Wallerstein's WSA. In fact, his thesis found favour with neither luminary.

At this point Arrighi's analysis diverges quite sharply from those accounts and from his own previous argument. Not only does he want to demonstrate that the epicentre of the world economy has shifted from West to East, but he has to substantiate the claim that this shift is epochal because it signals the possible end of the capitalist world economy and thus of capitalist history. When he wrote about Japan in the 1990s it was depicted as the key Eastern player during a period of declining US hegemony. But Japan was still very much a part of the Western capitalist 'archipelago' in the East. China, already on the rise when Arrighi wrote *The Long Twentieth Century*, was heir to different market traditions and working to a different model of growth, which he calls non-capitalist. If nothing else, this is a daring claim, so he has to justify his definition of China as non-capitalist and explain how it recovered so quickly from the depredations of the Great Divergence (and then Maoism) to stand increasingly centre-stage as a world economic power. Because China hardly figured in *The Long Twentieth Century*, these tasks are formidable.

Arrighi's position is that China's recent resurgence demonstrates Adam Smith's argument in *The Wealth of Nations* that free market fundamentalism is not the only way to better the economic fortunes of a country. China followed a 'natural' path of development based largely on agricultural and then industrial production for a domestic market. Commerce with other nations was of secondary importance, although overseas trading networks between China and maritime Asia can be seen from the thirteenth century onwards and contributed to economic growth that peaked in the late eighteenth century. This model contrasts with the 'unnatural' course followed by core European nations that advocated international movement of commercial capital and long-distance trade. Both Smith and Arrighi understand that these paths are not discrete. Thus in China's history, as well as today, non-capitalist market economics intersect with capitalist market imperatives. In the current intersection lies the prospect for a Smithian calculus.

The collapse of China and the whole of East Asia began with the Opium Wars in the mid-nineteenth century and lasted for over a century. China's re-emergence as an economic force began with US-led efforts to reconstruct Japan after World War II. It then benefited from the signal success of Japan in the 1960s and 1970s and from the relative decline in US influence during the same period. When US industry adopted Japanese organizational and production models, the importance of subcontracting networks and buyer-led commodity chains increased dramatically, along with competition between big capitalist businesses vying for international markets. One of the main beneficiaries in this realignment of sourcing and production was the 'overseas Chinese capitalist diaspora' (Arrighi, 2007, 348), and Arrighi stresses the role played by the expatriate Chinese business community in linking foreign buyers to suppliers who could manufacture goods cheaply and quickly for global markets. This, he says, was a pattern of commerce characteristic of late imperial China, one that continues as the dominant business form in Taiwan and Hong Kong.

So China's spectacular rise owes as much, if not more, to domestic and regional traditions and practices as to international capital and the strategy of global retailers. This is less a romantic version of how contemporary China has achieved prominence than an interpretation based on a particular reading of its history. Moreover, it allows Arrighi to gloss over the draconian labour policies, trade protectionism and other authoritarian measures put in train by the Chinese state post-Mao. While it may be that he is over-egging the peculiar or peculiarly regional features of Chinese political economy, as well as their effects, his main purpose – to distance what occurred there from anything resembling neo-liberal doctrine made practice through the Washington Consensus formula for development – bears consideration. In the process, he addresses criticisms of his earlier work from Gunder Frank (2005), who objected to Arrighi's model of East Asian development and Chinese resurgence as too Eurocentric. That said, it remains difficult to judge the purchase of Arrighi's prescription for a world-market society built around 'greater equality and mutual respect among peoples of European and non-European descent that Smith foresaw and advocated 230 years ago' (2007, 379), as opposed to a model of hegemonic succession.

Arrighi offers a critique of capitalism as a world-system; indeed as *the* modern world-system, but one inflected with a more pluralist feel as regards the significance of non-capitalist market forces, and geographically. Our third sceptical intervention has its provenance in constructivist critiques of the inevitability of neo-liberal globalization. In this respect, the body of work produced by Colin Hay since 2000 or so is significant. His is a critical account of the 'inevitability' of capitalist convergence and offers a refined, though still ideological statement on the theme that globalization is a duplicitous social construction (2004; 2006).

Hay's corpus is not sceptical in the way that most second wave critics of globalization would recognize. He shares with more conventional sceptics the insistence that the globalization hypothesis is proven only when global capitalist convergence is discernible and sustained. But his argument, and that of other third wave theorists, is that while much of the evidence does not support a globalization hypothesis, the more theoretically interesting datum is that the discourse of some political and economic elites still tries to justify precisely that. This position is presented as a significant modification to brute structuralist and materialist accounts of what constitutes globalization, because it introduces, or reintroduces, consciousness, ideas and agency to the explanatory account.

In fact, and certainly on first reading, the argument resembles a sophisticated rebranding of the Marxian notion of 'false consciousness', in that the pro-globalization rhetoric of elites, or else their resignation over its inevitability, is seen as an ideological mask for the prosecution of perceived class interests, or an expression of the abstract or imputed 'interests' of capital. In an exchange with Steven Lukes, Hay has criticized the very idea of false consciousness, but he does not, or maybe cannot, dispense with the concept entirely when trying to explain the supportive stance on liberal globalization attributed to Tony Blair and other leaders of social democratic parties and governments in the 1990s (Hay and Coates, 2002).

At that time, the language of inevitable globalization and the necessity of taking up neo-liberal formulas for economic success were articles of faith (Hay and Watson, 2003; for a different view see Lukes, 2005). But even if these actors really were unable to comprehend the allegedly deleterious effects of neo-liberal globalization, their decisions still have to be construed as agential if, on Hay's account, terribly mistaken. Either this, or they failed even to recognize the inherent conflict of interests that resided in their rhetorical and policy support for market-driven capitalism when set against the interests of their domestic constituencies. Which failure, of course, leaves them as either falsely conscious or wittingly true to their class interests. As an ideological position such an argument is understandable, but as a piece of social science it is problematic, because there seems no way in which actual decisions and rhetoric can be distinguished from the sense that agents may have been gulled by an ideological sleight of hand, display a necessary attachment to explicit interests or, in serving the 'needs' of capital, somehow conform to a set of abstract functional requirements.

These problems aside, the sceptical position adopted by Hay is well worth examining, especially where it questions the belief that there is a single global economy, however conceptualized. His emphasis is on the ways in which the global convergence implied and prescribed by neo-liberal economics is still mediated by powerful local, national and regional factors and by contingency, including, of course, how far political elites embrace or resist the ideology of neo-liberalism. Hay and other authors (1999; 2000; 2002) have examined the extent to which economic and welfare diversity or convergence is the most compelling hallmark of capitalist development in the contemporary world economy. Hay in particular has argued that it is very hard to find firm evidence of the kind of convergence that a globalization hypothesis requires, especially where this bears on the declining vitality and autonomy of welfare states in Europe (Hay, 2000; 2006). On the basis of evidence collected between 1960 and 2000 he suggests that rather than the expected convergence of European social models, as reflected in a number of indicators of the health of welfare nationalism, diversity rules.

This is not to say that European states have been immune from the pressures of economic neo-liberalism, or that they have been free to adopt, or else tried to adopt, common policies aimed at reforming welfare provision. Rather, continued variation in outcomes suggests two things. First, the process of neo-liberalism is not as immutable or as monolithic as its apologists have claimed and embedding it successfully in widely different contexts – some with powerful collectivist traditions, others with liberal histories and regimes – was always going to be harder than the mythology proclaimed. Second, such convergence as can be observed, or might be observed in the future, has little to do with globalization and more to do with conditions and constraints evident within the EU economic and governance space.

Of these constraints, the processes of regional economic integration in general, and of monetary union in particular, are drivers of common policy trajectories, but still produce variable outcomes. Quite rightly in the light of his constructivist thesis, Hay does not want to predict creeping neo-liberalism as the necessary consequence of European constraints, any more than he can allow that there are implacable global ones. Policy convergence is seen as neo-liberal in inspiration and intent, but neither globalization nor Europeanization actually entails neo-liberalization. While this is obviously a nuanced position, it might be considered a piece of special pleading necessary to sustain an intriguing, but partial, argument about the role of ideas and the place of agency in constructing globalization.

Hay's thesis fits well with our fourth sceptical position, which also turns on the extent to which globalization has the capacity to alter (transform or eclipse) previously distinct (though not discrete) models of capitalism (Hall and Soskice, 2001; Esping-Andersen, 1990; 1999). The Nordic states have been held to exemplify the kind of exceptionalism that combines market openness and social inclusiveness (Steinmo, 2003). Exceptionalism is manifest in the quite modest cutbacks to welfare provision in Norway, Sweden and Finland during the 1990s and, more recently, the motif seems justified by the superior economic record of the region throughout much of the early 2000s. In part, such phenomenal successes seem to follow from resistance to rampant neo-liberalism, an opposition grounded in the policy preferences of ruling social-democratic parties or governing coalitions. Their policies express powerful and enduring cultural traditions that valorize cooperation, community and attendance to welfare as the constitutive rules of Nordic societies (Ryner, 2010; Giddens, 1997).

Also pertinent to the matter of Nordic exceptionalism is the 'varieties of capitalism' (VoC) approach to the integration of the world economy. Although this approach is quite strongly inflected with normative positions on the desirability and sustainability of welfare nationalism in the face of global rationalism, its provenance resides in organization theory and the economics of the firm. The approach treats corporate social responsibility as an arena where differences across nations provide insights into patterns of convergence and divergence in capitalist practices (Hall and Soskice, 2001; Yamamura and Streeck, 2003).

The VoC approach identifies two main capitalist models that are differentiated by the extent to which any political economy is or is not 'coordinated'. The first is the *coordinated market economy*, cognate with the Nordic models described above and, just possibly, the Chinese version described by Arrighi. The model favours a political economy based on non-market relations, collaboration, commitment and informal deliberation. The second is the *liberal market economy*, which demonstrates arm's-length competitive relations, formal contracting and the operation of supply and demand in line with price sensitivity (Hall and Soskice, 2001). Liberal market economies have fluid labour markets that ensure good access to stock market capital. In turn, firms and capital use switchable assets to drive innovation in different market sectors. The profit motif is paramount. By contrast, in coordinated market economies there is long-term employment, enduring and consensual ties between firms and banks, an emphasis on long-term investment and incremental innovation.

The value of the VoC approach is to highlight the importance of particular institutional complementarities and clusters that govern the relations between capital and labour, and thus delineate models of capitalism. Couched at the level of the firm, the approach points to the significance of national peculiarities in moderating global pressures. It is also noteworthy because it identifies the ways in which the institutional structures of a particular political economy offer firms comparative advantage. Of course, the globalist argument is that countries and firms must either adopt market principles or metaphorically – and sometimes literally – shut up shop. Let's turn to neo-liberalism as a trope for globalization, appearing as its avatar and the bane of self-styled progressive visions of a global future.

Neo-Liberalism and Global Capitalism

Neo-liberal economic doctrine translated into practice is the touchstone for discussions of contemporary globalization. Previously we reviewed the dogma as an ideology of capitalism and as a philosophical treatise based on the theme of negative liberty. Many opponents of neo-liberalism treat its borderless market logic and stark policy alternatives as the embodiment of a regressive globalist ideology. This ideology turned a philosophy of individual needs and how to fulfil them into an economic doctrine and then into a political project aimed at advancing or restoring hegemonic power globally (Harvey, 2003; 2005b; Lechner, 2009). Before we engage with critical accounts, let's canvass those sympathetic to the dogma.

From outside the academy Thomas Friedman has promoted the neo-liberal formula for global economic integration in the pages of the *New York Times* and in best-selling books such as *The Lexus and the Olive Tree* (1999) and *The World Is Flat* (2005). Friedman, along with fellow journalist Martin Wolf (2004), is an unabashed apologist for economic globalization as a dislocating, but ultimately progressive force. Their wholehearted espousal of neo-liberal dogma has put them in the front line of hyper-globalist thinking, and the opprobrium that attaches to their work in some quarters results from their successful popularization of the strong globalization/liberalization thesis. Both provide quite grand visions of history and of contemporary society that are a world away from the middle-range empiricism of much current IPE and the hand-wringing accounts of many anti-/alter-globalists. Therein lies their strengths and undoubted weaknesses.

In both *Lexus* and, with a different gloss, *The World Is Flat*, Friedman offers a no-holds-barred version of globalization as a world economic system unlike any previous incarnation. Not only is the pattern of global integration that emerged in the 1990s on a scale that dwarfs previous episodes of global integration, but its intensity is 'turbo-charged' (1999, xviii). If the degree and scale of economic integration are unprecedented, so too is its growing reliance on information and communication technologies that compress space and time. Yet Friedman is not an out-and-out de-territorialist, at least not in his first book, because he sees American economic power (based on speed of translation from innovative design to market) and its geo-political and cultural dominance on the world stage as prime drivers in the shift to an integrated world political economy. Echoing the sentiments of some students of cultural globalization, Friedman equates globalization with speed – in communication of course, and in the more rapid movement of goods, capital and people. A truly globalized world is being made and it comprises a felicific balance between states, between states and markets and between individuals and both.

In *The World Is Flat*, Friedman offers a particular gloss on this more generalized account of world-making practices. Speed remains the dynamic, and in the phase of globalization since the year 2000, which he calls 'globalization-3' (2005, 10), what had previously been a process involving states and then businesses transmutes to a condition in which individuals become consciously and actively global, primarily through the affordances of the internet. New technologies further compress and 'flatten' the world. Cognate developments occur in business practices through lean and flexible 'out' or 'around' sourcing, and supply chains become increasingly bespoke, as individuals use the internet to construct and maintain their own lifestyles through networks of suppliers, entertainment providers and friendship groups; all without let or hindrance from the bonds of place. Markets are crucial to all this, but they take on a much more decentralized and less institutional or corporate look. Realizing effective demand, the core tenet of all market ideology and practice, becomes more reflexive than at any time in the history of capitalism.

Martin Wolf offers a no less resolute picture of economic globalization, albeit one that is rather more austere than Friedman's version. In his well-received *Why Globalization Works* (2004), Wolf insists on the progressive force of free market economics, drawing on the insights of Adam Smith, David Ricardo and Friedrich von Hayek. Like Friedman, but with a more measured gait and rather less panache, Wolf offers a rounded defence of the political economy of globalization. His defence rests on three main tenets. First, though hardly novel, is the idea that liberal market democracies offer the best chance of good governance. Second, and not unrelated, is the claim that liberal globalization is not only the best vehicle for adding to the sum of human wealth and happiness, but is capable of underwriting world peace. This argument owes a good deal to Kant's seminal claim that democracies do not go to war with each other (Kant, 1836). Finally, and on the back of the first two contentions, Wolf suggests that the reflex opposition of the anti-/alter-globalization movement is misplaced.

Both authors provide robust arguments in favour of market-driven globalization, and each is aware of the need to locate purely economic factors in the context of the broader political and cultural economies of global change. Neither author is an economic reductionist, although Friedman's work has been caricatured as such. At the same time, as with all globalist accounts, the empirical purchase of the evidence presented, let alone the credibility of the whole thesis, is contestable from a variety of political and intellectual standpoints. Friedman and Wolf's accounts rely on necessary connections between liberal market economics, democratization, social progress and material well-being. Such claims simply rehearse all the principles of modernization theory and invite the same objections about corroborating evidence. So, without wishing to use these authors as straw men, it is time to reflect on the various 'discontents' of neo-liberal globalization.

Impassioned and Dispassionate Critiques of Neo-Liberal Globalization

Theorists and activists who criticize neo-liberal capitalism muster as a fairly broad church. We will group critical and alternative positions as *basically reformist*, *activist/empirical radical*, *neo-Marxist*, those derived from *critical IPE* and finally *constructivist*. There is some overlap between categories, except perhaps between the first and all the others.

Basically reformist

In this first category, the conceit is to pillory the institutions of global economic governance while retaining a belief in the potential efficacy of market solutions to the financial problems of states, to uneven development and to inequalities. Authors such as Joseph Stiglitz (1998; 2003) are reformist, yet remain wedded to the positivist methodologies of classical economics. At the same time such reformers cannot be labelled neo-classical fundamentalists because, like John Maynard Keynes before them, they support a humanized or more permissive version of orthodox theory. The departure from the ontological assumptions of classical theory lies in the willingness of writers like Stiglitz to question the classical model of rational-utilitarian actors making transactions in closed systems and to take this model as 'applicable to all human behavior' (Becker, 1976, 8). In fact, the neo-classical formula that is the basis of neo-liberal economics itself departs from the political economy of Adam Smith and John Stuart Mill, because it cleaves to a highly abstract model of an economy whose properties are discoverable only by the application of unbending rules of causality and mathematical precision. Keynes and others favoured a more permissive approach than is allowed by classical orthodoxy, one in which economy and society are no longer deemed ontologically separate. Practical issues, contingency and unintended consequences intrude on the neat schema of rational fundamentalism.

This background is necessary for our analysis because Stiglitz is a mainstream economist, not one schooled in the traditions and concerns that continue to exercise international political economists with a provenance in IR (see also Soros, 1998; 2008; Krugman, 1990; 1996; Rodrik, 1997; 2011). At the same time, he traffics a much more heterodox economics than can be found in the mainstream of neo-classical theory, and has carried this heterodoxy into a critique of global neo-liberalism (Patomäki, 2006). Across three books (2002; 2003; 2006), Stiglitz offers a diagnosis of the ills of neo-liberal globalization made in America's image and proposes a curative for the maladies he discerns. The analytical thrust of his 2002 essay *Globalization and Its Discontents* was not to castigate free market globalism entirely – he recognizes the gains afforded by globalization in some areas of development and in the alleviation of poverty – but to point up the partial nature of its success and its potential to wreak havoc in transitional economies subject to its disciplines. In this regard he is vastly critical of neo-liberal ideology enshrined in the Washington Consensus and delivered through the policy prescriptions of the IMF and the World Bank.

In the case of the Asian financial crisis in the late 1990s, Stiglitz views IMF intervention as catastrophic. By encouraging and, in some cases, requiring greater openness to flows of capital, the IMF precipitated a run of debilitating actions. In a liminal financial climate, Asian banks borrowed dollars, lent them to local businesses, and were exposed when, after further economic slow-down, these companies could not repay their debts. In turn, currency decline made for even bigger dollar debts, completing a less than virtuous circle. The IMF's remedy was to call for even more openness and for stringent policies of debt reduction to be effected in countries whose economies were in dire need of stimulation, not further slow-down. This is an enduring theme in Stiglitz' critique.

The core of Stiglitz' argument over this period is that, for all the evidence of a more interconnected and interdependent world, the neo-liberal formula for freeing up markets is too blunt an instrument and too callous an ideology to do service in countries with quite different recovery needs and, of course, with different patterns of state intervention and cultural traditions. In *The Roaring Nineties*, published in 2003, he rides the wave of criticism over America's 'mismanagement' of globalization and debilitating flirtation with neo-conservative dogma abroad and protectionist trade policy at home, all dressed up as a necessary defence of American national interest and of the health of the world economy.

Overall, Stiglitz remains ambivalent about market-led globalization. He is concerned about its relative failure to reduce world poverty substantially and alarmed by the extent to which it has impeded the progress of some marginal and transitional economies, mainly in the global South. He is also exercised about the degree to which free market doctrine has been subsumed in the (largely unsuccessful) attempt to shore up American power. At the same time, he believes in the progressive force of free market capitalism, and in his third major book, *Making Globalization Work* (2006), brings this 'centrist neo-liberal' reformism to bear on exactly that goal.

Stiglitz' plan for making globalization work contains some fairly imprecise, but widely bruited, prescriptions for more effective institutions of global governance to bridge the gap between rampant economic integration and still grudging and piecemeal political globalization. To be fair, he is rather more exact when identifying policy and issue areas in which better governance is needed than are some of the more vapid prescriptions of new cosmopolitan thinkers. But, as usual, the devil lies both in the detail of what regulation would look like and in whether it would attract compliance. The policy areas are a catalogue of the ascribed ills of market globalization and, *inter alia*, take in the need for a more effective regime for international development, involving a balance of governments and markets. He also looks for changes in the trade regime that amount to rich countries and the multilateral institutions that are their voice giving up any semblance of 'economic and political conditionality' (2006, 47). Key to this reform would be the removal of tariff barriers on trade in agricultural products between poor and rich countries.

Debt forgiveness is part of a package of measures designed to introduce more responsibility in the behaviour of peripheral borrowers and core lenders, while the parlous state of the global commons impels Stiglitz to propose an alternative system for reducing carbon emissions, one based on a global tax on households and businesses. This, he argues, would improve on the contentious policy of national targets for reducing emissions that is subject to so much default. On intellectual property, he suggests that a new regime should be introduced to protect innovation in the developing world and insulate dependent populations against the interests and depredations of corporate globalizers. Finally, he invests in the need for stronger instruments of corporate responsibility, and this reform area encompasses more rigorous competition policy, codes of corporate governance that are enforceable world-wide and better regulation of the global banking system.

Stiglitz and like-minded thinkers make a powerful case against neo-liberal globalism, albeit that they underplay the ways in which neo-liberal policies have been mediated already by the action or inaction of state and corporate elites. In practice, implementation of any policy is always more reflexive than ideology or intentionality prescribe, and that is true of neo-liberalism as a global policy script. Notably, China's embrace of free market principles has been used by party elites to shore up their own position, foster a materially aspirant middle class and reduce rural poverty. Ideologically inflected constructivism sees this as a sell-out to market liberalism, or a case of elites internalizing the neo-liberal dogma, but it may well appear as a development no-brainer when faced with the exigencies of governing in hard times.

Of course, it is always very difficult to separate world-views of some intensity from careful analysis and cautious inference. Which brings us to the discontent exhibited by activists and those 'empirical radicals' referred to above. Activist discourses around globalization, especially neo-liberal globalization, are various. They are voiced not only by public intellectuals in the West (Klein, 2000; 2007; George, 2004; Monbiot, 2003; Hardt and Negri, 2000; 2004; 2009) but by radicals in the developing world (Bello, 2002; 2008; Marcos, 2002). Much activist writing on globalization suffers from an understandable failure to reach beyond its own constituency and sections of the academy, but some interventions have attracted widespread audiences.

Activist/empirical-radical critiques

An air of radical chic attaches to some of the positions taken under this rubric, notably those touched by the romance of the global justice movement (GJM), where their thinking resonates with some of the 'new' iconic issues on the Western civil society policy map: climate change, poverty reduction, debt relief, anti-war rhetoric and reform of the banking system. However, there is much that divides thinkers and activists and more that divides all of them from most academic research on this theme. Certainly there is no unifying ideology, although, for the most part, they may be seen as part of a 'global left' ensemble. At a high level of generality there are areas of common cause, such as a belief in cosmopolitan virtues and the protection of human dignity.

And of course, all are focused on the deleterious effects of neo-liberalism, even where they address different features and advocate different solutions to its ills. Walden Bello, writing out of the Marxist tradition, sees liberal globalization as irredeemable. Instead he advocates 'deglobalization' – a form of cultural, political and, of course, economic autarky (2002, 113). His is a particularly ascetic form of localism and is based on the kind of romantic and primitive Marxism that all but rejects the world in its current guise. His solution springs in part from a deep pessimism about the potential for reformist, and certainly social-democratic, solutions to global inequalities (2008). On the face of it, this is not a formula that attracts the governments of many developing countries, while many un-co-opted social movements also shy away from such an uncompromising denial of capitalist modernity (Marcos, 2002).

Naomi Klein has produced elegant diatribes against those features of economic governance that underpin branded consumerism and disaster capitalism (2000; 2002; 2007). *No Logo* (2000) is a powerful indictment of corporate power, although it is not about globalization per se. In it Klein mines the terrain worked by students of cultural globalization and critics of consumer culture. Here and in subsequent work, her thesis relies on a set of conceptual and empirical givens that supply an immediate emotional and intellectual frisson, but are probably too crudely drawn to provide more than a taster for a thoroughgoing critique of neo-liberalism.

Klein works with three main assumptions that provide coherence to her critique, but are overstated, occasionally to the point of caricaturing her advocacy. In part this springs from treating globalization as no more than an American strategy, rather than a universal script, and in seeming to believe that American interests account for all the ills of globalization. The first assumption traffics a very conspiratorial account of neo-liberal capitalism and of neo-liberal capitalists. For Klein, neo-liberalism is a totalizing creed and its adherents – in policy circles and on the boards of corporations – are the unquestioning devotees of a single dogma. This reasoning is just the flip side of hyper-globalist thinking and is based on a set of very selective cases and an admittedly impressive range of aperçus and human-interest stories. It also departs from a good deal of sceptical analysis that uses hard, long-term and comparative data to show that globalization is of variable intensity and impacts differentially on situated actors.

Klein's second assumption is to treat corporate power as monolithic and irresistible. In this her depiction of the consumer is monumentally dismissive. Consumers seem to have no agency; they are forever lost in and depleted by the lure of global brands. Now, consumerism may be the leitmotif of fast capitalism, but consumers (including audiences) are not blank pages, simply written on by the arbiters of popular tastes. Finally, and this too is a statement about agency, albeit collective agency, Klein identifies and applauds the emergence of an anti-/alter-globalization movement that is portrayed as self-evidently anti-corporate and immanently democratic.

There are echoes here of the open prescriptions for a practical global citizenship to be realized through struggle found in some strains of new cosmopolitanism (Archibugi, 2008a). Hardt and Negri's increasingly qualified romance with the idea of a global multitude (2000; 2004; 2008) also resonates with Klein's enthusiasm for bottom-up and participatory opposition. Of course, for Hardt and Negri, the politics conjured breaks with the lineage of radical opposition found in reformist and Marxist models of emancipatory action. Conventional modes of activism and the identities tied to them are seen as inapplicable to the global age. At the same time, globalization still reduces to an elemental struggle between networked corporations and networked protestors/citizens, but the novelty lies in the setting: a postmodern cultural and political economy of empire.

So, as a final iteration of activist/empirical-radical discontent, we should consider the work of Michael Hardt and Antonio Negri (2000; 2004; 2008; Browning, 2005; 2011); work alluded to throughout this book, hardly ever with approbation. The point to stress here is that although they offer an impossibly naive thesis about the existence and emancipatory potential of the global multitude, the real burden of their argument lies in claiming that the key concepts of *Multitude* and *Empire* are not prefigured in any social theory, or in line of descent from previous types of political mediation. In a way, they too discern a hyper-globalist world, but strenuously deny its logic as bruited in neo-liberal arguments. Instead, empire is globalization without the determination. In fact, it is barely a bio-political and economic *order* at all, but one that is decentred, networked and processual.

In a neat – probably too neat – complementarity, multitude is likewise de-centred and networked; conveniently spawned by empire, yet its nemesis in waiting. No presumptions are made about the type or location of politics conducted under its mantle; anyone, anywhere, can play. While this is highly seductive as a radical account of what others would call capitalist globaliza-tion and of opposition to it, it is allusive and, for all that Hardt and Negri invoke many instances of mobilization, evidentially light. Even to hold the idea of a global multitude together as the expression of an alternative glo-bality, they are forced to ignore history, particularity and many other condi-tions and exigencies which compromise the logic of collective action and curb normative intent.

Hardt and Negri offer an exotic alternative to both hyper-globalist accounts and other radical positions still rooted in what they see as outdated dogma, or reliant on a poor topographical map of world order and the power dynam-ics that invest it. In fact all the radical accounts we have canvassed have looked beyond a critique of actually existing capitalism to prescribe 'other worlds', alternative globalizations and, occasionally, de-globalization. Interestingly, Hardt and Negri deny any kind of dialectical relationship between empire and its seeming antithesis in the global multitude. The rela-tionship is clearly antagonistic but, as Gary Browning points out (2011), they are at some pains to distance their argument from the historical and philo-sophical dialectics of both Hegel and Marx. Yet their history clearly moves in a progressive direction, although the promise of emancipation from empire is realizable only through the complete success of the multitude. Both con-structs are seen as universal in character. So theirs is a historical grand nar-rative by any other name.

The conceit in Hardt and Negri's work is to offer a post-Marxist account of social change. In particular, they claim to supersede Marx's ideas on capital, including those on the nature of production. In postmodern empire, material production is inseparable from the immateriality of social and cultural worlds. Indeed, the production of things is increasingly overtaken by the production of information, and this is dispersed and bespoke. There is, they say, 'an informational colonization of being' (2000, 51), and this syncs with work on the postmodern economy of signs and on the networked information society, found in other strands of sociology and cultural studies. It marries too with widely accepted ideas about the social and cultural consequences of the transition from a Fordist to a post-Fordist cultural economy. The key Marxian category of *labour* commutes from manual labour, with its organizational expression in a politics predicated on the continued existence of the proletariat, to a more diffuse field of practice populated by a much wider constituency of agents. The material basis of Marx's economic analysis is called into question as the social contours of capitalist societies undergo change. Because production (and for that matter consumption) is not constrained by time or space, the upshot is a networked global economy, or a universal *biopower*.

Browning says that Hardt and Negri's critique of Marx actually understates their debt to the latter's treatment of the capacity of capital to recreate itself, adapt to changing circumstances and overcome or postpone immanent crisis tendencies. The scope of that debate exceeds the remit of this book, but it provides an appropriate link to the third category of 'discontents' identified, namely neo-Marxist critiques of neo-liberal capitalism; a spirited, but not uniform category.

Neo-Marxist critiques

Neo-liberalism is the villain of the piece for most neo-Marxist treatments of globalization, and the critique exhibits a number of strands. First is the normative or ideological objection to the concept and operation of a self-regulating market. Second is a critique of the ways in which land, capital and especially labour become mere commodities in ever widening markets. Third is the complaint that the main effect of disembedding economic relations from particular social contexts has been to disadvantage marginal populations further, sometimes because of a decline in social protection, often through condemning them to chastening poverty. In all these instances, the critique assumes that the ills produced by market fundamentalism will conjure an antithesis and that, harsh as neo-liberalism's eventual crisis will be, its denouement presages a fairer, more progressive globality. All the hallmarks of the Marxian dialectic are present in playing out and overcoming the 'awful logic' of neo-liberalism.

In *Bonfire of Illusions* (2010), Alex Callinicos reprises a theme developed over a decade or so of strenuous anti-globalist and anti-capitalist interventions (2003; 2009). His argument identifies twin crises in neo-liberal capitalism. These appear first in Russia's renewed challenge to American hegemony, especially to the spread of NATO as the strategic expression of that preponderance, and second in the financial crisis that blossomed in 2007–8. Both these crises are interpreted as severe qualifications of the already threadbare assumption that US imperialism (the second Gulf War and Afghanistan) can sustain the liberal-capitalist order by ensuring the conditions necessary for uninterrupted market fundamentalism. In this endeavour he also attacks the naive optimism of the early Fukuyama (1992) with his prognosis of a pacific world order based on the twin universals of liberal democracy and liberal capitalism.

Callinicos' longer-term assessment of the threatened, if not parlous, state of global capitalism and of depleted US power echoes the anti-imperialist credo of David Harvey's work on imperialism (2003; 2005b). There are strong similarities too with Ellen Meiskens-Wood's analysis in *Empire of Capital* (2003). Uniquely, *Bonfire* is a classic statement of that strain of Marxist thinking called the international socialist tendency (IST), and its interpretation of the unfolding crisis of capitalism and hegemonic power makes for an intriguing blend of geo-political and economic analysis. Callinicos' emphasis on the importance of what he calls the 'financialization' of capitalism in recent decades is, in many ways, unexceptionable. He notes the precarious nature of the financial architectures whose demise tumbled the world into financial chaos and whose legacies are still felt. Then he charts the ways in which the culture of speculation and easy accumulation of debt has depleted the lives of many ordinary people. His theoretical contribution to understanding the woes of global capitalism at this conjuncture rests on three assumptions. First is the venerable notion of an immanent crisis of accumulation, with a consequent tendency for the rate of profit to fall. Second is the particularly unstable condition of the financial system, and third is the willingness of core states to encourage credit bubbles as the over-heated engines of economic growth.

In addition, and pertinent to one of the valence issues of globalization research, Callinicos divines a tendency for individual states to play a more central role in determining capitalist dynamics and in altering the world's geo-political balance. The Russian intervention in Georgia in 2008, Chinese–US relations and – one might suppose – even the withdrawal of states from market regulation as a functional response to crisis can all be taken as exemplifying this trend. Obviously, much of this is at one with the broader 'states matter' thesis and with depictions of the new imperialism as a reaction to declining US hegemony, as well as a response to the renewed crisis of accumulation.

Against this charge is the argument offered in Bill Robinson's theory of globalized capitalism, itself a sustained critique of neo-liberal globalization from a resoundingly anti-capitalist standpoint. Robinson does not rely on a reworked theory of imperialism to provide sympathetic agency in the guise of US foreign policy. His thesis develops the analytical frameworks found throughout his work: the transnationalization of production and finance delivered through the agency of a TNCC and the global reach of the TNS (2008; 2004).

In *Latin America and Global Capitalism* (2008), Robinson provides a regional focus on the process of global capitalist expansion whereby new 'external' areas of the world are incorporated into the system of commodity production and capitalist market relations, and in which 'capitalist or commodity production replaces pre- or noncapitalist forms of production' (2008, 62). When discussing China we underlined the need to be sceptical of both neo-liberal claims about inevitable convergence and the scope for outright autarky. Robinson exercises at least some of this caution when dealing with Latin America's accommodation to global constraints. At the same time, he is committed to the cause of democratic-socialist emancipation, but sees little in the way of a sound social-democratic critique of capitalism.

Much of the book is a detailed and convincing analysis of earlier periods of developmental capitalism in Latin America, of the growth of flexible labour and of the changing mechanisms of global capital accumulation as played out in the region. Robinson too discerns a crisis of neo-liberalism at the outset of the twenty-first century, and reflects on the potential for popular resistance to take advantage of any dislocations. For our purposes, it is his rejection of classical Marxist theories of imperialism as unsuited to understanding current globality that is of most interest. He says that such theories have caricatured the world order and 'confused capitalist competition with state competition, and conflated disarray, factionalism . . . among transnational capitalist groups and global elites with nation-state rivalries' (2008, 68). This claim rests entirely on his ability to ground empirically the twin concepts of the TNCC and TNS, and on this we have already expressed some reservation in chapter 7.

Critical IPE, constructivism and the capitalist world economy

IPE emerged in the 1970s as a counterpoint to neo-realism and theories of liberal interdependence. As it appeared in the work of Robert Cox (1981; 1987) and then Stephen Gill and David Law (1988), IPE – re-labelled global political economy – looked to shift the focus of inquiry from the behaviour of states and a few other collective actors to the underlying socio-economic processes and structures that sustain and transform them. Over the years, and especially in the UK, some parts of Europe and Canada, the sub-discipline has been in dispute over the ontological focus of inquiry. These disputes turn on whether the research emphasis should be on identifying and explaining the motivations and actions of agents in the world economic system, or on the historical processes that have determined world economic order (Bruff and Tepe, 2011; Shields et al., 2011).

As a body of knowledge and an approach to its acquisition, IPE should not be burdened with attempting a theory of capitalism per se, any more than it is exercised principally by globalization as a cause or a consequence of capitalist expansion. Nonetheless, as Ian Bruff points out, since the early 1980s a progression (his term) towards a more refined grasp of globalization has taken place as IPE embraced the realm of ideas and motivations, mainly as a way of rounding out accounts of the material basis of world order. The shift towards a more questioning stance on the relationships between material and ideational factors has spawned an eponymous 'critical' IPE whose embrace of neo-Gramscian ideas has been wholehearted, but remains contentious. This much we canvassed in chapters 1 and 2. In what follows we will rehearse the views of some proponents of critical IPE.

Robert Cox's initial contribution to these debates drew on the world-systems approach of Immanuel Wallerstein, although he and Gill and Law see a much more integrated global political economy than is countenanced in Wallerstein's oeuvre. Cox, in particular, objects to Wallerstein's structural-functional interpretation of the emergence of a single capitalist world economy over the past 500 years. Instead, Cox draws on the more obvious Marxian legacy found in the key historicist concepts of relations of production, social class, forms of state, historic blocs and hegemony (1981; 1987; 1993). Writing in 1987, he examined the formation of different relations of production, social forces and forms of state in world history, and how they have affected the making of the contemporary world. In this regard he offers an innovative approach to the rise and then the crisis of the Bretton Woods system for managing the world economy.

At the heart of this endeavour, and threaded through pretty much all subsequent literature out of critical IPE, is a set of neo-Gramscian tenets. Neo-Gramscians aim to explain changes in forms of state and in the way the capitalist world economy is governed. The focus of their critique has been the neo-liberal revolution in economics and how it has been instantiated in thought and deed by its main apologists in core states, corporations and multilateral institutions (Gill, 1990; 1995; 2000; also Rupert, 1998). Their aim is to reveal the ideologies and power relations that sustain this order, a laudable aim and one in which the quality of empirical evidence on the balance of constraint between material factors (economy, warfare) and ideas is crucial to explanation. Of course, Cox was suitably modest in this intent, saying that all he was trying to do was to apply some useful concepts from Gramsci to invigorate IR theory.

Neo-Gramscians share with Marx the notion that agency and structure are interdependent, even mutually constitutive, which syncs with the ideal of a multidimensional theory of globalization. But how one demonstrates the relationship beyond its obvious plausibility is enduringly hard. In an early critique of neo-Gramscianism applied to IPE, Heikki Patomäki (2006) is quite scathing about the actual gains from its 'critical' variant. He opines that, in addition to the relative absence of developed research designs, including a lack of causal hypotheses, most neo-Gramscian accounts are light on empirical evidence, preferring a more casual and interpretative approach to selected illustrative material. Globalization sceptics would take this as a paradigm statement on the temper of pretty much all globalization research. Patomäki's remedy is not to dismiss neo-Gramscian IPE, but to call for a marriage between it and more thoroughly scientific critical realism.

Critical IPE offers some very nuanced accounts of what is often depicted as a uni-dimensional and over-determined process. For that alone its contribution to the study of global capitalism, as well as to the study of non-capitalist globalization, is noteworthy. Treatments of capitalism as a global system require attention to historical detail, to structural constraints and to crisis tendencies. They also need the insights provided by interpretative analysis. Ideologies are enacted through discourse, while ideational structures frame action. The problem for research continues to be how to theorize and then demonstrate the articulation of these two fields.

Conclusion

In this chapter we have explored the idea and the practice of capitalism as a global system through the scholarship of those who are often categorized as hyper-globalist (neo-liberal), sceptical or transformationalist. The extant themes – capitalism as *the* global system or just *a* global system, the existence or otherwise of a fully integrated global economy, the historical uniqueness of the present conjuncture, the potential for disruption of crisis proportions, and the balance between material and non-material forces in structuring capitalism – have given a specific gloss to globalization theory that can be dangerously exclusive. Much of the work examined here is caught up in its own radical or disciplinary agenda, while work that tries to escape such constraints can be methodologically naive and conceptually underdeveloped. Of course, we could say much the same about the balance of research we have covered in this book. But the study of globalization as an economic phenomenon and its equation with capitalist expansion still exercises too narrowing an influence on the study of global integration: 'necessary, but not sufficient' comes to mind as a judgement on the subtle – and not so subtle – kinds of economism found in much of the work we have explored. In the final chapter of the book, we step away from work out of the mainstream and introduce ideas less constricted in their understanding of globalization and in how to study it.

CHAPTER 9

All Change: Critical Globalization Studies or a Social Science of Globality?

In this chapter we will offer a critical summation of scholarship on the global. After identifying a novel and still under-used approach to global complexity, one that is full of transformative intent, we will locate the study of globalization in attempts to theorize social change, especially as reflected in the debates over modernity. The strengths and weaknesses of contemporary scholarship canvassed throughout the book are summarized and the contours of a critical social science of globality outlined. Globalization remains a compelling idea, and the appropriation of the concept in so many discourses is witness to its enduring appeal and purchase on the social-scientific imagination. But as we know, because it is convenient shorthand for the way we live now, it has occasioned more than its share of slovenly usage.

In such appropriation, scholarly precision – over concept specification, about causation and with regard to how far the concepts of globalization, globalism and globality impact on the scope and conduct of normal science – is often the victim. A good deal of academic debate on globalization is notable only because it rehearses either (hyper-)globalist or sceptical positions and is hortatory and/or adversarial in its mode of address. In turn, transformationalist thinking carries a whiff of romance and the promise of danger, but is increasingly resigned to an Aristotelian balancing act between the first two positions. The upshot is certainly a lively set of exchanges, but too often conducted out of disciplinary and ideological bunkers. Sceptical accounts rehearse a stern defence of existing knowledge communities, organized around disciplines for the most part, but visible too in some ideologies and theories of history and social change. All this parades as a fascinating burlesque, but its effects on scholarship of the global and on the prospects for 'rethinking' social science are still enervating.

Of course, all academic debate moves to such conceits and rhythms, and scientific progress is often achieved through the steady accretion of new knowledge and incremental undoing of the old. Perhaps the main problem with the concept of globalization is that its conceptual scope is not limited and may not be limitable. As such, it does not designate an agreed curriculum for investigation. Its potential as a game-breaker in the transformation of the social and historical sciences is still vitiated by the sheer inclusiveness of the concept, and by the continuing hold of disciplinary agendas and methodo-logical nationalism on the framing of questions that guide investigation and the conduct of research.

Globalization implies connectivity and institutionalization. Fundamentally, it is about change, even transformation. In the lexicon of much social science, change has been approached through attention to social stability, or through its antithesis, crisis. Globalization scholarship hints at other ways of compre-hending change, but, as we have seen, rarely delivers. Let's begin our final reflections by considering the possibility of abrogating conventional under-standings of change and stability in search of a social science of the global. We will canvass arguments that jettison assumed relations of time and space and of agency and structure. Implicit – at least implicit – in this scholarship is the need for social-scientific investigation of globalization to start some distance away from the usual ontological suspects, and for critical studies of globality to take the matter of transformation seriously, not just as a horta-tory device or a convenient label for a group of scholars.

Here are the main questions we have considered. First, is globalization the primary driver of massive and disjunctive social change? Second, are recent dramatic changes in world politics and economics part of the unfolding of world history, of universalized modernity slouching to its denouement, or do they presage something quite other? Finally, can the idea of the world being made into a single place, and demonstrating a systematic rather than a jobbing unicity, be taken seriously? To address these questions we have to look more closely at the transformations implied by the concept of glo-balization and delivered in some, but only some, of the scholarship we have examined. We will consider work that transcends or dissolves the antinomies of order or disorder and stability or change that often govern such inquiry. In this regard, it will be argued that complexity theory offers a very controversial interpretation of social action, let alone of globalization, but one that holds out great promise for students of globalization (Urry, 2003; 2005).

Globalization as Order, Disorder or Both?

The idea of order is central to most accounts of social change, especially those reliant on functionalist reasoning. Even theories of crisis start with order and explore the ways in which immanent contradictions, structural or agential constraints and contingency precipitate a challenge to the organizational principles, and thus the integrity, of any social formation. In turn, the resolution of crisis may produce a return to stasis, social transformation, or a reflexive modification in usual practices and forms. In hyper-globalist research, globalization as process suggests a *telos*, that of universalization, which is fashioning the world into a single place; a world quite other than that defined by territory and territoriality.

In this scenario, transformation inaugurates a kind of 'global modern' (Pasha, 2010), one that achieves the universalization of capitalism and the Western cultural account, but at terminal cost to a raft of other modernist givens, notably territoriality. In other discourses, globalization constitutes a rupture with modernity, rather than being some re-spatialized apotheosis of the modern. Where a rupture or transformation is entertained, a more fluid postmodernity unencumbered by modernist icons such as states and bounded societies, the centred self and systemic rationality, is a possible outcome. On the one hand globalization predicates singularity, perhaps even uniformity; but on the other hand it signals fracture, even chaos, with alarm bells ringing about an actual or impending crisis of modernity. It is in the latter guise that its transformative thrust is most palpable.

Complexity theory and global (dis)order

Complexity theory applied to the study of globalization has its origins elsewhere. Its provenance includes physics, the mathematics of chaos, economics and those social sciences employing network approaches to understand human mobility, communication and risk as features of an interconnected world (Lash and Urry, 1994; Urry, 2000; 2003; Castells, 2000a; Dicken et al., 2001; Giddens, 1990; Walby, 2008). In *Sociology beyond Societies*, John Urry (2000) develops the common theme that social life can no longer be contained or theorized as confined to territorial societies. Once the 'scale, range and depth' of a multitude of mobile and global processes are taken into account (2003, ix), the location and nature of the social are problematized, along with ways of thinking about them.

Later, in 'The complexities of the global' (2005), Urry rightly points out that the use of complexity theory is implicit in the treatments of globalization and modernity found in work by Giddens (1990), Harvey (1989), Castells (2000a) and Hardt and Negri (2000). Beck (Beck and Willms, 2003) also describes various boomerang effects (complex relationality) when corporations and states generate consequences that return to haunt them because they are part of complex systems where everyone is inside and outside at the same time. There are also strong connections with Luhmann's systems theory (Luhmann, 1983; Albert, 2007). Complexity science examines systems that adapt and evolve as they self-organize over time, and this is a tenet of that strain of systems theory called autopoiesis (Urry, 2003). The key feature of autopoietic systems is that their autonomy and ability to survive are dependent on the ways they interact with the increasingly complex environments they inhabit. These environments act as sources of disturbance, even chaos. Contra classical sociology with its emphasis on the natural state of order, in complex systems the potential for disharmony is always present and its appearance not pathological but routine.

Complexity theory contributes to our understanding of global process by discerning parallels between the change from classical physics to quantum physics in the late twentieth century and the emergence of systemic globality in the same period. Classical physics was based on absolute notions of time and space, on the solidity of matter and on immutable laws of motion. Quantum physics treats with an indeterminate world in which the boundaries of time and space are not absolute and any 'laws' are subject to chance and contingency (Prigogene, 1997). In other words, the systems are non-linear, with order and disorder seen as integral elements of all physical and social phenomena. Moreover, there is no consistent relationship between cause and effect. Applied to the study of globalization, especially to its theorization, these insights have some purchase, although they are obviously controversial. John Urry offers a preliminary argument on the ways in which complexity theory helps us understand the diverse material worlds implicated in globalization.

In *Global Complexity* (2003), Urry unpacks the emergent properties of the global. On the way to that goal he offers a three-part critique of much of the social science of globalization. The burden of this critique will be familiar from other work we have examined, but it is worth repeating. First, he notes its failure to break out of the national, the societal and the territorial as the basis of social inquiry. Second, he registers the tendency for the global 'level' to be taken for granted and for globalization to be depicted as the force through which sub-global actors come to identify with the global. Last, because it is taken for granted as an exogenous constraint, globalization becomes a kind of reified structure, with individuals, associational actors, localities, regions and states seen as agents whose stance towards globalization is either accommodation or resistance.

Instead Urry prescribes the social science of globalization as a theory of connections, arguing that 'there is no agency, no macro or micro levels and no system and no life-world' (2003, 122), because each of these notions presumes that there are entities with separate and distinct essences that are brought into 'external juxtaposition with each other' and with the 'linear metaphor of scales, such as that stretching from micro to macro'. Such formulations should be replaced by a 'metaphor of connections' (2003, 122). For many theorists of globalization the metaphor would be apposite, but in this radical guise it remains problematic for accounts still reliant on the steadfastness of national and territorial ontologies.

The radical core of Urry's thinking about global complexity is that phenomena usually denoted by terms such as 'local', 'global' and 'identity' have to be rethought as a 'constellation of complex, reflexive systems and self-organizing exchanges and transactions linked to wider systems of power and influence' (Hand and Sandywell, 2002, 46). This avoids the implication that interaction between an integrated and relatively stable global system and derivative or otherwise subordinate local and networked actors is configured by the immanent qualities of structures and agents. In Urry's formulation, globalization commutes from being the over-determined effect of capitalist relations, cultural domination or hegemonic aspiration to a 'heterogeneous field of world-making practices' (Hand and Sandywell, 2002, 213). These practices have a powerful, even necessary emergent quality that is revealed in the imbrication of local and global, through the interplay of global scapes and contingent glocal actors and through various 'networks, fluids and governance institutions' (Urry, 2003, 103). For critics this still seems very allusive, but it affords a number of insights useful for the study of global complexity.

First, agency retains its centrality in explaining global dynamics, but not as part of an analytic dualism that reduces questions about relationality and reflexivity to arguments about shades of dominance. Admittedly, one of the complaints about Urry's complexity thesis, seen too in the critique of Luhmann's systems analysis, is that the agency conjured is pretty anodyne, with what are actually enduring questions about the distribution of power and resources, or about consciousness, parlayed into the much more forgiving notion of 'complex relationality'. Second, in global complexity, the ontological autonomy of local systems is modified by the variety of formal and informal networks – interdiscursive, economic, political, religious and so on – that cross both phenomenal and imagined boundaries. In global complexity, agents (individual and collective) not only interact with a dominant – and possibly territorial – set of cultural and structural properties, but with intersecting, overlapping and sometimes contradictory sets and the identities and power relations tied to them.

The result, and this bears repetition, is to problematize what constitutes a political sphere, and still more, a social and cultural order. Actually, there is a resonance here with 'new' cosmopolitan thinking from writers such as David Held, although Urry has no normative agenda on the re-spatialization of interest and affect. If anything, his ideas sync best with Appadurai's imagery of fluid global scapes and contingent glocal actors, and that is a telling indicator of its strengths and its weaknesses. Perhaps the main strength of Urry's account of global complexity is that he blends the analysis of globalization and complexity theory so well that he goes some way to making a convincing case that globalization is inexplicable without it.

As with Appadurai's equally challenging schematic for understanding globalization, the need is for more sustained empirical application of the core concepts. In recent work on different types of mobilities and on global 'fluids' such as travelling peoples, tourists and refugees, as well as on the mechanics of network interaction, Urry and his co-researchers are addressing the complaint that complexity theory is much too light on empirical evidence to render service in a theory of transformative globality. At the same time, complexity theory finds few takers in other strands of theorizing the global. Although Urry mentions work on the formation and operation of the TNCC as exemplifying a particular type of global fluid, the progenitors of that account of capitalist expansion tend to give complexity theory short shrift.

John Gray describes the current state of the globe as 'an intractably disordered world' (2001) and as Urry notes, 'complexity' 'provides some metaphors, concepts and theories essential for analyzing such intractable disorderliness' (2005, 83). And Urry's complaint, that many existing global analyses lack the kind of conceptualization necessary for examining these 'strangely ordered systems that are complex, rich and non-linear, involving multiple negative and positive feedback loops' (2005, 83), has much to recommend it. This is especially true if one retains the core of his prescription for globalization research, which calls for understanding globalization as a theory of connections. In this prescription he echoes a good deal of more conventional work on connectivity, as well as research from the wilder shores of globalization theory.

Critical Globalization Studies as a Science of Globality

Or perhaps not so wild, since complexity theory meets some of the tenets of that critical globalization scholarship that we outlined in chapter 1. It dismisses simple and often misleading binaries such as state and society, local and global, agency and structure. It is multidimensional in that it does not discriminate between economics, politics and culture as exclusive and theoretically sufficient drivers of global complexity and global change. It has little time for the kind of compartmentalization that follows from rigid adherence to 'levels' of analysis, and it has no disciplinary pretensions to uphold. Finally, it is not ideologically inflected. It is, in short, a telling critique of much of the social science of globalization as that has emerged throughout this book.

Of course, with the possible exception of the last point, much the same might be said of that other meta-theory of social action applied to globalization, namely constructivism and its offspring, structuration theory. Neither meta-theory passes full muster on all accounts, but each makes globalization explicable in ways difficult for all structuralist positions and those that are entirely action-centred. Regrettably, complexity theory does not attend much to history. And tracing historical processes, and being able to track globalization through careful periodization, is what globalization theory aspires to. Too often for comfort, constructivism falls back on crude empiricist phenomenology.

Complexity theory and those theories that discern a postmodern future, if not a postmodern globality, sit rather uneasily in the wider pantheon of global theory, even if we set aside hyper-globalist knockabout. There is also an unremitting presentism in complexity approaches that syncs with postmodern scepticism about historical grand narratives and with any critique of the neat teleology found in some theories of modernization. But as we have seen, global theory still invests a great deal in the idea of the modern as either a point of rupture with a non-global past, or the locus of transformation to something that is deemed to be quite other, though rarely completely anti-categorical.

Few global theories want to elevate globalization (as process) to the status of a modernist grand narrative and equally few want to dispense with modernist givens altogether. The protracted, if elemental, debate over the state and the future of the state, so central to many of the narratives of globalization we have explored, is illustrative of this dilemma, even if it takes on a more limited and instrumental hue when estimating state strength or capacities in face of globalizing pressures. In early hyper-globalist accounts and in some of the sceptical responses to those excesses, the real charge in the 'decline of the state' debate was and, to some extent, remains the transformative impact of globalization on institutional, philosophical and quotidian modernity.

At various points we have voiced the suitably careful refrain that states matter, but sometimes they do not, or will not. This tension rather glibly illustrates an important dilemma for globalization theory as regards modernity, and that is whether to jump one way or the other, or to sit judiciously on the fence. The properly cautious answer, bruited by Gary Browning (2011), is that modernity remains important 'unfinished business' for research on globalization and that most global theorists understand as much. But with a view to audience satisfaction rather than social-scientific caution, electing for straightforward teleology or outright scepticism plays a whole lot better than trying to explain the messy interweave of agency and structure, or contingency, while keeping at least a casual eye on history; all in search of good explanation.

Browning also suggests that while most global theorists reject modernist grand narratives on historical directionality and postmodernist conceits on the ineluctable variety of experience, globalization is still treated as the 'defining navigational mechanism' (2011, 114) that directs the general course of history and, in some cases underscores a palpable normative agenda. His is a useful observation because it gets to the heart of the issue we have rehearsed at some length; namely, what is global theory trying to explain? At the same time, the related distinction drawn by Justin Rosenberg (2000; 2005) between *globalization theory* and *theories of globalization*, to designate a gap between treating globalization as a (the) causal factor in social change and seeing it as a dependent variable, is overdrawn, as a description of both the ways in which most global theory has been couched, simplifying how worlds are made, and how theories of such worlds are, or should be, constructed.

World-making practices are both reflexive and recursive. Where simple causation gives way to multiple causation and where the intermediation of other variables complicates the causal sequence is not always clear, even where such variables can be quantified, or just specified. So that even if one started with a simple model of cause and effect, over time, the balance of factors and the linearity of causation is likely to be modified. But with so many potential variables clustered under the umbrella of globalization and with its constellation and scope being so variable over time, treating it as a look-alike for a grand narrative of social change might – and here Rosenberg is right – be poor social science, or at best premature. In fact, the scholarship of globalization has become increasingly cautious and self-conscious over the years; more middle-range in its attention to empirical detail, to escape just that charge. But the consequences are not always as beneficial as one might suppose.

Because, for all that admirable caution, it could be argued that what sets the concept of, and scholarship on, globalization apart – what provides its real frisson – is the promise of a paradigm shift and a two-way transforma-tion: first an observed transformation in the actual conduct of affairs in the world and in the way that the world is (dis)ordered; second a transformation in social-scientific knowledge about that world, such that the taken-for-granted nature of disciplinary divides, the hold of methodological national-ism on the scientific imagination and the tendency to compartmentalize existence into discrete spheres of activity – and then to ascribe explanatory precedence to one or other of these – are all renounced. The difficulty with realizing such promise lies in part in the sheer naivety of an all-embracing concept like globalization and partly in the obduracy of existing systems of knowledge as these have construed the world. Hyper-globalist theory rather tarnished the respectable, if over-blown, intention to effect a paradigm shift, leading to charges of 'globaloney' (Veseth, 2005), and there is still a sense among sceptics that transformationalists are really lambs who have inadvert-ently strayed from the fold. Of course, sceptics would aver that globalization is all smoke and mirrors anyway, which is something of a limiting case where the subject matter of a book like this is concerned.

The more modest idea that the study of globalization constitutes a 'positive problem shift' in the social sciences remains potent, but carries less of a burden of expectation (Lakatos, 1970). Yet too much scholarship remains committed to putting the genie back in the bottle, or to normalizing its radical promise by trying to demonstrate that globalization is not worth examination just because it offends the ontology and epistemology of specific branches of knowledge. Perhaps we should expect these difficulties in a schol-arship that not only works at the intersection of disciplines as Sassen advises, but looks to cross them in pursuit of fuller explanation of social phenomena.

Arguably, the main point of globalization studies is to overcome the per-ceptual and intellectual barriers that surround individual academic disci-plines, but this is a hard environment in which to operate and, because it is one step removed from the real action – what globalization looks like when it globalizes and what its effects are – somewhat abstract too. Globalization scholarship must needs traffic in both camps, but rarely does so, because the imperative to execute a meta-theory of social action and social change often takes back seat to the perceived, and understandable, need to demonstrate something concrete *in* and *about* global processes. Of course, there is the counter-imperative, which is to deny that globalization exists, or if it does, that there are any consequences for usual social science or usual politics. So how should we sum up on the social science of globalization as this has unfolded across the book?

First, there is a powerful transformative dynamic in key areas of globalization scholarship and in the very idea of globalization. The most obvious example is the claim to discern transformations of space and time – and thus of social life – as experienced by situated and mobile actors. The force of the concept 'space-time compression' and its import for the organization of political, social and economic life are widely acknowledged. But too often the concept is reduced to a simple, descriptive account of geography or a convenient aphorism to convey simultaneity, rather than being at the core of a theory of social process and change. To be sure, the literature, especially transformationalist literature, is full of concepts that inform this theme – time-space distanciation, 'flat' world, global scapes, cellular globality and the like. But perhaps Justin Rosenberg is correct to say that while these concepts are potent, their translation into a convincing theory of globality is pending. Even their operationalization and use in more modest and empirically grounded research on processes of global extent has been patchy.

Second, and closely related, is the critique of rational-territorialist assumptions about the basis of social life and order that constitute normal social science. Seen in the growing unwillingness to view the world as organized into discrete and hierarchical scales, this critique achieves something near apotheosis in ideas about networked globality and in the prospect of a globalized world being made through the interplay of networks and borders, where the understanding of both concepts extends beyond purely geographical connotations and legal boundaries to embrace virtual and affective signifiers of belonging (Axford, 2007a). Here too the transformative force of the thesis is properly qualified by the relative dearth of empirical investigation – although that is being remedied – and by the frantic rowing back from the charge of hyper-globalism seen in the use of more cautious language like 'de-nationalization' (Sassen, 2006). As we have noted, the durability of the territorial state as an actor still imprints much social science, which is structured around its ontological centrality. Because of this, the more qualified language of repositioning, rather than the absolutes of demise or transformation, may be apposite. More corrosive of the 'territorial trap' is the wide acceptance that the locus and boundaries of society and of community cannot be taken for granted as congruent with national territory and territoriality.

Third, the language of globalization as either continuous or discontinuous with, or in various ways parasitic on, modernity remains central to work on globalization as historical process. The debates about multiple modernities and civilizations remind us that history matters, that seemingly novel forms and practices may have historical antecedents, and that attention to social change in pre-modern times is a useful, even necessary, antidote to 'chrono-fetishism' and Western-centrism. Here, work from comparative macro history, the micro histories of Braudel and others, and strands of post-colonial theory stand as important sources of knowledge on globalizations in the plural. Of course, we should remain wary of evolutionary arguments and of teleology applied to global processes.

Fourth, historical insights and comparative data show that globalization is not now and, even in previous moments, was never a uni-modal process. Rather, any sense of the global, of globality, as implying or requiring singularity is not about what Bayart calls 'uniformization'. Caricatured and otherwise jaundiced accounts of globalization would cavil at this claim because of the need to demonstrate homogeneity as a necessary outcome of the process. In its absence, say sceptics, the globalization hypothesis must fail. Even some normative critics of globalization see an unremitting and regressive pattern of homogenization, damaging to diversity and of locality. But the balance of findings tends to the counter-intuitive and thus unsatisfactory conclusion that globalization implies and delivers the simultaneous production of sameness and difference – unsatisfactory because, aesthetically, globalization as a totalizing and universalizing process delivers more bangs per buck than equivocation about its variable and contingent impact on identities; or else comes to the conclusion that it is relativizing and essentializing at one and the same time.

Transformative accounts of a growing, possibly modal, globality see no theoretically debilitating contradiction in pointing to the systematic oneness of the world, especially in matters of consciousness, and recognizing that reflexive agents experience these things in different ways and enact them differently. At the same time, there is little doubt that apart from normative and/or ideological thinking, the implied universality of globalization has been tempered, even deliberately played down where it can be interpreted as the universalization of the Western cultural account. Empirical-analytical research on the ways in which elements of that account and its material avatars have been indigenized by aboriginals may also prefer the notion that cultures and civilizations meet in a fruitful and domination-free fusion or creolization of difference. This too can be portrayed as a feature of globalization; at least of a progressive variant.

Fifth, this sensible qualification of theoretical and polemical excess suggests an opening out of disciplinary redoubts, but is that the case? Certainly there are areas of commonality in the research focus across disciplines and sub-fields. This is partly because such issues as territoriality, modernity and the agency–structure dualism surface in many of the fields that conduct globalization research. At the same time, important and enduring differences in the interpretation of globalization and its use in explanations of social change exist because of ideological stance, disciplinary rules and methodological preferences. It is not necessary to rehearse these in detail, but they include differences in how globalization is defined (indeed, whether it is countenanced at all), over its origins and provenance, about what causes globalization (itself a narrowing of focus, from the more theoretically bold 'what does globalization cause?'), over the primary and contributory drivers of globalization, and on whether and how the process might be understood from a normative perspective. While such variety is not debilitating and is by no means unique to globalization research, it does rather complicate the search for a multidimensional and inter- or non-disciplinary approach to the subject.

Of course, it is possible to take such goals as having no more than hortatory force. But, as we have noted, the very idea of globalization implies the absence of boundaries and invites a scholarship that is committed to the same ends. Throughout this book we have noted scholarship that tries to ignore or collapse disciplinary differences, abjures uni-dimensional thinking and strives for a synthesis of social-scientific imagination when describing and explaining new worlds. But these accounts often remain highly abstract or allusive, as witnessed in Appadurai's intuitively powerful notion of global scapes and Giddens' structurationist approach to global integration, along with Urry's call for a theory of connections. Mostly they are marginal to mainstream scholarship on globalization. Such authors receive almost obligatory mention in research across the academic spectrum, but very rarely are their ideas applied in empirical investigation, except in some areas of social anthropology, network analysis and – rather less so – communication studies. Some of this reluctance must have to do with the very broad-brush ideas they traffic; still more perhaps with a continuing reluctance to entertain the possibility of a paradigm shift.

In other respects the most intuitively appealing ideas in globalization research – interdisciplinarity, mutual constitution and space-time distanciation – are notoriously difficult to operationalize. We may applaud calls for a synthesis of perspectives and epistemologies when trying to understand globalization, but delivery is something else. Even moving beyond basically connectivist understandings of globalization and treating it as more than a form of intensified exchange remains difficult in some scholarship. World polity theory has made the leap to construing globalization as a socio-cultural phenomenon, but many of the contributions from constructivism and ideational neo-Gramscian theory find themselves unable to shake off the trammels of vulgar Marxism and the state-centrism of conventional IR.

Finally, the academic study of globalization has undoubtedly suffered from its own form of concept compression and conflation, which has proved debilitating in the development of a sound scholarship. Earlier we delineated the analytical advantages in distinguishing globalization as process from globalization as ideology, and both from globality as condition or system. By contrast, in early accounts globalization appeared as a reified structure, with individuals, groups, localities, regions and so on all reified as agents. Globality, on the other hand, is a constitutive framework, but one that is mutable and unfinished. And it is the sheer breadth of the notion of globality as a constitutive framework for social action that plays very easily into the hands of those who argue that unless research on the global sticks to measurable connectivity it becomes vacuous. So we are left with the question: what should critical globalization studies and a social science of globality look like? Let's start with some more general points.

First, a critical scholarship of globalization and globality can and should be an inclusive knowledge community. There is no single 'right' way to study globalization, and this is both strength and weakness: strength because it opens up, or should open up, scholarship to new ways of thinking about the limits of disciplinarity, the sanctity of discrete levels of analysis, the agency–structure dualism and so on; weakness because where anyone can play, many want to play by their own rules and to keep the ball. Much innovative work still suffers from the weaknesses identified by Justin Rosenberg – lack of precise definition, failure to specify indicators and to generate hypotheses capable of being set against empirical evidence – but there are compensating strengths found mainly in the recognition that increasing facets of social life are identifiable and explainable only through reference to global affordances, global consciousness and the enactment of global relations – to globality. At its least demanding this would lead to the hypothesis that global consciousness is a factor in configuring social relationships, although definitional imprecision about what constitutes globalization, let alone globality, still dogs rigorous testing.

Second, such scholarship must pay attention to Rosenberg's call for greater definitional precision on what constitutes globalization. This must not limit the spheres of existence where the observer might examine globalization as process, or globality as condition, but, at the least, will avoid the kind of lexical conflation we have referenced throughout.

Third is the insistence that 'order' in the global system should not be seen as evidence of its organic unity, or as the result of a functional fit between parts of a system, with each enshrined in the dogma that social, biological and physical systems have to be ordered. Rather, what we have is a negotiated and contingent condition arising from the articulation of local subjects and structures with more encompassing global ones. The growing density and extensiveness of these articulations and connections carry the possibility of systemic disorder as much as they conform to the requirements of a functional order. Of course, this is a matter of consciousness as well as of connection. Processes of globalization not only make it more difficult for societal systems and networks of individuals to effect closure, but actually open up new imaginaries, 'new practices and new institutions' (Friedman, 1993, 86).

Fourth, as James Mittelman and Bill Robinson advocate, critical studies of globality must demonstrate a concern with *reflexivity*. This, as Mittelman tells us (2004, 24), is 'an awareness of the relationship between knowledge and specific material and political conditions'. To be reflexive is to subscribe to an approach that is rooted in a historical perspective and thus shows concern with the historicity of globalization. As a result, both presentism and treating globalization as embracing all of world history are avoided. Reflexivity also refers to the interplay between acting *in* the world and awareness that actions have effects *on* the world, as well as on knowledge about it. This insight informs the debate about whether globalization is the cause or consequence of social change and cautions that, while researchers need to be clear about what version of causality they are investigating, there is no simple model of cause and effect at work.

Fifth, globalization research should aspire to a thoroughgoing interdisciplinarity. We have laboured the point that social life cannot be partitioned easily or usefully into discrete zones of experience, and nor should its study. The research examined here demonstrates that, good intentions or not, this is a hard row to hoe and yet it is essential for a critical understanding of the global. As Robinson notes, the 'opposition of political economy to cultural analysis ... is a false dualism that obscures rather than elucidates the complex reality of global society, insofar as our material existence as humans is always, of necessity, only possible through the construction of a symbolic order and systems of meaning' (2005, 16) – so, reflexivity again. Many commentators on globalization understand this intellectually, but they seldom follow through in their research. Instead they reproduce the certainties of methodological territorialism and disciplinary non-recognition.

Sixth is the need for a truly multidimensional approach to globalization-globality; one that does not start from the a priori assumption that one sphere of existence is anterior to, or immanently more powerful for explanatory purposes than, another. It is perhaps obvious that treating cultural and economic factors as mutually constitutive, and their relationship as reflexively ordered, will require stepping outside the usual confines of disciplinary research and risking the jibes of true believers. As we have described, where this has been attempted, approbation is widespread; but take-up in actual empirical research remains very limited.

Seventh, the intuitively appealing idea of mutual constitution needs to be given more purchase through middle-range empirical studies of the kind undertaken by Giulianotti and Robertson (2009). Otherwise it stays as abstract as ever and subject to the same objections mustered against Giddens' structurationist approach to social constitution.

Eighth, much of the above could be entertained and prosecuted through more rigorous attention to what may be the most credible meta-construction of a globalized world: the dialectic between borders, networks and mobilities (Axford, 2007a). A dialectical approach identifies how dimensions of social reality may be analytically separate, yet constitutive of each other as aspects of more 'encompassing process' (Robinson, 2005, 17). Issues of mobility and connectivity are increasingly canvassed when discussing global themes like terrorism, commodity chains, elite mobility and transnational activism.

This approach has three telling advantages. First of all, it expresses the ontology of a globalized world. There is no support for rooting analysis either in analytically separate territorial nationalisms or in the kind of data used in standard cross-national comparisons, both of which just reproduce usual science applied to the global. Second, the dialectic of networks and borders abjures the language of scales and admits the possibility, indeed the existence, of multi-scalar and a-scalar modalities and identities. Because of these two advantages, third, it offers some purchase on ways to theorize and to investigate the interaction of personal and global, long a goal of interdisciplinary theorists and proponents of multidimensional studies of globality.

Finally, globalization as either promise or spectre carries a powerful normative charge. The conflation of normative and empirical-analytical approaches to the study of globalization is something of a feature of research in the field. This does not mean that there is, or can be, a neat disjunction between the two. However understood, globalization takes place in the phenomenal world and its trammels shape consciousness, while affect as well as cognition infuses consciousness and action. Social science must pay due attention to these factors in assessing the promise of new worlds.

Transformation is the most powerful term in the global studies lexicon and means different things to different commentators. It may be interpreted as no more than incremental, possibly secular changes in a set of indicators, or a narrative about the unfolding of different, but routine, processes. Alternatively, transformation may be immanent in the playing out of contested histories, perhaps in the ways in which self-ascribed civilizations brush against each other or collide, as the engines of large-scale change. We might even view it as no more than an ideological rallying cry in the politics of resistance to or support for change; a strategic and normative goal. Meanwhile, all kinds of transformative actions can be buried in the routines of those who reproduce, but also change, their lives in the interstices of larger and sometimes unseen processes. All these should be the stuff of globalization-globality studies, and they are only partly served by contemporary scholarship, for all its richness. Taken in the round, we have a full and compelling agenda for a concept that remains at the core of social-scientific inquiry and progress, rather than one that has been relegated to its margins, or overtaken by the surge of events.

Bibliography

Abbeloos, J-F. and Vanhaute, E. (2011): Cutting the Gordian knot of world history: Giovanni Arrighi's model of the great divergence and convergence. *Journal of World-Systems Research*, xvii(1), 89–106.

Abdelal, R. E. (2007): *Capital Rules: The Construction of Global Finance*. Cambridge, MA: Harvard University Press.

Abrams, P. (1982): *Historical Sociology*. Ithaca, NY: Cornell University Press.

Abu-Lughod, J. (1971): *Cairo: 1001 Years of the City Victorious*. Princeton, NJ: Princeton University Press.

Abu-Lughod, J. (1989): *Before European Hegemony: The World System A.D. 1250–1350*. New York, NY: Oxford University Press.

Abu-Lughod, J. (2007): The challenge of comparative case studies. *City*, 11(3), 399–404.

Adam, B. (1994): Perceptions of time. In T. Ingold (ed.), *Companion Encyclopedia of Anthropology: Humanity, Culture and Social Life*. London: Routledge.

Adams, J., Clemens, E. and Shola Orloff, A. (2003): *Social Theory, Modernity, and the Three Waves of Historical Sociology*. Russell Sage Foundation Working Paper 206.

Adorno, T. W. (ed.) (1991): *The Culture Industry: Selected Essays on Mass Culture*. London: Routledge.

Adorno, T. W., Albert, H., Dahrendorf, R., Habermas, J., Pilot, H. and Popper, K. R. (1976) [1969]: *The Positivist Dispute in German Sociology* (trans. G. Adey and D. Frisby). London: Heinemann.

Agamben, G. (1998): *Homo Sacer: Sovereign Power and Bare Life* (trans. D. Heller-Roazen). Palo Alto, CA: Stanford University Press.

Agamben, G. (2005): *State of Exception* (trans. K. Attell). Chicago, IL: University of Chicago Press.

Agnew, J. (1994): The territorial trap: The geographical assumptions of international relations theory. *Review of International Political Economy*, 1(1), 55–71.

Agnew, J. (2005): *Hegemony: The New Shape of Global Power*. Philadelphia, PA: Temple University Press.

Agnew, J. (2009): *Globalization and Sovereignty*. Lanham MD: Rowman and Littlefield.

Ajami, F. (1993): The summoning. *Foreign Affairs*, 72(4), 2–9.

Ajami, F. (2006): *The Foreigner's Gift: The Americans, the Arabs and the Iraqis in Iraq*. New York, NY: Free Press.

Albert, M. (2007): Globalization theory: Yesterday's fad or more lively than ever? *International Political Sociology*, 1(3), 165–82.

Albert, M. (2009): Globalization and world society theory: A reply. *International Political Sociology*, 3(1), 126–8.

Albert, M., Jacobson, D. and Lapid, J. (eds.) (2001): *Identities, Borders, Orders: Rethinking International Relations Theory.* Minneapolis, MN: University of Minnesota Press.

Albrow, M. (1996): *The Global Age: State and Society Beyond Modernity.* Cambridge: Polity.

Albrow, M. (2007a): A new decade of the global age, 1996–2006. *Globality Studies Journal,* 8.

Albrow, M. (2007b): Situating global social relations. In I. Rossi (ed.), *Frontiers of Globalization Research: Theoretical and Methodological Approaches.* New York, NY: Springer.

Al-e Ahmad, J. (1962): *Occidentosis: A Plague from the West.* Paris: Clandestine.

Amin, A. (2002): Spatialities of globalisation. *Environment and Planning A,* 34(3) 385–99.

Amin, A. and Thrift, N. (1997): *Globalization, Institutions, and Regional Development in Europe.* Oxford: Oxford University Press.

Amin, S. (1989): *Eurocentrism.* New York, NY: Monthly Review Press.

Anderson, B. (1983): *Imagined Communities.* London: Verso.

Anderson, P. (1974): *Lineages of the Absolutist State.* London: New Left Books.

Anderson, P. (2000): Renewals. *New Left Review,* 1(1), 5–24.

Anderson-Gold, S. (2001): *Cosmopolitanism and Human Rights.* Chicago, IL: University of Chicago Press.

Anheier, H., Kaldor, M. and Glasius, M. (eds.) (2005): *Global Civil Society 2004/5.* London: Sage.

Antonio, R.J. (2007): The cultural construction of neo-liberal globalization. In G. Ritzer (ed.), *The Blackwell Companion to Globalization.* Malden, MA: Blackwell.

Appadurai, A. (1990): Disjuncture and difference in the global cultural economy. In M. Featherstone (ed.), *Global Culture: Nationalism, Globalization and Modernity.* London: Sage.

Appadurai, A. (1993): *The Production of Locality.* Paper presented at the ASA IV Decennial Conference, Oxford, July.

Appadurai, A. (1998): *Modernity at Large: Cultural Dimensions of Globalization.* Minneapolis, MN: University of Minnesota Press.

Appadurai, A. (2006): *Fear of Small Numbers: An Essay on the Geography of Anger.* New York, NY: Columbia University Press.

Appelbaum, R. and Robinson, W. I. (eds.) (2005): *Critical Globalization Studies.* London: Routledge.

Appiah, K. (2006): *Cosmopolitanism: Ethics in a World of Strangers.* London: Allen Lane.

Archer, M. (1988): *Culture and Agency: The Place of Culture in Social Theory.* Cambridge: Cambridge University Press.

Archer, M. (2007): Social integration, system integration and global governance. In I. Rossi (ed.), *Frontiers of Globalization Research: Theoretical and Methodological Approaches.* New York: Springer.

Archibugi, D. (2008a): *The Global Commonwealth of Citizens: Towards Cosmopolitan Democracy.* Princeton, NJ: Princeton University Press.

Archibugi, D. (2008b): A league of democracies or a democratic United Nations? *Harvard International Review,* 30(2).

Archibugi, D. and Held, D. (2011): *Cosmopolitan Democracy: Paths and Agents.* Paper presented at the ISA Annual Convention, Montreal, 16–19 March.

Archibugi, D., Koenig-Archibugi, M. and Marchetti, R. (eds.) (2011): *Global Democracy: Normative and Empirical Perspectives.* Cambridge: Cambridge University Press.

Ardener, E. (1989): The construction of history: 'Vestiges of creation'. In E. Tonkin, M. MacDonald and M. Chapman (eds.), *History and Ethnicity.* London: Routledge.

Arjomand, S. and Tiryakian, E. (eds.) (2004): _Rethinking Civilizational Analysis_. London: Sage.

Arnason, J. (1989): Civilization, culture and power: Reflections on Norbert Elias' genealogy of the West. _Thesis_, 11(24), 44–70.

Arnason, J. (2003): _Civilizations in Dispute: Historical Questions and Theoretical Traditions_. Leiden: Brill.

Arnason, J. (2008): Civilizational analysis: A paradigm in the making. In _Encyclopedia of Life Support Systems_, at http://www.eolss.net/Eolss-sampleAllChapter.aspx

Arnason, J. P., Eisenstadt, S. N. and Wittrock, B. (eds.) (2005): _Axial Civilizations and World History_. Leiden: Brill.

Arrighi, G. (1994): _The Long Twentieth Century: Money, Power and the Origins of Our Times_. London: Verso.

Arrighi, G. (2005): Hegemony unravelling: 1. _New Left Review_, 32.

Arrighi, G. (2007): _Adam Smith in Beijing: Lineages of the Twenty-First Century_. London: Verso.

Arrighi, G. and Zhang, L. (2009): Beyond the Washington consensus: A new Bandung? In J. Shefner and P. Fernandez Kelly (eds.), _Globalization and Beyond: New Examinations of Global Power and Its Alternatives_. Pittsburgh, PA: Penn State University Press.

Axford, B. (1995): _The Global System: Economics, Politics and Culture_. Cambridge: Polity.

Axford, B. (1999): Globalization. In A. Halcli, G. K. Browning and F. Webster (eds.), _Understanding Contemporary Society_. London: Sage.

Axford, B. (2001): The transformation of politics or anti-politics. In B. Axford and R. Huggins (eds.), _New Media and Politics_. London: Sage.

Axford, B. (2004): Global civil society or networked globality? _Globalizations_, 1(2), 249–65.

Axford, B. (2005): Critical globalization studies and a network perspective on global civil society. In R. Appelbaum and W. Robinson (eds.), _Critical Globalization Studies_. London: Routledge.

Axford, B. (2006): The dialectic of borders and networks in Europe: Reviewing 'topological presuppositions'. _Comparative European Politics_, 4(2), 160–82.

Axford, B. (2007a): In at the death? Reflections on Justin Rosenberg's 'post-mortem' on globalization. _Globalizations_, 4(2), 171–91.

Axford, B. (2007b): Editorial. Special issue: _Borders and Networks in the Global System. Globalizations_, 4(3), 321–7.

Axford, B. (2009): Network Europe and the information society. In C. Rumford (ed.), _The Sage Handbook of European Studies_. London: Sage.

Axford, B. (2012): Mere connection: Do communication flows compensate for the lack of world society? In G. Peter and R. M. Krausse (eds.), _Selbstbeobachtung der Modernen Gesellschaft und die neuen Grenzen des Soczialen_. Frankfurt: Springer.

Axford, B. and Huggins, R. (2007): The European information society: A new public sphere? In C. Rumford (ed.), _Cosmopolitanism and Europe_. Liverpool: Liverpool University Press.

Axford, B. and Huggins, R. (2010): The telemediatization of cricket: Commerce, connectivity and culture in the post-television age. In C. Rumford and S. Wagg (eds.), _Cricket and Globalization_. Newcastle: Cambridge Scholars.

Axford, B. and Huggins, R. (eds.) (2011): _Cultures and/of Globalization_. Newcastle: Cambridge Scholars.

Axtmann, R. (ed.) (2003): _Understanding Democratic Politics: Concepts, Institutions, Movements_. London: Sage.

Baba, M. and Hill, C. (2006): The globalization of anthropology. *NAPA Bulletin*, 25(1), 1–13.

Badie, B. and Birnbaum, P. (1983): *The Sociology of the State*. Chicago, IL: University of Chicago Press.

Balibar, E. (1999): *Europe as Borderland*. The Alexander von Humboldt Lecture in Human Geography, University of Nijmegen, Netherlands.

Ballantyne, T. (ed.) (2002): *Orientalism, Racial Theory and British Colonialism*. London: Palgrave.

Barber, B. (1995): *Jihad vs. McWorld*. New York, NY: Times Books.

Barber, B. (2007): *Consumed: How Markets Corrupt Children, Infantilize Adults and Swallow Citizens Whole*. New York, NY: Norton.

Barrett, D. and Kurzman, C. (2004): Globalizing social movement theory: The case of eugenics. *Theory and Society*, 33, 487–527.

Barry, A. (2001): *Political Machines: Governing a Technological Society*. London: Athlone Press.

Bartelson, J. (2009a): *Visions of World Community*. Cambridge: Cambridge University Press.

Bartelson, J. (2009b): Is there a global society? *International Political Sociology*, 3(1), 112–15.

Bauman, Z. (1998): *Globalization: The Human Consequences*. New York, NY: Columbia University Press.

Bauman, Z. (2000): *Liquid Modernity*. Cambridge: Polity.

Bauman, Z. (2005): *Liquid Life*. Cambridge: Polity.

Bayart, J-F. (2007): *Global Subjects: A Political Critique of Globalization*. Cambridge: Polity.

Bayly, C. (2002): 'Archaic' and 'modern' globalization. In A. G. Hopkins (ed.), *Globalization in World History*. New York, NY: Norton.

Beck, U. (1992): *Risk Society: Towards a New Modernity*. London: Sage.

Beck, U. (1996a): *The Reinvention of Politics: Rethinking Modernity in the Global Social Order*. Cambridge: Polity.

Beck, U. (1996b): *What is Globalization?* Cambridge: Polity.

Beck, U. (2005): *Power in the Global Age*. Cambridge: Polity.

Beck, U. (2006): *Cosmopolitan Vision*. Cambridge: Polity.

Beck, U. (2008): *World at Risk*. Cambridge: Polity.

Beck, U. and Beck-Gernsheim, E. (2002): *Individualization: Institutionalized Individualism and its Social and Political Consequences*. London: Sage.

Beck, U. and Grande, E. (2007): *Cosmopolitan Europe*. Cambridge: Polity.

Beck, U. and Grande, E. (2010): Varieties of second modernity: extra-European and European experiences and perspectives. *British Journal of Sociology*, 61(3), 406–638.

Beck, U. and Lau, C. (2005): Second modernity as a research agenda: Theoretical and empirical explorations in the 'meta-change' of modern society. *British Journal of Sociology*, 56(4), 525–57.

Beck, U. and Sznaider, N. (2006): Unpacking cosmopolitanism for the social sciences: A research agenda. *British Journal of Sociology*, 57(1), 1–23.

Beck, U. and Willms, J. (2003): *Conversations with Ulrich Beck*. Cambridge: Polity.

Becker, G. (1976): *The Economic Approach to Human Behavior*. Chicago, IL: University of Chicago Press.

Bell, D. (2003): Globalization and history: Reflections on temporality. *International Affairs*, 79(4), 801–15.

Bello, W. (2002): *De-Globalization: Ideas for a New World Economy*. London: Zed Books.

Bello, W. (2008): *Dark Victory: The United States and Global Poverty*. Amsterdam: Transnational Institute.

Benhabib, S. (2002): Unholy wars. *Constellations*, 9(1), 34–45.

Benhabib, S. (2005): Is European multiculturalism a paper tiger? *Philosophia Africana*, 8(2), 111–15.

Bennison, A. K. (2002). Muslim universalism and Western globalization. In A. G. Hopkins (ed.), *Globalization in World History*. New York, NY: Norton.

Berger, J. and Huntington, S. (eds.) (2002): *Many Globalizations: Cultural Diversity in the Contemporary World*. Oxford: Oxford University Press.

Bergesen, A. (1990): Turning world-system theory on its head. *Media, Culture and Society*, 7(2), 67–83.

Berkovich, N. (1999): *From Motherhood to Citizenship: Women's Rights and International Organizations*. Baltimore, MD: Johns Hopkins University Press.

Berry, C. (2008): *International Political Economy, the Globalisation Debate and the Analysis of Globalisation Discourse*. Working Paper, University of Warwick, Centre for the Study of Globalisation and Regionalisation, Coventry.

Bhabha, H. (1989): *The Location of Culture*. London: Routledge.

Bhabha, H. (1990): *Nation and Narration*. London: Routledge.

Bhabha, H. (2005): Interview on *Towards a Global Cultural Citizenship*. *Hindu Literary Review*, 3 July.

Bhagwati, J. (2005): *In Defence of Globalization*. New York, NY: Oxford University Press.

Bhaskar, R. (1998): *The Possibility of Naturalism* (3rd edition), London: Routledge.

Billig, M. (1995): *Banal Nationalism*. London: Sage.

Blaut, J. M. (1993): *The Colonizer's Model of the World: Geographical Diffusionism and Eurocentric History*. New York, NY: Guilford.

Boli, J. (1989): *New Citizens for a New Society: The Institutional Origins of Mass Schooling in Sweden*. Oxford: Pergamon.

Boli, J. and Lechner, F. (2005): *World Culture: Origins and Consequences*. Malden, MA: Blackwell.

Boli, J. and Petrova, V. (2007): Globalization today. In G. Ritzer (ed.), *The Blackwell Companion to Globalization*. Malden, MA: Blackwell.

Boli, J. and Thomas, G. (1999): *Constructing World Culture: International Nongovernmental Organizations since 1875*. Stanford, CA: Stanford University Press.

Boli, J., Thomas, G., Meyer, J. W. and Ramirez, F. (eds.) (1987): *Institutional Structure: Constituting State, Society and the Individual*. Beverly Hills, CA: Sage.

Bourdieu, P. (1977): *Outline of a Theory of Practice*. Cambridge: Cambridge University Press.

Bourdieu, P. (1991): *Language and Symbolic Power*. Cambridge, MA: Harvard University Press.

Braudel, F. (1979): *Civilisation matérielle, économie et capitalisme, 15e–18e siècle* (trans. S. Reynolds, 3 vols.). Paris: Armand Colin.

Braudel, F. (1981–94): *Civilization and Capitalism* (3 vols.). London: Collins.

Breidenbach, J. and Zukrigl, I. (2000): Cultural battle or McWorld? *Deutschland*, 3, 40–3.

Brenner, N. (1998): Global cities, glocal states: Global city formation and state territorial restructuring in contemporary Europe. *Review of International Political Economy*, 5(2), 1–37.

Brenner, N. (1999): Beyond state-centrism? Space, territoriality and scale in globalization studies. *Theory and Society*, 28, 39–78.

Brenner, N. (2001): The limits to scale: Methodological reflections on scalar structuration. *Progress in Human Geography*, 25(4), 591–614.

Brenner, N. (2004): *New State Spaces, Urban Governance and the Rescaling of Statehood*. Oxford: Oxford University Press.

Brenner, N. and Elden, S. (2009): Henri Lefebvre on state, space, territory. *International Political Sociology*, 3, 353–77.

Brenner, R. (1977): The origins of capitalist development: A critique of neo-Smithian Marxism. *New Left Review*, 104, 25–92.

Broad, R. (2002): *Global Backlash: Citizen Initiatives for a Just World Economy*. Lanham, MD: Rowman and Littlefield.

Brown, C. (2007): Reimagining international society and global community. In D. Held and A. McGrew (eds.), *Globalization Theory: Approaches and Controversies*. Cambridge: Polity.

Browning, G.K. (2005): A globalist ideology of post-Marxism? Hardt and Negri's *Empire*. *Critical Review of International Social and Political Philosophy*, 8(2), 193–208.

Browning, G.K. (2011): *Global Theory from Kant to Hardt and Negri*. Basingstoke: Palgrave.

Bruff, I. (2005): Making sense of the globalisation debate when engaging in political economy analysis. *British Journal of Politics and International Relations*, 7(2), 261–80.

Bruff, I. and Tepe, D. (2011): What is critical IPE? *Journal of International Relations and Development*, 14(3), 354–8.

Buchanan, J. (1969): *The Collected Works of James M. Buchanan. Vol. 6: Cost and Choice: An Inquiry in Economic Theory*. Indianapolis, IN: Liberty Fund.

Bulkeley, H.A. (2005): Reconfiguring environmental governance: Towards a politics of scales and networks. *Political Geography*, 24, 875–902.

Bull, H. (1968): Strategic studies and its critics. *World Politics*, 20(4), 593–605.

Bull, H. (1977): *The Anarchical Society: A Study of Order in World Politics*. London: Macmillan.

Bull, H. (1990): The importance of Grotius in the study of international relations. In H. Bull, B. Kingsbury and A. Roberts (eds.), *Hugo Grotius and International Relations*. Oxford: Clarendon.

Buzan, B. (2004): *From International to World Society? English School Theory and the Social Structure of Globalisation*. Cambridge: Cambridge University Press.

Buzan, B. (2010): Globalization and identity: Is world society possible? *Journal of Zhejiang University (Humanities and Social Sciences)*, 40(5), 5–14.

Callinicos, A. (2002): *Against the Third Way*. Cambridge: Polity.

Callinicos, A. (2003): *New Mandarins of American Power: The Bush Administration's Plans for the World*. Cambridge: Polity.

Callinicos, A. (2005): Imperialism and global political economy. *International Socialism*, 108.

Callinicos, A. (2007): Does capitalism need the state system? *Cambridge Review of International Affairs*, 20(4), 533–49.

Callinicos, A. (2009): *Imperialism and Global Political Economy*. Cambridge: Polity.

Callinicos, A. (2010): *Bonfire of Illusions: The Twin Crises of the Liberal World*. Cambridge: Polity.

Cameron, A. and Palan, R. (2004): *Imagined Economies of Globalization*. London: Sage.

Campbell, D. (1995): Political prosaics, transversal politics and the anarchical world. In M. Shapiro and H. Alker (eds.), *Challenging Boundaries: Global Flows, Territorial Identities*. Minneapolis MN: University of Minnesota Press.

Carr, E.H. (1961): *What is History?* Harmondsworth: Penguin.

Caselli, M. (2008): Measuring . . . what? Notes on some globalization indices. *Globalizations*, 5(3), 383–404.

Castells, M. (1989): *The Informational City: Information Technology, Economic Restructuring, and the Urban Regional Process*. Oxford: Blackwell.

Castells, M. (1991): *The Informational City* (paperback edition). Oxford: Blackwell.

Castells, M. (2000a) [1996]: *The Information Age: Economy, Society and Culture. Vol. I: The Rise of the Network Society* (2nd edition). Oxford: Wiley-Blackwell.

Castells, M. (2000b) [1998]: *The Information Age: Economy, Society and Culture. Vol. III End of Millennium*. Oxford: Wiley-Blackwell.

Castells, M. (2001): European unification in the age of the network state. *Open Democracy*, at http://www.ucc.ie/social_policy/Castell_European_Unification.htm

Castells, M. (2004a) [1997]: *The Information Age: Economy, Society and Culture. Vol. II: The Power of Identity*. Oxford: Wiley-Blackwell.

Castells, M. (ed.) (2004b): *The Network Society: A Cross-Cultural Perspective*. Cheltenham: Edward Elgar.

Castells, M. (2006): *Mobile Communication and Society: A Global Perspective*. Cambridge, MA: MIT Press.

Castells, M. (2008): The new public sphere: Global civil society, communication networks, and global governance. *Annals of the American Academy of Political and Social Science*, 616(1), 78–93.

Castells, M. (2009): *Communication Power*. Oxford: Oxford University Press.

Cerny, P. (1999): Globalising the political and politicising the global: Concluding Reflections on international political economy as a vocation. *New Political Economy*, 4(1), 147–62.

Cerny, P. (2010): *Rethinking World Politics: A Theory of Transnational Neopluralism*. Oxford: Oxford University Press.

Chandhoke, N. (2005): How global is global civil society? *Journal of World Systems Research*, XI(2), 355–71.

Chandler, D. (2004): Building global civil society 'from below'? *Millennium: Journal of International Studies*, 33, 313–39.

Chandler, D. (2007): Deriving norms from 'global space': The limits of cosmopolitan approaches to global civil society theorizing. *Globalizations*, 4(2), 283–98.

Chandler, D. (2009): Critiquing liberal cosmopolitanism? The limits of the biopolitical approach. *International Political Sociology*, 3(1), 53–70.

Chandler, D. (2010): *International Statebuilding: The Rise of Post-Liberal Governance*. Abingdon: Routledge.

Chandler, D. and Baker, G. (2005): *Global civil Society: Contested Futures*. Abingdon: Routldege.

Chase-Dunn, C. (1989): Comparing world-systems: Toward a theory of semiperipheral development. *Comparative Civilizations Review*, 19, 29–66.

Chase-Dunn, C. (1992): Theoretical approaches to world-systems analysis. In C. Polychroniou (ed.), *Perspectives and Issues in International Political Economy*. Westport, CT: Praeger.

Chase-Dunn, C. (1998): *Global Formation: Structures of the World-Economy* (2nd edition). New York, NY: Rowman and Littlefield.

Chase-Dunn, C. (2007): Sociocultural evolution and the future of world society. *World Futures*, 63(5–6), 408–24.

Chase-Dunn, C. and Boswell, T. (2000): *Spiral of Capitalism and Socialism: Towards Global Democracy*. Boulder, CO: Lynne Rienner.

Chase-Dunn, C. and Gills, B. (2005): Waves of globalization and resistance in the capitalist world system: Social movements and critical globalization studies. In R. Appelbaum and W. Robinson (eds.), *Critical Globalization Studies*. London: Routledge.

Chaudhuri, K.N. (1990): *Asia before Europe: Economy and Civilisation of the Indian Ocean From the Rise of Islam to 1750*. Cambridge: Cambridge University Press.

Cheah, P. (2006): *Inhuman Conditions: On Cosmopolitanism and Human Rights*. Cambridge, MA: Harvard University Press.

Chernilo, D. (2006): Social theory's methodological nationalism: Myth and reality? *European Journal of Social Theory*, 9, 5–22.

Clark, I. (2003): Legitimacy in a global order. *Review of International Studies*, 29, 75–95.

Clark, I. (2011): *Hegemony in International Society*. Oxford: Oxford University Press.

Clifford, J. (1988): *The Predicament of Culture: Twentieth Century Ethnography, Literature and Art*. Cambridge, MA: Harvard University Press.

Cohen, B. (2007): The transatlantic divide: Why are American and British IPE so different? *Review of International Political Economy*, 14(2), 197–219.

Cohen, B. (2008): *International Political Economy: An Intellectual History*. Princeton, NJ: Princeton University Press.

Cohen, B. (2009): *Currency and State Power*. Paper prepared for a conference to honour Stephen D. Krasner, Stanford University, 4–5 December.

Cohen, R. (2007): Creolization and cultural globalization: The soft sounds of fugitive power. *Globalizations*, 4(2), 369–85.

Colas, A. (2005): Imperious civility: Violence and the dilemmas of global civil society. *Contemporary Politics*, 11(2–3).

Colas, A. (2007): *Empire*. Cambridge: Polity.

Connolly, W. (2002): *Neuropolitics: Thinking, Culture, Speed*. Minneapolis, MN: University of Minnesota Press.

Corbridge, S. and Agnew, J. (1995): *Mastering Space: Hegemony, Territory and International Political Economy*. London: Routledge.

Cowen, T. (2002): *How Globalization is Changing the World's Cultures*. Princeton, NJ: Princeton University Press.

Cox, K., Low, M. and Robinson, J. (eds.) (2008): *The Sage Handbook of Political Geography*. London: Sage.

Cox, M. and Quinn, A. (2008): Hard times for soft power? America and the Atlantic community. In D. Held and H. L. Moore, *Cultural Politics in the Global Age*. London: One World.

Cox, R.W. (1981): Social forces, states and world orders: Beyond international relations theory. *Millennium: Journal of International Studies*, 10(2), 126–55.

Cox, R.W. (1987): *Production, Power and World Order: Social Forces and the Making of History*. New York, NY: Columbia University Press.

Cox, R.W. (1989): Production, the state and change in world order. In E. Czempiel and J. N. Rosenau (eds.), *Global Changes and Theoretical Challenges*. Toronto: Maxwell Macmillan.

Cox, R.W. (1993): The global political economy and social choice. In S. Gill (ed.), *Gramsci, Historical Materialism and International Relations*. Cambridge: Cambridge University Press.

Crack, A. (2007): Transcending borders? Reassessing public spheres in a networked world. *Globalizations*, 4(3), 241–54.

Crack, A. (2008): *Global Communication and Transnational Public Spheres*. New York, NY: Palgrave.

Crossley, P. (2008): *What is Global History?* Cambridge: Polity.

Cutler, A.C. (1999): Private authority in international trade relations: The case of maritime transport. In C. Cutler, D. Haufler and M. Porter (eds.), *Private Authority and International Affairs*. London: Routledge.

Cutler, A.C. (2003): *Private Power and Global Authority: Transnational Merchant Law in the Global Political Economy*. Cambridge: Cambridge University Press.

Cutler, A.C. (2005): Critical globalization studies and international law under conditions of postmodernity and late capitalism. In W. Robinson and R. Applebaum (eds.), *Critical Globalization Studies*. New York, NY: Routledge.

Dahl, R. (1963): *Who Governs? Democracy and Power in the American City*. New Haven, CT: Yale University Press.

Delanty, G. (2005) [1997]: *Social Science: Philosophical and Methodological Foundations* (2nd edition). Minneapolis, MN: University of Minnesota Press.

Delanty, G. (2006): The cosmopolitan imagination: Critical cosmopolitanism and social theory. *British Journal of Sociology*, 57(1), 25–47.

Delanty, G. (2009): *The Cosmopolitan Imagination: The Renewal of Critical Social Theory*. Cambridge: Cambridge University Press.

Denemark, R. (2009): World system history: Arrighi, Frank and the way forward. *Journal of World-System Research*, 15(2), 233–42.

Denemark, R., Friedman, J., Modelski, G. and Gills, B. (2000): *World System History*. London: Routledge.

Der Derian, J. and Shapiro, M. (eds.) (1989): *Intertextual Relations: Postmodern Readings of World Politics*. Washington, DC: Lexington Books.

Derrida, J. (1976): *Of Grammatology* (trans. G. C. Spivak). Baltimore, MD: Johns Hopkins University Press.

Dessler, D. (1989): What's at stake in the agent–structure debate? *International Organization*, 34(3), 441–73.

Deudney, D. (1999): Regrounding realism: Anarchy, security and changing material contexts. *Security Studies*, 10(1), 1–45.

Devezas, T., Modelski, G. and Thompson, W. R. (eds.) (2007): *Globalization as an Evolutionary Process*. Abingdon: Routledge.

Dicken, P. (2011): *Global Shift: Mapping the Changing Contours of the World Economy* (6th edition). London: Guilford.

Dicken, P., Kelly, P.F., Olds, K. and Wai-Chung Yeung, H. (2001): Chains and networks, territories and scales: Towards a relational framework for analysing the global economy. *Global Networks*, I(2), 89–112.

Dobson, A. (2006): Thick cosmopolitanism. *Political Studies*, 54, 165–84.

Drainville, R. (1994): International political economy in the age of open Marxism. *Review of International Political Economy*, 1(1), 105–32.

Drainville, R. (2004): *Contesting Globalization: Space and Place in the World Economy*. London: Routledge.

Drori, G.S., Meyer, J.W., Ramirez, F. and Schofer, E. (2003): *Science in the Modern World Polity: Institutionalization and Globalization*. Palo Alto, CA: Stanford University Press.

Drori, G. S., Meyer, J. W. and Hwang, H. (eds.) (2006): *Globalization and Organization: World Society and Organizational Change*. Oxford: Oxford University Press.

Durkheim, E. (1912): *The Elementary Forms of Religious Life* (trans C. Cosman). Oxford: Oxford University Press.

Dustin, D. (2007): *The McDonaldisation of Social Work*. Aldershot: Ashgate.

Eade, J. (ed.) (1997): *Living the Global City*. London: Routledge.

Easton, D. (1969): The new revolution in political science. *American Political Science Review*, LX111(4), 1051–73.

Eckholm, K. and Friedman, J. (2008): *Modernities, Class, and the contradictions of Globalization: The Anthropology of Global Systems*. Los Angeles, CA: Altamira Press.

Edkins, J. and Vaughn-Williams, N. (eds.) (2009): *Critical Theorists in International Relations*. London: Routledge.

Edwards, M. (ed.) (2011): *The Oxford Handbook of Civil Society*. Oxford: Oxford University Press.

Eisenstadt, S. M. (ed.) (1986): *The Origins and Diversity of Axial Age Civilizations*. Albany, NY: State University of New York Press.

Eisenstadt, S.M. (1987): *European Civilization in Comparative Perspective*. Oslo: Scandinavian University Press.

Eisenstadt, S.M. (1996): *Japanese Civilization: A Comparative View*. Chicago, IL: University of Chicago Press.

Eisenstadt, S.M. (1998): Modernity and the construction of collective identities. *International Journal of Comparative Sociology*, 39(1), 13–58.

Eisenstadt, S.M. (2000): Multiple modernities. *Daedalus*, 129, 86–104.

Eisenstadt, S.M. (2004): The dialogue between cultures or between cultural interpretations of modernity: Multiple modernities on the contemporary scene. *Protosociology*, 20, 201–17.

Eisenstadt, S.M. (2006): Cultural models and political systems. *European Journal of Political Research*, 34(1), 1–22.

Eisenstadt, S.M. (2009): Contemporary globalization, New intercivilizational visions and hegemonies: Transformation of nation-states. *Protosociology*, 26, 7–19.

Elias, N. (1969): *The Civilizing Process. Vol. I: The History of Manners*. Oxford: Blackwell.

Elias, N. (1982): *The Civilizing Process. Vol. II: State Formation and Civilization*. Oxford: Blackwell.

Elias, N. (1994): *Reflections on a Life* (trans. E. Jephcott). Cambridge: Polity.

Elster, J. (1989): *The Cement of Society: A Study of Social Order*. Cambridge: Cambridge University Press.

Esping-Andersen, G. (1990): *The Three Worlds of Welfare Capitalism*. Princeton, NJ: Princeton University Press.

Esping-Andersen, G. (1999): *Social Foundations of Postindustrial Economies*. Oxford: Oxford University Press.

Evans, P., Rueschemeyer, D. and Skocpol, T. (eds.) (1985): *Bringing the State Back In: New Perspectives on the State as Institution and Social Actor*. Cambridge: Cambridge University Press.

Falk, R. (1995): *On Humane Governance: Toward a New Global Politics – The World Order Models Project Report of the Global Civilization Initiative*. Pittsburgh, PA: Penn State University Press.

Falk, R. (1999): *Predatory Globalization: A Critique*. Cambridge: Polity.

Falk, R. (2001): *Human Rights Horizons: The Pursuit of Justice in a Globalizing World*. London: Routledge.

Falk, R. (2002): *Reframing the International: Law, Culture, Politics*. London: Routledge.

Falk, R. (2005): Reimagining the governance of globalization. In R. Appelbaum and W. I. Robinson (eds.), *Critical Globalization Studies*. London: Routledge.

Featherstone, M. (1990): Global culture: An introduction. *Theory, Culture and Society*, 7, 1–14.

Featherstone, M. (2006): Genealogies of the global. *Theory, Culture and Society*, 23(2–3), 387–419.

Ferguson, N. (2004): *Colossus: The Rise and Fall of the American Empire*. New York, NY: Basic Books.

Fine, R. (2007): *Cosmopolitanism*. London: Routledge.

Flint, C. and Taylor, P.J. (2007): *Political Geography: World-Economy, Nation-State and Locality* (5th edition). Harlow: Longman.

Fossum, B. and Schlesinger, P. (eds.) (2007): *The European Union and the Public Sphere: A Communicative Space in the Making?* London: Routledge.

Foucault, M. (1970): *The Order of Things*. London: Tavistock.

Foucault, M. (1977): *Discipline and Punish*. London: Allen Lane.

Foucault, M. (2004): *Death and the Labyrinth*. London: Continuum.

Foucault, M. (2006): *The History of Madness*. London: Routledge.

Frank, A.G. (1969a): *Latin America: Underdevelopment or Revolution?* New York, NY: Monthly Review Press.

Frank, A.G. (1969b): *Capitalism and Underdevelopment in Latin America*. New York, NY: Monthly Review Press.

Frank, A.G. (1992): *The Centrality of Central Asia*. Amsterdam: VU University Press.

Frank, A.G. (1998): *Global Economy in the Asian Age*. Berkeley, CA: University of California Press.

Frank, A.G. and Gills, B. (1993): *The World-System: Five Hundred Years or Five Thousand?* London: Routledge.

Fraser, N. (1981): Foucault on modern power: Empirical insights and normative confusions. *Praxis International*, 1(3), 272–87.

Fraser, N. (1987): Rethinking the public sphere: A contribution to the critique of actually existing democracy. In C. Calhoun (ed.), *Habermas and the Public Sphere*. Cambridge MA: MIT Press.

Fraser, N. (1997): *Justice Interruptus: Critical Reflections on the 'Postsocialist' Condition*. New York, NY: Routledge.

Fraser, N. (2003): From discipline to flexibilization: rereading Foucault in the shadow of globalization. *Constellations*, 10(2), 160–71.

Fraser, N. (2008): *Scales of Justice: Reimagining Political Space in a Globalizing World*. New York, NY: Columbia University Press.

Fraser, N. (2009): Feminism, capitalism and the cunning of history. *New Left Review*, 56, 97–117.

Fraser, N. (2010): Will feminism be articulated to the left or to the right? Interview by European Alternatives, at http://mrzine.monthlyreview.org/2010/fraser170410.html

Friedman, J. (1993): Order and disorder in global systems: A sketch. *Social Research*, 60(2), 205–34.

Friedman, J. (2000): Globalization, class and culture in global systems. *Journal of World-Systems Research*, 6(3), 636–56.

Friedman, J. (2006): *Globalization and Violence. Vol. III: Globalizing War and Intervention*. London: Sage.

Friedman, J. (2007): *Modernities, Class and the Contradictions of Globalization*. Walnut Creek, CA: Altamira Press.

Friedman, J. and Randeira, S. (2004): *Worlds on the Move: Globalization, Migration and Cultural Security*. London: Tauris.

Friedman, T. (1999): *The Lexus and the Olive Tree: Understanding Globalization*. New York, NY: Anchor Books.

Friedman, T. (2005): *The World Is Flat: A Brief History of the Twenty-First Century*. New York, NY: Anchor Books.

Friedman, T. and Chase-Dunn, C. (eds.) (2005): *Hegemonic Declines: Present and Past*. Boulder, CO: Paradigm Press.

Friedman, T., Denemark, R., Gills, B. and Modelski, G. (2000): *World System History: The Science of Long Term Change*. London: Routledge.

Fukuyama, F. (1992): *The End of History and the Last Man*. New York, NY: Free Press.

Fukuyama, F. (1996): *Trust: The Social Virtues and the Creation of Prosperity*. New York, NY: Free Press.

Fukuyama, F. (2011): *The Origins of Political Order: From Prehuman Times to the French Revolution*. New York, NY: Profile.

Gaventa, J. and Edwards, M. (2006): *Global citizen action*. Boulder CO: Lynne Rienner.

Geertz, C. (1973): *The Interpretation of Cultures*. New York, NY: Basic Books.

George, J. (1994): *Discourses of Global Politics: A Critical (Re)Introduction to International Relations*. Boulder, CO: Lynne Rienner.

George, S. (2004): *Another World Is Possible, If . . .* London: Verso.

Giddens, A. (1984): *The Constitution of Society: Outline of the Theory of Structuration*. Cambridge: Polity.

Giddens, A. (1990): *The Consequences of Modernity*. Cambridge: Polity.

Giddens, A. (1992): *The Transformation of Intimacy: Sexuality, Love and Eroticism in Modern Societies*. Cambridge: Polity.

Giddens, A. (1997): *The Third Way: The Renewal of Social Democracy*. Cambridge: Polity.

Giddens, A. (1999): *Runaway World: How Globalization is Reshaping Our Lives*. London: Profile.

Gill, S. (1990): Hegemonic leadership, transnational capital and global order. In D. Rapkin (ed.), *International Political Economy Yearbook, 1990: World Leadership and Hegemony*. Boulder, CO: Lynne Rienner.

Gill, S. (1995): The global panopticon? The neo-liberal state, economic life and democratic surveillance. *Alternatives*, 20, 1–49.

Gill, S. (2000): *The Constitution of Global Capitalism*. Paper presented at the International Studies Association Convention, Chicago.

Gill, S. (2008): *Power and Resistance in the New World Order* (2nd edition). London: Palgrave Macmillan.

Gill, S. (2009): *American Hegemony and the Trilateral Commission*. Cambridge. Cambridge University Press.

Gill, S. and Law, D. (1988): *The Global Political Economy: Perspectives, Problems and Policies*. Brighton: Harvester Wheatsheaf.

Gills, B. (ed.) (2010): *Globalization in Crisis: Rethinking Globalizations*. London: Routledge.

Gills, B. and Thompson, W. R. (eds.) (2006): *Globalization and Global History*. London: Routledge.

Gilpin, R. (1987): *The Political Economy of International Relations*. Princeton, NJ: Princeton University Press.

Gilpin, R. (2000): *The Challenge of Global Capitalism*. Princeton, NJ: Princeton University Press.

Gilpin, R. (2001): *Global Political Economy: Understanding the International Economic Order*. Princeton, NJ: Princeton University Press.

Gilroy, P. (1994): Black cultural politics: An interview with Paul Gilroy by Timmy Lott. *Found Object*, 4, 46–81.

Ginzberg, C. (1980): *The Cheese and the Worms: The Cosmos of a Sixteenth Century Miller*. Baltimore, MD: Johns Hopkins University Press.

Ginzberg, C. (1983): *The Night Battles: Witchcraft and Agrarian Cults in the Sixteenth and Seventeenth Centuries*. Baltimore, MD: Johns Hopkins University Press.

Giulianotti, R. and Robertson, R. (2006). Futbol, globalizacion y glocalizacion: Un analisis sociologico del juego mundial. *Revista Internacional di Sociologia*, LXIV(45), 9–35.

Giulianotti, R. and Robertson, R. (2007): *Globalization and Sport*. Oxford: Blackwell.

Giulianotti, R. and Robertson, R. (2009): *Globalization and Football*. London: Sage.

Glasius, M., Kaldor, M. and Anheier, H. (eds.) (2006): *Global Civil Society 2005/6*. London: Sage.

Glatzer, M. and Rueschmeyer, D. (eds.) (2005): *Globalization and the Future of the Welfare State*. Pittsburgh, PA: University of Pittsburgh Press.

Globalizations (2005): Special issue: *Empire or Cosmopolis*, 2(1).

Globalizations (2007): Special issue: *Cultures of Globalization: Coherence, Hybridity, and Contestation*, 4(1).

Globalizations (2010): Special issue: *Globalization and Crisis*, 7(1–2).

Gouldner, A. (1978): *The Two Marxisms*. New York, NY: Oxford University Press.

Gowan, P. (2003): Instruments of empire. *New Left Review*, 21, 147–53.

Gowan, P. (2004): Europe and the new imperialism. *Labour Focus on Eastern Europe*, 75–6, 113–41.

Gramsci, A. (1971): *Selections from the Prison Notebooks*. London: Lawrence and Wishart.

Gray, J. (2000): *The Two Faces of Liberalism*. Cambridge: Polity.

Gray, J. (2001): Goodbye to globalisation. *Guardian*, 27 February at http://www.guardian.co.uk/world/2001/feb/27/globalisation

Gray, J. (2002): *Straw Dogs: Thoughts on Humans and Other Animals*. London: Granta.

Gray, J. (2009): *False Dawn: The Delusions of Global Capitalism*. Cambridge: Polity.

Gregory, D. (2006): Troubling geographies. In N. Castree and D. Gregory (eds.), *David Harvey: A Critical Reader*. Oxford: Blackwell.

Grotius, H. (1925) [1625] *De jure belli ac pacis libri tres [On the Law of War and Peace]* (trans. F. W. Kelsey with A. E. R. Boak and H. A. Sanders). Oxford: Oxford University Press.

Guilhot, N. (2008): The realist gambit: Postwar American political science and the birth of IR theory. *International Political Sociology*, 2(4), 281–304.

Guillen, M.F. (2001): Is globalization civilizing, destructive or feeble? Five key debates in the social science literature. *Annual Review of Sociology*, 235–60.

Gullick, J. (2004): A critical appraisal of Peter Gowan's 'Contemporary intra-core relations and world-systems theory': A capitalist world-empire or U.S.–East Asian geo-economic integration? *Journal of World-Systems Research*, 10(2), 503–15.

Gulmez, D. (2010): Stanford school on sociological institutionalism: A global-cultural approach. *International Political Sociology*, 4(3), 253–70.

Gurvitch, G. (2003): *The Spectrum of Social Time*. Dordrecht: Reidel.

Guzzini, S. and Leander, A. (eds.) (2006): *Constructivism and international Relations: Alexander Wendt and His Critics*. London: Routledge.

Haas, E. (1958): *The Uniting of Europe*. Palo Alto, CA: Stanford University Press.

Haas, E. (1961): International integration: The European and the universal process. *International Organization*, 15(3), 366–92.

Habermas, J. (2001): *The Postnational Constellation*. Cambridge MA: MIT Press.

Habermas, J. (2003): *The Future of Human Nature*. Cambridge: Polity.

Habermas, J. (2006): *The Divided West*. Cambridge: Polity.

Hafez, K. (2007): *The Myth of Media Globalization*. Cambridge: Polity.

Hafner-Burton, E.M. and Tsutsui, K. (2005): Human rights in a globalizing world: The paradox of empty promises. *American Journal of Sociology*, 100(5), 1373–411.

Hall, P.A. and Soskice, D. (2001): *Varieties of Capitalism: The Institutional Foundations of Comparative Advantage*. Oxford: Oxford University Press.

Hall, P.A. and Taylor, R.C.R. (1996): Political science and the three new institutionalisms. *Political Studies*, 44, 936–57.

Hall, R. (1999): *National Collective Identity: Social Constructs and International Systems*. New York, NY: Columbia University Press.

Hall, S. (1971): *People and Culture: A Critique*. Working Papers in Cultural Studies, 1. Birmingham: CCCS.

Hall, S. (1992): The question of cultural identity. In S. Hall, D. Held and T. McGrew (eds.), *Modernity and its Futures*. Cambridge: Polity.

Hall, S. (1996): Cultural studies: Two paradigms. In J. Munns, and E. Ragan (eds.), *A Cultural Studies Reader: History, Theory, Practice*. London: Longman.

Hand, M. and Sandywell, B. (2002): E-topia as cosmopolis or citadel: On the democratizing and de-democratizing logics of the internet, or, towards a critique of the new technological fetishism. *Theory, Culture and Society*, 19(1–2), 197–225.

Hannerz, U. (1992a): *Flows, Boundaries and Hybrids: Keywords in Transnational Anthropology*. Oxford: Transnational Communities Programme.

Hannerz, U. (1992b): *Cultural Complexity: Studies in the Social Organization of Meaning*. New York, NY: Columbia University Press.

Hannerz, U. (1996): *Transnational Connections: Culture, People, Places*. London: Routledge.

Hannerz, U. (2006): Foreign correspondents as flaneurs: Journalists' views of urban life in the global ecumene. In G. H. Lenz, F. Ulfers and A. Dallmann (eds.), *Toward a New Metropolitanism*. Heidelberg: Universitätsverlag Winter.

Hardt, M. and Negri, A. (2000): *Empire*. Cambridge, MA: Harvard University Press.

Hardt, M. and Negri, A. (2004): *Multitude: War and Democracy in the Age of Empire*. New York, NY: Penguin.

Hardt, M. and Negri, A. (2009): *Commonwealth*. Cambridge, MA: Belknap Press of Harvard University Press.

Harris, J. (2005): To be or not to be: The nation-centric world under globalization. *Science and Society*, 69(3), 329–40.

Harris, J. (2006): *The Dialectics of Globalization: Economic and Political Conflict in a Transnational World*. Newcastle: Cambridge Scholars.

Harris, J. (ed.) (2009): *The Nation in the Global Era*. London: Brill.

Harvey, D. (1969): *Explanation in Geography*. London: Edward Arnold.

Harvey, D. (1973): *Social Justice and the City*. London: Edward Arnold.

Harvey, D. (1982): *The Limits to Capital*. Oxford: Blackwell.

Harvey, D. (1985): *Consciousness and the Urban Experience*. Oxford: Blackwell.

Harvey, D. (1989): *The Condition of Postmodernity*. Oxford: Blackwell.

Harvey, D. (2000): *Spaces of Hope*. Edinburgh: Edinburgh University Press.

Harvey, D. (2001): *Spaces of Capital: Towards a Critical Geography*. Edinburgh: Edinburgh University Press.

Harvey, D. (2003): *The New Imperialism*. Oxford: Oxford University Press.

Harvey, D. (2005a): *The New Imperialism* (reissue of Harvey 2003 with an afterword). Oxford: Oxford University Press.

Harvey, D. (2005b): *A Brief History of Neoliberalism*. Oxford: Oxford University Press.

Hay, C. (1999): *The Political Economy of New Labour*. Manchester: Manchester University Press.

Hay, C. (2004): Common trajectories, variable paces, divergent outcomes? Models of European capitalism under conditions of complex economic interdependence. *Review of International Political Economy*, 11(2), 231–62.

Hay, C. (2006): What's globalisation got to do with it? Economic interdependence and the future of European welfare states. *Government and Opposition*, 41(1), 1–23.

Hay, C. (2007): Constructivist institutionalism. In R. A. W. Rhodes, S. Dimaggio Binder and B. Rockman (eds.). *The Oxford Handbook of Political Institutions*. Oxford: Oxford University Press.

Hay, C. and Coates, D. (2002): The internal and external face of New Labour's political economy. *Government and Opposition*, 36(4), 447–71.

Hay, C. and Marsh, D. (eds.) (2000): *Demystifying Globalisation*. London: Macmillan.

Hay, C. and Rosamond, B. (2002): Globalisation, European integration and the discursive construction of economic imperatives. *Journal of European Public Policy*, 9(2), 147–67.

Hay, C. and Smith, N. (2008): Mapping the political discourse of globalisation and European integration in the UK and Ireland empirically. *European Journal of Political Research*, 47(3), 359–82.

Hay, C. and Watson, M. (2003): The discourse of globalisation and the logic of no alternative: Rendering the contingent necessary in the political economy of New Labour. *Policy and Politics*, 31(3), 289–305.

Hayes, D. and Wynyard, R. (eds.) (2002): *The Mcdonaldization of Higher Education*. Westport, CT: Bergin and Garvey.

Held, D. (2003): *Cosmopolitanism: A Defence*. Cambridge: Polity.

Held, D. (2004): *Global Covenant: The Social Democratic Alternative to the Washington Consensus*. Cambridge: Polity.

Held, D. (2005): Principles of the cosmopolitan order. In G. Brock and H. Brighouse (eds.), *The Political Philosophy of Cosmopolitanism*. Cambridge: Cambridge University Press.

Held, D. (2010): *Cosmopolitanism: Ideals and Realities*. Cambridge: Polity.

Held, D. and Archibugi, D. (1995): *Cosmopolitan Democracy: An Agenda for a New World Order*. Cambridge: Polity.

Held, D. and Koenig-Archibugi, M. (eds.) (2005): *Global Governance and Public Accountability*. Oxford: Blackwell.

Held, D. and McGrew, A. (2002): *Globalization/Anti-Globalization* (fully revised 2nd edition 2007). Cambridge: Polity.

Held, D. and McGrew, A. (eds.) (2007): *Globalization Theory: Approaches and Controversies*. Cambridge: Polity.

Held, D. and Moore, H. (eds.) (2008): *Cultural Politics in a Global Age: Uncertainty, Solidarity, and Innovation*. Oxford: Oneworld.

Held, D., Archibugi, D. and Koehler, M. (1998): *Re-Imagining Political Community: Studies in Cosmopolitan Democracy*. Cambridge: Polity.

Held, D., McGrew, A. and Perraton, J. (1999): *Global Transformations: Politics, Economics and Culture*. Cambridge: Polity.

Helmig, J. and Kessler, O. (2007): Space, boundaries and the problem of order: A view from systems theory. *International Political Sociology*, 1(3), 240–56.

Herman, E. S. and McChesney, R. W. (1997): *The Global Media: The New Missionaries of Corporate Capitalism*. Washington, DC: Cassell.

Hicks, J. (1989): *A Market Theory of Money*. Oxford: Oxford University Press.

Hindess, B. and Hirst, P. (1975): *Pre-Capitalist Modes of Production*. London: Routledge and Kegan Paul.

Hirst, P. (2001): *War and Power in the 21st Century*. Cambridge: Polity.

Hirst, P. and Held, D. (2002): Globalisation: The argument of our time. *Open Democracy* debate, 22 January, at http://www.opendemocracy.net/globalization-vision_reflections/article_637.jsp

Hirst, P. and Thompson, G. (1996): *Globalization in Question: The International Economy and the Possibilities*. Cambridge: Polity.

Hirst, P. and Thompson, G. (2000): *Globalization in Question: The International Economy and the Possibilities* (2nd edition). Cambridge: Polity.

Hirst, P., Thompson, G. and Bromley, S. (2009): *Globalization in Question: The International Economy and the Possibilities* (3rd edition). Cambridge: Polity.

Hjavard, S. (2008): The mediatization of society: A theory of the media as agents of social and cultural change. *Nordicom Review*, 29(2), 105–34.

Hobden, S. and Hobson, J. (2002): *The Historical Sociology of International Relations*. Cambridge: Cambridge University Press.

Hobson, J. (2006): East and West in global history. *Theory, Culture and Society*, 23(2–3), 408–10.

Hobson, J. (2007a): Reconstructing international relations through world history: Oriental globalisation and the global dialogic conception of inter-civilisational relations. *International Politics*, 44(4), 414–30.

Hobson, J. (2007b): Deconstructing the Eurocentric Clash of civilizations: De-Westernizing the West by acknowledging the dialogue of civilizations. In M. Hall and P. T. Jackson (eds.), *Civilizational Identity*. New York, NY: Palgrave Macmillan.

Hobson, J., Lawson, G. and Rosenberg, J. (2010): Historical sociology. In R. A. Denemark (ed.), *The International Studies Encyclopedia. Vol. 6*. Oxford: Wiley-Blackwell.

Holton, R. (2005): *Making Globalization*. London: Palgrave.

Holton, R. (2008): *Global Networks*. London: Palgrave.

Holton, R. (2009): *Cosmopolitanisms*. London: Palgrave.

Hoogvelt, A. (1998): *Globalisation and the Post-Colonial World*. Basingstoke: Macmillan.

Hopkins, A. G. (ed.) (2002): *Globalization in World History*. New York, NY: Norton.

Hopkins, A. G. (ed.) (2006): *Global History: Interactions Between the Universal and the Local*. Basingstoke: Palgrave Macmillan.

Huntington, S. (1996): *The Clash of Civilizations and the Remaking of World Order*. London: Free Press.

Huntington, S. (2004): *Who Are We? The Challenges to America's National Identity*. New York, NY: Simon and Schuster.

Hutnyk, J. (ed.) (2006): *Celebrating Transgression: Method and Politics in Anthropological Studies of Cultures*. Oxford: Berghahn Books.

Ikenberry, J. (2010): The liberal international order and its discontents. *Millennium*, 38(3), 1–13.

Ikenberry, J. (2011): *Liberal Leviathan: The Origins, Triumph, Crisis, and Transformation of the American World Order*. Princeton, NJ: Princeton University Press.

Inglehart, R. (1977): *Silent Revolution: Changing Values and Political Styles Among Western Publics*. Princeton, NJ: Princeton University Press.

Inglehart, R. and Norris, P. (2009): *Cosmopolitan Communications: Cultural Diversity in a Globalized World*. New York, NY: Cambridge University Press.

Inglis, D. and Robertson, R. (2008): The elementary forms of globality: Durkheim and the emergence and nature of global life. *Journal of Classical Sociology*, 8(1), 5–25.

International Political Sociology (2009): Forum on global society, 3(1).

Ireyi, A. and Mazlish, B. (eds.) (2005): *The Global History Reader*. Abingdon: Routledge.

Jackson, P., Crang, P. and Dwyer, C. (2004): *Transnational Spaces*. London: Routledge.

Jaeger, H.M. (2007): Global civil society and the political depoliticization of global governance. *International Political Sociology*, 1(3), 257–77.

James, P. (2006): *Globalism, Nationalism, Tribalism: Bringing Theory Back In*. London: Sage.

Jameson, F. (1991): *Postmodernism, or, The Cultural Logic of Late Capitalism*. London: Verso.

Jameson, F. (2001): *A Singular Modernity: Essay on the Ontology of the Present*. London: Verso.

Jaspers, K. (1949): *The Origin and Goal of History*. New York, NY: Philosophical Society.

Jessop, B. (1990): *State Theory: Putting the Capitalist State in Its Place*. Cambridge: Cambridge University Press.

Jessop, B. (2000): The crisis of the national spatio-temporal fix and the tendential ecological dominance of globalizing capital. *International Journal of Urban and Regional Research*, 24, 323–60.

Jessop, B. (2003): Informational capitalism and empire: The post-Marxist celebration of US hegemony in a new world order. *Studies in Political Economy*, 71/2, 39–58.

Jessop, B. (2004): Multi-level governance and multi-level metagovernance: Changes in the European Union as integral moments in the transformation and reorientation of contemporary statehood. In I. Bache and M. Flinders (eds.), *Multi-Level Governance*. Oxford: Oxford University Press.

Jessop, B. (2007): *State Power: A Strategic-Relational Approach*. Cambridge: Polity.

Jessop, B. and Sum, N-L. (2006): *Beyond the Regulation Approach: Putting the Capitalist Economy in its Place*. London: Edward Elgar.

Jessop, B., Brenner, N., Jones, M. and MacLeod, G. (eds.) (2003): *State/Space: A Reader*. Oxford: Blackwell.

Jessop, B., Brenner, N. and Jones, M. (2008): Theorizing socio-spatial relations. *Environment and Planning D: Society and Space*, 26(3), 389–401.

Jones, A. (2010): *Globalization: Key Thinkers*. Cambridge: Polity.

Journal of World-Systems Research (2009): Book review symposium on Giovanni Arrighi's *Adam Smith in Beijing*, 15(2).

Journal of World-Systems Research (2010): Special issue: *From the Global to the Local: Social Forums, Movements, and Place*, 16(1).

Kaldor, M., Albrow, M., Anheier, H. and Glasius, M. (eds.) (2007): *Global Civil Society 2006/7*. London: Sage.

Kallinikos, J. (2004): Networks as alternative forms of organization: Some critical remarks. Unpublished paper, London School of Economics, London.

Kant, I. (1836): *Metaphysical Works of the Celebrated Immanuel Kant* (trans. J. Richardson). Ithaca, NY: Cornell University Library.

Kant, I. (2008): *The Critique of Practical Reason*. New York, NY: Wilder.

Katzenstein, P. (ed.) (1996): *The Culture of National Security: Norms and Identity in World Politics*. Ithaca, NY: Columbia University.

Keane, J. (2003): *Global Civil Society*. Cambridge: Polity.

Keane, J. (2008): *The Life and Death of Democracy*: London: Free Press.

Kearney, M. (1995): The local and the global: The anthropology of globalization. *Annual Review of Anthropology*, 24, 547–65.

Keck, M. and Sikkink, K. (1998): *Activists Beyond Borders*. Ithaca, NY: Cornell University Press.

Kennedy, P. (1989): *The Rise and Fall of the Great Powers: Economic Change and Military Conflict 1500–2000*. London: Fontana.

Keohane, R. (1986): *Neorealism and Its Critics*. New York, NY: Columbia University Press.

Keohane, R. (2001): Governance in a partially globalized world. *American Political Science Review*, 95(1), 1–13.

Keohane, R. (2009): The old IPE and the new. *Review of International Political Economy*, 16(1), 34–46.

Keohane, R. and Hoffman, S. (1991): *The New European Community: Decisionmaking and Institutional Change*. Boulder, CO: Westview Press.

Keohane, R. and Nye, J. (1997): *Power and Interdependence: World Politics in Transition* (2nd edition). Boston: Little, Brown.

Keohane, R. and Nye, J. (2000): Globalization: What's new? What's not new? (And so what?). *Foreign Policy*, 188, 104–19.

Keselleck, M. (2002): *Critique and Crisis: Enlightenment and the Pathogenesis of Modern Society*. Cambridge, MA: MIT Press.

Khor, M. (2001): *Rethinking Globalization: Critical Issues and Policy Choices*. London: Zed Books.

Kiely, R. (2005): *The Clash of Globalisations: Neo-Liberalism, the Third Way and 'Anti-Globalisation'*. Leiden: Brill.

Klein, N. (2000): *No Logo: No Space, No Choice, No Jobs*. Montreal: Knopf.

Klein, N. (2002): *Fences and Windows: Dispatches from the Front Lines of the Globalization Debate*. Montreal: Knopf.

Klein, N. (2007): *The Shock Doctrine: The Rise of Disaster Capitalism*. Montreal: Knopf.

Knorr-Cetina, K. (2007): Microglobalization. In I. Rossi (ed.), *Frontiers of Globalization Research: Theoretical and Methodological Approaches*. New York, NY: Springer.

Knorr-Cetina, K. and Bruegger, U. (2002): Traders' engagement with markets: A postsocial relationship. *Theory, Culture and Society*, 19(5–6), 161–85.

Koenig-Archbugi, M. (2010): Is global democracy possible? *European Journal of International Relations: Online First*, 16 June.

Kompridis, N. (2005): Normativizing hybridity/neutralizing culture. *Political Theory*, 33(3), 318–43.

Kondratieff, N.D. (1979) [1935]: The long waves in economic life. *Review of Economic Statistics*, 17, 105–15.

Kraidy, M.M. (2005): *Hybridity, or the Cultural Logic of Globalization*. Philadelphia, PA: Temple University Press.

Krasner, S. (ed.) (1983): *International Regimes*. Ithaca, NY: Cornell University Press.

Krasner, S. (1994): International political economy: Abiding discord. *Review of International Political Economy*, 1(1), 13–19.

Kratchowil, J. and Ruggie, J. (1986): The state of the art or the art of the state. *International Organization*, 40, 753–76.

Krishnaswamy, R. and Hawley, J. (eds.) (2008): *The Postcolonial and the Global*. Minneapolis, MN: University of Minnesota Press.

Krucken, G. and Drori, S. (eds.) (2009): *World Society: The Writings of John W. Meyer*. Oxford: Oxford University Press.

Krugman, P. (1990): *Rethinking International Trade*. Cambridge MA: MIT Press.

Krugman, P. (1996): *The Self-Organizing Economy*. Oxford: Blackwell.

Krugman, P. (1999): *The Return of Depression Economics*. Oxford: Oxford University Press.

Krugman, P. (2007): *The Conscience of a Liberal*. New York, NY: Norton.

Kumar, K. (1999): Modernization and industrialization. In M. Waters (ed.), *Modernity: Critical Concepts. Vol. 1: Modernization*. London: Routledge.

Kuus, M. and Agnew, R. (2008): Theorizing the state geographically: Sovereignty, subjectivity, territoriality. In K. Cox, J. Robinson and M. Low (eds.), *The Handbook of Political Geography*. London: Sage.

Lacher, H. (2006): *Beyond Globalization: Capitalism, Territoriality and the International Relations of Modernity*. London: Routledge.

Lakatos, I. (1970): *Criticism and the Growth of Knowledge*. New York, NY: Cambridge University Press.

Lash, S. (2007): Power after hegemony. *Theory, Culture and Society*, 24(3), 55–78.

Lash, S. and Lury, C. (2007): *Global Culture Industry: The Mediation of Things*. Cambridge: Polity.

Lash, S. and Urry, J. (1994): *Economies of Signs and Space*. London: Sage.

Lawson, G. (2005): Rosenberg's ode to Bauer, Kinkel and Willich. *International Politics*, 42(3), 381–9.

Leach, E. (1954): *The Political Systems of Highland Burma*. London: Athlone Press.

Leander, A. (2009): Globalization theory: Feeble . . . and hijacked. *International Political Sociology*, 3, 109–12.

Lechner, F. (2001): Cultural aspects of the modern world-system. In P. Beyer (ed.), *Religion in the Process of Globalization*. Wurtzburg: Ergon.

Lechner, F. (2009): *Globalization: The Making of World Society*. Malden, MA: Wiley-Blackwell.

Lechner, F. and Boli, J. (2005): *World Culture: Origins and Consequences*. Oxford: Blackwell.

Lee, G. and Preyer, G. (eds.) (2004): World-systems analysis: Contemporary directions and research. *Protosociology*, 20, 1–257.

Lefebvre, H. (1974): *The Production of Space*. Paris: Anthropos.

Lewellen, T. (2002): *The Anthropology of Globalization: Cultural Anthropology Enters the 21st Century*. Westport, CT: Bergin and Garvey.

Leyshon, A. and Thrift, N. (1997): *Money/Space: Geographies of Monetary Transformation*. London: Routledge.

Linklater, A. (1998): *The Transformation of Political Community: Ethical Foundations of the Post-Westphalian Era*. Cambridge: Polity.

Linklater, A. (1999): *The Transformation of Political Community Towards 'A Cosmopolitan System of General Political Security'*. Occasional paper 55. York University, Canada.

Lissandrello, E. (2003): *Cross-border Regions in European Context: When 'Territoriality' Is an Outcome of Networks Interaction*. Paper presented at the third joint congress, ACSP-AESOP, Leven, Belgium, 8–12 July.

Lock, A. and Strong, T. (2010): *Social Constructionism: Sources and Stirrings in Theory and Practice.* Cambridge: Cambridge University Press.

Luhmann, N. (1981): *Politische Theorie im Wohlfahrtsstaat.* Munich: Olzog. (English translation, with essays from *Soziologische Aufklärung 4: Political Theory in the Welfare State,* Berlin: de Gruyter, 1990.)

Luhmann, N. (1983): *Soziale Systeme: Grundriß einer allgemeinen Theorie.* Frankfurt: Suhrkamp. (English translation: *Social Systems,* Stanford, CA: Stanford University Press, 1995.)

Luhmann, N. (1997): *Die Gesellschaft der Gesellschaft.* Frankfurt: Suhrkamp.

Luhmann, N. (2000): *The Reality of the Mass Media.* Stanford, CA: Stanford University Press.

Lukes, S. (2005): *Power: A Radical View* (2nd edition). Basingstoke: Palgrave Macmillan.

Lury, C. and Lash, S. (2008): *The Global Culture Industry.* Cambridge: Polity.

Mackinder, H.J. (1907): On thinking imperially. In M. E. Sadler (ed.), *Lectures on Empire.* London: privately printed.

Maliniak, D. and Tierney, M.J. (2009): The American school of IPE. *Review of International Political Economy,* 16(1), 6–33.

Mann, M. (1986): *The Sources of Social Power. Vol. 1.* New York, NY: Cambridge University Press.

Mann, M. (1988): *States, War and Capitalism.* Oxford: Blackwell.

Mann, M. (1993): *The Sources of Social Power. Vol. 2.* New York, NY: Cambridge University Press.

Mann, M. (1996): Neither nation-states nor globalism. *Environment and Planning,* 28, 1960–4.

Mann, M. (1997): Has globalization ended the rise of the nation state? *Review of International Political Economy,* 4(3), 272–96.

Mann, M. (2003): *Incoherent Empire.* London: Verso.

Mann, M. (2006): Response to my critics. Special forum on the work of Michael Mann. *Millennium,* 34(2), 476–550.

Marcos, S. (2002): *Our Word Is Our Weapon.* New York, NY: Seven Stories Press.

Marcos, S. (2009): *Neoliberalism, Globalization and the Mainstream Media.* Youtube, at http://www.youtube.com/watch?v=g_npZFVHUzo

Martell, L. (2007): The third wave in globalisation theory. *International Studies Review,* 9, 173–96.

Marx, K. (1967) [1867]: *Grundrisse.* London: Penguin.

Marx, K. (1975): *Collected Works.* New York, NY: International.

Marx, K. (2006) [1852]: *The Eighteenth Brumaire of Louis Bonaparte.* Project Gutenberg e-book 1346.

Massey, D. (1991): A global sense of place. *Marxism Today,* 38, 24–9.

Massey, D. (2005): *For Space.* London: Sage.

Maturana, H.R. and Varela, S.J. (1980): *Autopoiesis and Cognition: The Realization of the Living.* Dordrecht: Reidel.

Mauss, M. and Durkeim, E. (1998) [1913]: Note on the notion of civilization. In J. Rundell and S. Mennell (eds.), *Classical Readings in Culture and Civilization.* London: Routledge.

Mazlish, B. (1998): Comparing global history to world history. *Journal of Interdisciplinary History,* xxviii(3), 385–95.

Mazlish, B. and Buultjens, R. (eds.) (1993): *Conceptualizing Global History.* Boulder, CO: Westview Press.

McAdam, D., Tarrow, S. and Tilly, C. (eds.) (2001): *Dynamics of Contention*. Cambridge: Cambridge University Press.

McChesney, H. (2006): The new global media. In E. P. Bucy (ed.), *Living in the Information Age: A New Media Reader* (2nd edition). Belmont, CA: Wadsworth Thomson Learning.

McMichael, P. (2001): Sleepless since Seattle: What is the WTO about? *International Political Economy*, 7(3), 466–74.

McMichael, P. (2004): *Development and Change: A Global Perspective* (3rd edition). Thousand Oaks, CA: Pine Forge Press.

McNeill, J. R. and McNeill, W. (eds.) (2003): *The Human Web: A Bird's-Eye View of World History*. New York, NY: Norton.

Mearsheimer, J. (1994): The false promise of international institutions. *International Security*, 19(3), 5–49.

Mearsheimer, J. (2006): Interview. *International Affairs*, 20(1 and 2): 105–23, 231–43.

Meiskens-Wood, E. (2003): *Empire of Capital*. London: Verso.

Melucci, A. (1996): *Challenging Codes: Collective Action in the Information Age*. Cambridge: Cambridge University Press.

Meyer, J.W. (1982): Political structure and the world economy. *Contemporary Sociology*, 11(3), 263–6.

Meyer, J.W. (2001): The European Union and the globalization of culture. In S. S. Anderson (ed.), *Institutional Approaches to the European Union*. Oslo: Arena.

Meyer, J.W. (2004): Standardizing and globalizing the nation-state. *Sophia AGLOS News*, 5, 4–11.

Meyer, J.W. (2007): Globalization: Theory and trends. *International Journal of Comparative Sociology*, 48(4–5), 261–73.

Meyer, J.W. and Drori, G. (2006): *Scientization: Making a World Safe for Organizing*. Cambridge: Cambridge University Press.

Meyer, J.W. and Jepperson, R. (2000): The 'actors' of modern society: The cultural construction of social agency. *Sociological Theory*, 18(1), 100–20.

Meyer, J.W. and Schofer, E. (2005): The world-wide expansion of higher education in the twentieth century. *American Sociological Review*, 70, 898–920.

Meyer, J.W., Boli, J. and Thomas, G. (1987): Ontology and rationalization in the Western cultural account. In G. Thomas, J. W. Meyer, J. Boli and F. Ramirez (eds.), *Institutional Structure*. London: Sage.

Meyer, J.W., Boli, J., Thomas, G. and Ramirez, F. (1997): World society and the nation-state. *American Journal of Sociology*, 103(1), 144–81.

Miege, B. (1989): *The Capitalization of Cultural Production*. New York, NY: International General.

Miliband, R. (1969): *The State in Capitalist Society*. London: Weidenfeld and Nicolson.

Miliband, R. (1985): The new revisionism in Britain. *New Left Review*, I(150), 5–26.

Millennium: Journal of International Studies (2006): Special forum on the work of Michael Mann, 34(2).

Millennium: Journal of International Studies (2010): Special issue on liberal internationalism, 38(3).

Miller, T., Lawrence, G., Mckay, J. and Rowe, D. (1999): Modifying the sign: Sport and globalization. *Social Text*, 17(3), 15–33.

Mills, C.W. (2000) [1959]: *The Sociological Imagination*. Oxford: Oxford University Press.

Mittelman, J. (2004): *Whither Globalization? The Vortex of Knowledge and Ideology*. London: Routledge.

Mittelman, J. (2010): *Hyperconflict: Globalization and Insecurity*. Palo Alto, CA: Stanford University Press.

Modelski, G. (1988): *Long Cycles in World Politics*. Seattle, WA: University of Washington Press.

Modelski, G. (1990): Is world politics evolutionary learning? *International Organization*, 44, 1–24.

Modelski, G., Devezas, T. C. and Thompson, W. R. (eds.) (2008): *Globalization as Evolutionary Process: Modeling Global Change*. Abingdon: Routledge.

Mol, A. and Law, J. (1994): Regions, networks and fluids: Anaemia and social topology. *Social Studies of Science*, 24, 641–71.

Monbiot, G. (2003): *The Age of Consent*. London: Flamingo.

Moore, B. (1966): *Social Origins of Dictatorship and Democracy: Lord and Peasant in the Making of the Modern World*. Boston, MA: Beacon Press.

Morris, I. (2010): *Why the West Rules – For Now*. New York, NY: Profile Books.

Mosley, L. (2005): Globalization and the state: Still room to move? *New Political Economy*, 10 (3), 355–62.

Mouzelis, N. (1989): Restructuring structuration theory. *Sociological Review*, 37(4), 613–35.

Munck, R. (2006): Globalisation and contestation: A Polanyian problematic. *Globalizations*, 3(2), 175–86.

Munck, R. (2007): *Globalization and Contestation: The New Great Counter Movement*. London: Routledge.

Neumann, I. B. and Sending, O. J. (2010): *Governing the Global Polity: Practice, Mentality, Rationality*. Ann Arbor, MI: University of Michigan Press.

Newman, D. (2003): Boundary geopolitics: Towards a theory of territorial lines? In E. Berg and H. van Houtum (eds.), *Routing Borders: Between Territories, Discourses and Practices*. Aldershot: Ashgate.

Newman, D. (2005): The lines that continue to separate us: Borders in our 'borderless' world. *Progress in Human Geography*, 30(2), 143–61.

Noortmann, M. and Ryngaert, C. (2010): Introduction: Non-state actors in the world of states. In M. Noortmann and C. Ryngaert (eds.), *Non-State Actor Dynamics in International Law: From Law-Takers to Law-Makers*. Aldershot: Ashgate.

Nozick, R. (1974): *Anarchy, State, and Utopia*. New York, NY: Basic Books.

Nussbaum, M. (1996): *For Love of Country*. Boston, MA: Beacon Press.

Nye, J. (1990): Soft power: The means to success in world politics. *Foreign Policy*, 80, 153–71.

O'Hearn, D. (2009): The anthropology of globalization or the globalization of anthropology? *Identities*, 16(4), 492–510.

Ohmae, K. (1990): *The Borderless World: Power and Strategy in the Interlinked Economy*. London: Collins.

Ohmae, K. (2001): *The Invisible Continent: Four Strategic Imperatives of the New Economy*. New York, NY: Harper Business.

Oke, N. (2009): Globalizing time and space: Temporal and spatial considerations in discourses of globalization. *International Political Sociology*, 3(3), 310–26.

Ong, A. and Collier, S. (eds.) (2005): *Global Assemblages: Technology, Politics and Ethics as Anthropological Problems*. Malden, MA: Blackwell.

Orgad, S. (2012): *Media Representation and the Global Imagination*. Cambridge: Polity.

O'Tuathail, G. (1996): Political geography II: (Counter) revolutionary times. *Progress in Human Geography*, 20, 404–12.

O'Tuathail, G. (2003): Geopolitical structures and cultures: Towards conceptual clarity in the study of critical geopolitics. In L. Tchantouridze (ed.), *Geopolitical Perspectives on World Politics*. Winnipeg: Centre for Defence and Security Studies.

Parsons, T. (1966): *Societies: Evolutionary and Comparative Perspectives*. New York, NY: Prentice Hall.

Parsons, T. (1969): *Politics and Social Structure*. New York, NY: Free Press.

Pasha, M. (2010): In the shadows of globalization: Civilizational crisis, the 'global modern' and 'Islamic nihilism'. *Globalizations*, 7(1–2), 173–85.

Patomäki, H. (2003): Problems of democratising global governance: Time, space and the emancipatory process. *European Journal of International Relations*, 9(3), 347–76.

Patomäki, H. (2006): Realist ontology for futures studies. *Journal of Critical Realism*, 5(1), 1–31.

Patomäki, H. (2010a): After critical realism? The relevance of contemporary science. *Journal of Critical Realism*, 9(1), 59–89.

Patomäki, H. (2010b): The Tobin Tax and global civil society organizations: The aftermath of the 2008–9 financial crisis. *Ritsumeikan Annual Review of International Studies*, 1–18.

Pemberton, J.A. (2001): *Global Metaphors: Modernity and the Quest for One World*. London: Pluto Press.

Perkmann, M. and Sum, N-L. (2002): *Globalization, Regionalization and Cross-Border Regions*. Basingstoke: Palgrave.

Phipps, P. (2009): Globalization, indigeneity and performing culture. *Local-Global: Identity, Security, Community*, 6, 28–48.

Pieterse, J.N. (2003): *Globalization and Culture: Global Mélange*. Lanham, MD: Rowman and Littlefield.

Pieterse, J.N. (2005): Globalization as hybridization. In G. Meenakshi Durham and D. Kellner (eds.), *Media and Cultural Studies*. Oxford: Blackwell.

Pieterse, J.N. (2006): Oriental globalization. *Theory, Culture and Society*, 23(2–3), 391–4.

Pieterse, J.N. (2007): *Ethnicities and Global Multiculture: Pants for an Octopus*. Lanham, MD: Rowman and Littlefield.

Pieterse, J.N. (2008): *Is there Hope for Uncle Sam? Beyond the American Bubble*. London: Zed Books.

Pieterse, J.N. (2009): *Globalization and Culture: Global Mélange* (2nd edition). Lanham, MD: Rowman and Littlefield.

Polanyi, K. (1944): *The Great Transformation*. New York, NY: Rinehart.

Polanyi, K. (1945): *Origins of Our Time: The Great Transformation*. London: Gollancz.

Popper, K. (2002) [1957]: *The Poverty of Historicism*. London: Routledge.

Preyer, G. (2007): Introduction: The paradigm of multiple modernities. Special issue: *Shmuel N. Eisenstadt: Multiple Modernities – A Paradigma of Cultural and Social Evolution*. *Protosociology*, 24, 1–18.

Preyer, G. (2009): Editorial. Special issue: *Modernization in Times of Globalization 1*. *Protosociology*, 26/7.

Prigogene, I. (1997): *The End of Certainty: Time, Chaos and the Laws of Nature*. New York, NY: Free Press.

Protosociology (2004): Special issue: *World-Systems Analysis: Contemporary Directions and Research*, 24.

Protosociology (2009): Special issue: *Modernization in Times of Globalization 1*, 26/7.

Ramirez, F. (1987): Global changes, world myths, and the demise of cultural gender: Implications for the USA. In T. Boswell and A. Bergesen (eds.), *America's Changing Role in the World-System*. New York, NY: Praeger.

Ramirez, F. (2001): World society and the political incorporation of women. Special issue: *Gender Studies. Kolner Zeitxchrift fur Soziologie und Sozialpsychologie*, 63.

Ramirez, F. and Riddle, P. (1991): The expansion of higher education. In P. Altbach (ed.), *International Higher Education: An Encyclopedia*. New York, NY: Garland.

Ramirez, F., Soysal Y. N. and Shanahan, S. (1997): The changing logic of political citizenship: Cross-national acquisition of women's suffrage rights, 1890 to 1990. *American Sociological Review*, 62, 735–45.

Ramirez, F. et al. (1996): The nation-state, citizenship, and educational change: institutionalization and globalization. In W. K. Cummings and N. F. McGinn (eds.), *International Handbook of Education and Development: Preparing Schools, Students, and Nations for the Twenty-First Century*. New York, NY: Garland.

Raz, A. E. (1999): Glocalization and symbolic interactionism. *Studies in Symbolic Interactionism*, 22, 3–16.

Review of International Political Economy (1994): Special issue: *The Nature of International Political Economy*, 1(1).

Reynolds, D. (2002): American globalism: Mass, motion and the multiplier effect. In A. G. Hopkins (ed.), *Globalization in World History*. New York, NY: Norton.

Risse, T. (2007): Social constructivism meets globalization. In D. Held and A. McGrew (eds.). *Understanding Globalization: Theories and Controversies*. Cambridge: Polity.

Ritzer, G. (2004): *The Globalization of Nothing*. Thousand Oaks, CA: Sage.

Ritzer, G. (2007): *The Globalization of Nothing 2*. Thousand Oaks, CA: Sage.

Ritzer, G. (2010): *Globalization: A Basic Text*. Oxford: Wiley-Blackwell.

Ritzer, G. (ed.) (2011): *Globalization: The Essentials*. Oxford: Wiley-Blackwell.

Ritzer, G. (2012) [1993]: *The McDonaldization of Society* (7th edition). Thousand Oaks, CA: Sage.

Ritzer, G. and Liska, J. (1997): 'McDonaldization' and 'post-tourism': Complementary perspectives on contemporary tourism. In C. Rojek and J. Urry (eds.), *Touring Cultures: Transformations of Travel and Theory*. London: Routledge.

Robertson, R. (1992): *Globalization: Social Theory and Global Culture*. London: Sage.

Robertson, R. (1996): Globality, globalization and transdisciplinarity. *Theory, Culture and Society*, 13(4), 131–47.

Robertson, R. (2007a): Globalization and culture. In G. Ritzer (ed.), *The Blackwell Encyclopedia of Sociolology*. Vol. 4. Oxford: Blackwell.

Robertson, R. (2007b): Open societies, closed minds? Exploring the ubiquity of suspicion and voyeurism. *Globalizations*, 4(3), 339–416.

Robertson, R. (2009): Differentiational reductionism and the missing link in Albert's approach to globalization theory. *International Political Sociology*, 3(1), 119–22.

Robertson, R. and Chirico, J. (1985): Humanity, globalization and worldwide religious resurgence: A theoretical exploration. *Sociological Analysis*, 46, 219–42.

Robertson, R. and Giulianotti, R. (2005): Glocalization, globalization and migration: The case of Scottish football supporters in North America. *International Sociology*, 21(2), 171–98.

Robertson, R. and Inglis, D. (2004): Beyond the gates of the *polis*: Reworking the classical roots of classical sociology. *Journal of Classical Sociology*, 4(2), 165–89.

Robertson, R. and Inglis, D. (2008): The elementary forms of globality: Durkheim and the emergence and nature of global life. *Journal of Classical Sociology*, 8(1), 5–25.

Robertson, R. and Lechner, F. (1985): Modernization, globalization and the problem of culture in world-systems theory. *Theory, Culture and Society*, 2(3), 103–18.

Robertson, R. and Scholte, J. A. (eds.) (2006): *Encyclopedia of Globalization*. London: Routledge.

Robinson, W.I. (2001): Social Theory and Globalization: The Rise of a Transnational State, *Theory and Society*, 30 (2): 157–200.

Robinson, W.I. (2002): Global capitalism and nation-state centric thinking: What we don't see when we do see nation-states. Response to Arrighi, Mann, Moore, van der Pijl, and Wendt. *Science and Society*, 65(4), 500–8.

Robinson, W.I. (2004): *A Theory of Global Capitalism: Production, Class and State in a Transnational World*. Baltimore, MD: Johns Hopkins University Press.

Robinson, W.I. (2006): Reification and theoreticism in the study of globalization, imperialism, and hegemony: A comment on Kiely, Pozo, and Valladao. *Cambridge Review of International Affairs*, 19(3), 529–33.

Robinson, W.I. (2008): *Latin America and Global Capitalism: A Globalization Perspective*. Baltimore, MD: Johns Hopkins University Press.

Robinson, W.I. (2009): Saskia Sassen and the sociology of globalization: A critical appraisal. *Sociological Analysis*, 3(1), 5–29.

Robinson, W.I. (2011): Globalization and the sociology of Immanuel Wallerstein: A critical appraisal. *International Sociology*, 26(6), 723–45.

Robinson, W.I. and Harris, J. (2000): Toward a global ruling class? Globalization and the transnational capitalist class. *Science and Society*, 64(1), 11–54.

Rodrik, D. (1997): *Has Globalization Gone Too Far?* Washington, DC: Institute for International Economics.

Rodrik, D. (2000): How far will international economic integration go? *Journal of Economic Perspectives*, 14(1), 177–86.

Rodrik, D. (2006): *One Economics, Many Recipes: Globalization, Institutions, and Economic Growth*. Princeton, NJ: Princeton University Press.

Rodrik, D. (2011): *The Globalization Paradox: Democracy and the Future of the World Economy*. New York, NY: Norton.

Rodrik, D., Subramanian, A. and Trebbi, F. (2004): Institutions rule: The primacy of institutions over geography and integration in economic development. *Journal of Economic Growth*, 9(2), 131–65.

Roman, J. (2006): *Three Uses of Glocalization*. Paper presented at the 78th Congress of the Canadian Political Science Association, 1–3 June, York University, Toronto.

Rosamond, B. (2000): European integration and globalisation. In M. Jerneck and U. Niemann (eds.), *Asia and Europe: Regional Co-operation in a Globalising World*. Singapore: Asia-Europe Foundation.

Rosamond, B. (2003): Babylon and on: Globalization and international political economy. *Review of International Political Economy*, 10(4), 661–71.

Rosamond, B. (2006): Disciplinarity and the political economy of transformation: The epistemological politics of globalization studies. *Review of International Political Economy*, 13(3), 516–32.

Rosenau, J. (1990): *Turbulence in World Politics: A Theory of Change and Continuity*. Princeton, NJ: Princeton University Press.

Rosenau, J. (1997): *Along the Domestic–Foreign Frontier: Exploring Governance in a Turbulent World*. Cambridge: Cambridge University Press.

Rosenau, J. (2003): *Distant Proximities: Dynamics Beyond Globalization*. Princeton, NJ: Princeton University Press.

Rosenau, J. and Czempiel, E.O. (1992): *Governance Without Government: Order and Change in World Politics*. Cambridge: Cambridge University Press.

Rosenberg, J. (1994): *The Empire of Civil Society*. London: Verso.

Rosenberg, J. (2000): *The Follies of Globalisation Theory: Polemical Essays*. London: Verso.

Rosenberg, J. (2005): Globalisation theory: A post-mortem. *International Politics*, 42(1), 2–74.

Rosenberg, J. (2006): Why is there no international historical sociology? *European Journal of International Relations*, 12(3), 307–40.

Rosenberg, J. (2007): And the definition of globalization is . . . ? A reply to 'In at the death?' by Barrie Axford. *Globalizations*, 4(3), 417–21.

Rosow, S.J. (2003): Towards an anti-disciplinary global studies. *International Studies Perspective*, 4(1), 1–14.

Rossi, I. (ed.) (2007): *Frontiers of Globalization Research: Theoretical and Methodological Approaches*. New York, NY: Springer.

Roudometof, V. and Roberstson, R. (2005): Globalization, world-systems theory and the comparative study of civilizations: Issues of theoretical logic in world-historical sociology. In S. Sanderson (ed.), *Civilizations and World-Systems: studying World-Historical Change*. Walnut Creek, CA: Altamira Press.

Rueschmeyer, D. and Mahoney, M. (2003): *Comparative Historical Analysis in the Social Sciences*. New York, NY: Cambridge University Press.

Ruggie, J. (1982): International regimes, transactions, and change: Embedded liberalism in the postwar economic order. *International Organization*, 36, 379–415.

Ruggie, J. (1992): Multilateralism: The anatomy of an institution. *International Organization*, 46(3), 566–8.

Ruggie, J. (1993): Territoriality and beyond: Problematizing modernity in international relations. *International Organization*, 46, 139–74.

Ruggie, J. (1998): *Constructing the World Polity: Essays on International Institutionalization*. London: Routledge.

Ruggie, J. (2004): Reconstituting the global public domain: Issues, actors and practices. *European Journal of International Relations*, 10, 499–531.

Ruggie, J. (2005): American exceptionalism, exemptionalism and global governance. In M. Ignatieff (ed.), *American Exceptionalism and Human Rights*. Princeton, NJ: Princeton University Press.

Ruggie, J. (2006): *Winning the Peace: America and World Order in the New Era*. New York, NY: Columbia University Press.

Ruggie, J. (2008): *Embedding Global Markets: An Enduring Challenge*. Aldershot: Ashgate.

Rumford, C. (2008): *Cosmopolitan Spaces: Globalization, Europe, Theory*. Abingdon: Routledge.

Rumford, C. (ed.) (2009): *Sage Handbook of European Studies*. London: Sage.

Rumford, C. and Wagg, C. (eds.) (2010): *Cricket and Globalization*. Newcastle: Cambridge Scholars.

Rupert, M. (1998): *Producing Hegemony*. Cambridge: Cambridge University Press.

Ryner, M. (2010): An obituary for the 'Third Way': The financial crisis and social democracy in Europe. *Eurozine*, April, at http://www.eurozine.com/articles/2010-04-27-ryner-en.html

Sachs, J. (1997): *Development Economics*. Oxford: Blackwell.

Sanderson, S. (2005): World-systems analysis after thirty years: Should it rest in peace? *International Journal of Comparative Sociology*, 46, 179–213.

Sassen, S. (1988): *The Mobility of Labor and Capital: A Study in International Investment and Labor Flow*. Cambridge: Cambridge University Press.

Sassen, S. (1990): *Losing Control? Sovereignty in an Age of Globalization*. New York, NY: Columbia University Press.

Sassen, S. (1991): *The Global City: New York, London, Tokyo*. Princeton, NJ: Princeton University Press.

Sassen, S. (2006): *A Sociology of Globalization*. New York, NY: Norton.

Sassen, S. (2007): *Deciphering the Global: Its Scales, Spaces and Subjects*. London: Routledge.

Sassen, S. (2008) [2006]: *Territory, Authority, Rights: From Medieval to Global Assemblages* (2nd edition). Princeton, NJ: Princeton University Press.

Sassen, S. (2011) [1994]: *Cities in a World Economy* (4th edition). Thousand Oaks, CA: Pine Forge Press.

Schafer, W. (2007): Lean globality studies. *Globality Studies*, 7, May, at http://globality. cc.stonybrook.edu/?p=81

Schafer, W. (2009): Towards a critical global theory: Our Sisyphean task. A review of Eduardo Mendieta, 2008: *Global Fragments, Globalizations, Latinamericanisms and Critical Theory. Globality Studies Journal*, at http://globality.cc.stonybrook.edu/?p=112

Schmidt, V. H. (2006): Multiple modernities or varieties of modernity? *Current Sociology*, 54(1), 77–97.

Scholte, J. A. (2000): *Globalization: A Critical Introduction*. Basingstoke: Palgrave.

Scholte, J. A. (2003): *Global Civil Society and Global Finance*. Basingstoke: Palgrave.

Scholte, J. A. (2005a): *Globalization: A Critical Introduction* (2nd edition). Basingstoke: Palgrave.

Scholte, J. A. (2005b): Premature obituaries: A response to Justin Rosenberg. *International Politics*, 42(3), 390–9.

Scholte, J. A. (2008): *Civil Society and IMF Accountability*. CSGR Working Paper 244–08, May.

Schumpeter, J. O. (1976) [1942]: *Capitalism, Socialism and Democracy*. London: George Allen and Unwin.

Servaes, J. (2008): *Communication for Development and Social Change*. Thousand Oaks, CA: Sage.

Shaw, M. (2000): *Theory of the Global State*. Cambridge: Cambridge University Press.

Shaw, M. (2001): The historical transition of our times: The question of globality in historical sociology. In J. Hobson and S. Hobden (eds.), *Historical Sociology and International Relations*. Cambridge: Cambridge University Press. (Also *Cambridge Review of International Affairs*, XIV(2), 273–89.)

Shaw, M. (2003): The global transformation of the social sciences. In M. Kaldor, H. Anheier and M. Glasius (eds.), *Global Civil Society Yearbook 2003*. Oxford: Oxford University Press.

Shields, S., Bruff, I. and Macartney, H. (2011). 'Critical' and 'international political economy'. In S. Shields, I. Bruff and H. Macartney (eds.), *Critical International Political Economy: Dialogue, Debate and Dissensus*. Basingstoke: Palgrave Macmillan.

Silver, B. and Arrighi, G. (2001): Workers North and South. In L. Panitch and C. Leyes (eds), *Socialist Register 2001*, London: Merlin Press.

Singh Grewal, D. (2008): *Network Power: The Social Dynamics of Globalization*. New Haven, CT: Yale University Press.

Sklair, L. (1991): *Sociology of the Global System*. Baltimore, MD: Johns Hopkins University Press.

Sklair, L. (2001): *The Transnational Capitalist Class*. Oxford: Blackwell.

Sklair, L. (2002): The transnational capitalist class and global politics: Deconstructing the corporate–state connection. *International Political Science Review*, 23(2), 159–74.

Sklair, L. (2004): The end of capitalist globalization. In M. B. Steger (ed.), *Rethinking Globalism*. Lanham, MD: Rowman and Littlefield.

Sklair, L. (2007): Competing conceptions of globalization. In J. T. Roberts and A. B. Hite (eds.), *The Globalization and Development Reader*. Oxford: Blackwell.

Skocpol, T. (1979): *States and Social Revolutions*. Cambridge: Cambridge University Press.

Smith, A. (1990): *Nations and Nationalism*. Cambridge: Polity.

Smith, N. (2001): Marxism and geography in the Anglophone world. *Geographische Revue*, 2, 5–21.

Snyder, L.D. (1999): *Macro-History: A Theoretical Approach to Comparative World History*. Lewiston, NY: Edwin Mellen Press.

Soja, E. (1989): *Postmodern Geographies: The Reassertion of Space in Critical Social Theory*. London: Verso.

Sorenson, G. (2004): *The Transformation of the State: Beyond the Myth of Retreat*. Basingstoke: Palgrave Macmillan.

Sorensen, G. (2006): Liberalism of restraint and liberalism of imposition: Liberal values and world order in the new millennium. *International Relations*, 20(3), 251–72.

Soros, G. (1998): *The Crisis of Global Capitalism: Open Society Endangered*. New York: Public Affairs.

Soros, G. (2008): *The New Paradigm for Financial Markets: The Credit Crisis of 2008 and What it Means*. New York: Public Affairs.

Spengler, O. (1918): *The Decline of the West* (2 vols.). London: Allen and Unwin.

Spruyt, H. (1994): *The Sovereign State and Its Competitors*. Princeton, NJ: Princeton University Press.

Steger, M. (2002): *Globalism: The New Market Ideology*. Lanham, MD: Rowman and Littlefield.

Steger, M. (2005a): From market globalism to imperial globalism: Ideology and American power after 9/11. *Globalizations*, 2(1), 31–46.

Steger, M. (2005b): Five central claims of globalism. In D. Egan and L. Chorbajian (eds.), *Power: A Critical Reader*. Upper Saddle River, NJ: Prentice Hall.

Steger, M. (2007): Globalism. In R. Robertson and J-A. Scholte (eds.), *Encyclopedia of Globalization*. London: Routledge.

Steger, M. (2009): *Globalisms: The Great Ideological Struggle of the 21st Century* (3rd edition). Lanham, MD: Rowman and Littlefield.

Steinmo, S. (2003): Bucking the trend? The welfare state and the global economy: The Swedish case close up. *New Political Economy*, 8, 31–48.

Stiglitz, J. (1998): *Redefining the Role of the State: What Should It Do? How Should It Do It? And How Should These Decisions Be Made?* Paper presented at the Tenth Anniversary of MITI Research Institute, Tokyo, March.

Stiglitz, J. (2002): *Globalization and Its Discontents*. New York, NY: Norton.

Stiglitz, J. (2003): *The Roaring Nineties*. New York, NY: Norton.

Stiglitz, J. (2006): *Making Globalization Work*. London: Penguin.

Storper, M. (1997): *The Regional World*. London: Guilford.

Strange, S. (1996): *The Retreat of the State: The Diffusion of Power in the World Economy.* Cambridge: Cambridge University Press.

Strihan, A. (2005): *A Network-Based Approach to Regional Borders.* Fulbright Seminar, Vienna, 1–9 April.

Swyngedouw, E. (1992): The Mammon quest: 'Glocalization', interspatial competition and the monetary order: The construction of new scales. In M. Dunford and G. Kafkalas (eds.), *Cities and Regions in the New Europe: The Global–Local Interplay and Spatial Development Strategies.* London: Belhaven Press.

Swyngedouw, E. (2004): Scaled geographies: Nature, place, and the politics of scale. In R. McMaster and E. Sheppard (eds.), *Scale and Geographic Inquiry: Nature, Society and Method.* Oxford: Blackwell.

Tambakaki, P. (2009): Cosmopolitanism or agonism? Alternative visions of world order. *Critical Review of International Social and Political Philosophy*, 12(1), 101–16.

Tarrow, S. (2002): From lumping to splitting: Inside 'globalization' and 'resistance'. In J. Smith and H. Johnston (eds.), *Globalization and Resistance.* New York, NY: Rowman and Littlefield.

Taylor, P. (1994): The state as a container: Territoriality in the modern world-system. *Progress in Human Geography*, 18(2), 151–62.

Taylor, P. (2004): *World City Network: A Global Urban Analysis.* London: Routledge.

Taylor, P. and House, J. W. (eds.) (1984): *Political Geography: Recent Advances and Future Directions.* New York, NY: Rowman and Littlefield.

Taylor, P. and Knox, A. (eds.) (2005): *World Cities in a World System.* New York: Cambridge University Press.

Teschke, B. (2003): *The Myth of 1648: Class, Geopolitics and the Making of Modern International Relations.* London: Verso.

Thelen, H. (2004): *How Institutions Evolve.* Cambridge: Cambridge University Press.

Therborn, G. (1995): *European Modernity and Beyond: The Trajectory of European Societies.* London: Sage.

Therborn, G. (2000): Globalizations: Dimensions, historical waves, regional effects, normative governance. *International Sociology*, 15(2), 151–79.

Thomas, G. (2009): World polity, world culture, world society. *International Political Sociology*, 3(1), 115–19.

Thompson, G. (2000): *The Limits to Globalization: Taking Borders Seriously.* Working Paper, Milton Keynes, Open University.

Thompson, G. (2003): *Between Hierarchies and Markets: The Logic and Limits of Network Organization.* Oxford: Oxford University Press.

Thompson, G. (2007): The fate of territorial engineering: Mechanisms of territorial power and post-liberal forms of international governance. *International Politics*, 44(5), 487–512.

Thompson, G. (2010): The global regulatory consequences of an irrational crisis: Examining 'animal spirits' and 'excessive exuberances'. *Globalizations*, 7(1), 87–103.

Thrift, N. (2006): Space. *Theory, Society and Culture*, 23(2–3), 13–155.

Tilly, C. (1990): *Coercion, Capital and European States AD 990–1990.* Oxford: Blackwell.

Tilly, C. (2005): *Identities, Boundaries and Social Ties.* New York, NY: Paradigm Press.

Tilly, C. (2009): Europe transformed: 1945–2000. In C. Rumford (ed.), *Sage Handbook of European Studies.* London: Sage.

Tomlinson, J. (1999): *Globalization and Culture.* Cambridge: Polity.

Tomlinson, J. (2006): Globalization and cultural analysis. In D. Held and A. McGrew (eds.), *Globalization Theory: Approaches and Controversies*. Cambridge: Polity.

Tomlinson, J. (2007): *The Culture of Speed: The Coming of Immediacy*. London: Sage.

Toynbee, A. (1934–61): *A Study of History* (12 vols.). Oxford: Oxford University Press.

Toynbee, A. (1948): *Civilization on Trial*. Oxford: Oxford University Press.

Trentmann, F. (2004): Beyond consumerism: New perspectives on consumption. *Contemporary History*, 39(3), 373–401.

Trimberger, E. (1978): *Revolution from Above: Military Bureaucrats and Development in Japan, Turkey, Egypt and Peru*. New Brunswick, NJ: Transaction Books.

Trotsky, L. (1962): *The Permanent Revolution and Results and Prospects*. London: New Park.

Trotsky, L. (1964): *The Age of Permanent Revolution: A Trotsky Anthology* (ed. I. Deutscher). New York, NY: Dell.

Turner, B. (2006): *Vulnerability and Human Rights*. Pittsburgh, PA: Penn State University Press.

Turner, B. and Khonder, H. (2010): *Globalization: East and West*. London: Sage.

Urry, J. (2000): *Sociology beyond Societies: Mobilities for the Twenty-First Century*. Abingdon: Routledge.

Urry, J. (2003): *Global Complexity*. Cambridge: Polity.

Urry, J. (2005): The complexities of the global. *Theory, Culture and Society*, 22(5), 235–54.

van der Pilj, K. (1984): *The Making of an Atlantic Ruling Class*. London: Verso.

van der Pilj, K. (1998): *Transnational Classes and International Relations*. London: Routledge.

Vernon, R. (1971): *Sovereignty at Bay: The Multinational Spread of U.S. Enterprises*. New York, NY: Basic Books.

Veseth, M. (2005): *Globaloney: Unraveling the Myths of Globalization*. Lanham, MD: Rowman and Littlefield.

Virilio, P (1991): *The Aesthetics of Disappearance*. New York: Semiotext(e).

von Hayek, F. (1944): *The Road to Serfdom*: London: Routledge.

von Mises, L. (1963) [1919]: *Human Action: A Treatise on Economics*. Chicago: Henry Regnery.

Walby, S. (2008): *Globalization and Inequalities: Complexity and Contested Modernities*. London: Sage.

Walker, R.J.B. (1992): *Inside/Outside International Relations*. Cambridge: Cambridge University Press.

Wallace-Brown, G. (2008): Globalization is what we make of it: Contemporary globalization theory and the future construction of global interconnection. *Political Studies Review*, 6, 42–53.

Wallerstein, I. (1974): *The Modern World-System. Vol. I: Capitalist Agriculture and the Origins of the European World-Economy in the Sixteenth Century*. New York, NY: Academic Press.

Wallerstein, I. (1979): *The Capitalist World-Economy*. Cambridge: Cambridge University Press.

Wallerstein, I. (1980): *The Modern World-System. Vol. II: Mercantilism and the Consolidation of the European World-Economy, 1600–1750*. New York, NY: Academic Press.

Wallerstein, I. (1989): *The Modern World-System. Vol. III: The Second Great Expansion of the Capitalist World-Economy, 1730–1840s*. San Diego, CA: Academic Press.

Wallerstein, I. (1991): *Unthinking Social Science: The Limits of Nineteenth Century Paradigms*. Cambridge: Polity.

Wallerstein, I. (1993): *Historical Capitalism*. London: Verso.

Wallerstein, I. (1998): *Utopistics: Or, Historical Choices of the Twenty-First Century*. New York, NY: New Press.

Wallerstein, I. (2000): *The Essential Wallerstein*. New York, NY: New Press.

Wallerstein, I. (2003): *Decline of American Power: The U.S. in a Chaotic World*. New York, NY: New Press.

Wallerstein, I. (2006): *European Universalism: The Rhetoric of Power*. New York, NY: New Press.

Wallerstein, I. (2011): *The Modern World-System. Vol. IV: Centrist Liberalism Triumphant, 1789–1914*. Berkeley, CA: University of California Press.

Walters, W. and Haahr, J.H. (2005): *Governing Europe: Discourse, Governmentality and European Integration*. London: Routledge.

Waltz, K. (1979): *Theory of International Politics*. New York, NY: McGraw-Hill.

Waltz, K. (1999): Thoughts about virtual nuclear arsenals. *Washington Quarterly*, 20(3), 153–61.

Wapner, P. (1995): Politics beyond the state: Environmental activism and world civic politics. *World Politics*, 47(3), 311–40.

Weber, M. (1958): *The Protestant Ethic and the Spirit of Capitalism* (trans T. Parsons). London: Unwin.

Weber, M. (1968): *Economy and Society: An Outline of Interpretative Sociology* (trans G. Roth and D. Wittich). New York, NY: Bedminster.

Weiss, L. (1998): *The Myth of the Powerless State*. Ithaca, NY: Cornell University Press.

Weiss, L. (2000): Globalization and the myth of the powerless state. In R. Higgott (ed.), *The Political Economy of Globalization*. Cheltenham: Edward Elgar.

Weiss, L. (2005): The state-augmenting effects of globalisation. *New Political Economy*, 10(3), 345–53.

Weiss, L. (2006): Michael Mann, state power, and the two logics of globalisation. *Millennium*, 34(2), 529–41.

Wellman, B. (2008): Agency in social activity and ICT interactions: The role of social networks in time and space. *Tijdschrift voor Economische en Sociale Geografie*, 99(5), 562–83.

Wellman, B., Quan-Hasse, A., Chen, W., Hampton, H., Dias de Isla, I. and Miyata, K. (2003): The social affordances of the internet for networked individualism. *Journal of Computer Mediated Communication*. 8(3), at http://jcmc.indiana.edu/vol8/issue3/wellman.html

Wendt, A. (1987): The agent–structure problem in international relations theory. *International Organization*, 41(3), 335–70.

Wendt, A. (1992): Anarchy is what states make of it: The social construction of power politics. *International Organization*, 46(2), 391–425.

Wendt, A. (1994): Collective identity formation and the international state. *American Political Science Review*, 88, 384–96.

Wendt, A. (2003): Why a world state is inevitable: Teleology and the logic of anarchy. *European Journal of International Relations*, 9(4), 491–542.

Wendt, A. (2004): The state as person in international theory. *Review of International Studies*, 30(2), 289–316.

Wendt, A. (2006): Social theory as Cartesian science: An auto-critique from a quantum perspective. In S. Guzzini and A. Leander (eds.), *Constructivism and International Relations: Alexander Wendt and His Critics*. London: Routledge.

Wiener, A. (2008): *The Invisible Constitution of Politics: Contested Norms and International Encounters*. Cambridge: Cambridge University Press.

Wight, M. (1977): *Systems of States*. Leicester: Leicester University Press.

Williams, R. (1978): *Keywords*. London: Collins.

Williamson, J. (1989): What Washington means by policy reform. In J. Williamson (ed.), *Latin American Readjustment: How Much Has Happened*. Washington, DC: Institute for International Economics.

Wolf, E. (1982): *Europe and the People Without History*. Berkeley, CA: University of California Press.

Wolf, E. (1999): *Envisioning Power: Ideologies of Dominance and Power*. Berkeley, CA: University of California Press.

Wolf, M. (2004): *Why Globalization Works*. New Haven, CT: Yale University Press.

Woods, N. (2006): Bretton Woods institutions. In T. G. Weiss and S. Daws (eds.), *Oxford Handbook on the United Nations*. Oxford: Oxford University Press.

Worsley, P. (1984): *The Three Worlds: Culture and World Development*. Chicago, IL: University of Chicago Press.

Wright, E. O. (1989): Models of historical trajectory: An assessment of Giddens' critique of Marxism. In D. Held and J. B. Thompson (eds.), *Social Theory of Modern Societies: Anthony Giddens and his Critics*. Cambridge: Polity.

Yamamura, K. and Streeck, W. (eds.) (2003): *The End of Diversity? Prospects for German and Japanese Capitalism*. Ithaca, NY: Cornell University Press.

Index

223